The COMPLETE COOK

PLAIN AND PRACTICAL DIRECTIONS
FOR COOKING AND HOUSEKEEPING

The AMERICAN ANTIQUARIAN COOKBOOK Collection

This facsimile edition of *The Complete Cook* by J.M. Sanderson was reproduced by permission from the volume in the collection of the American Antiquarian Society (AAS), Worcester, Massachusetts. Founded in 1812 by Isaiah Thomas, a Revolutionary War patriot and successful printer and publisher, the Society is a research library documenting the life of Americans from the colonial era through 1876. AAS aims to collect, preserve, and make available as complete a record as possible of the printed materials from the early American experience. The cookbook collection includes approximately 1,100 volumes.

OTHER BOOKS IN
THE AMERICAN ANTIQUARIAN SOCIETY
COOKBOOK COLLECTION

1776-1876: The Centennial Cook Book and General Guide, by Mrs. Ella E. Myers

American Cookery, by Amelia Simmons

The American Family Keepsake, by The Good Samaritan

The American Vine-Dresser's Guide, by John James Dufour

Apician Morsels, by Dick Humelbergius Secundus

The Appledore Cookbook, by Maria Parloa

The Art of Dining, and the Art of Attaining High Health, by Thomas Walker

Baker's Guide, by John Weild

California Recipe Book, by Ladies of California

The Canadian Housewife's Manual of Cookery

Canoe and Camp Cookery, by Seneca

The Caroline Housewife, by Sarah Rutledge

The Compleat Housewife, by Eliza Smith

The Complete Confectioner, Pastry-Cook, and Baker, by Eleanor Parkinson

The Cook Book of Rare and Valuable Recipes

The Cook Not Mad

The Cook's Oracle and Housekeeper's Manual, by William Kitchiner, M.D.

The Cook's Own Book, and Housekeeper's Register, by Mrs. N.K.M. Lee

The Cooking Manual of Practical Directions for Economical Every-Day Cookery, by Juliet Corson

Cottage Economy, by William Cobbett

Confederate Receipt Book

Crumbs from the Round Table, by Joseph Barber

Dainty Dishes, by Lady Harriet E. St. Clair

Dairying Exemplified, by Josiah Twamley

De Witt's Connecticut Cook, and Housekeeper's Assistant, by Mrs. N. Orr

The Dessert Book, by A Boston Lady

Directions for Cookery, by Eliza Leslie

Directions for Cooking by Troops, in Camp and Hospital, by Florence Nightingale

Domestic French Cookery, by L.E. Audot

Every Lady's Cook Book, by Mrs. T. J. Crowen

Fifteen Cent Dinners for Families of Six, by Juliet Corson

The French Cook, by Louis Eustache Ude

The Frugal Housewife, by Susannah Carter

The Frugal Housewife, by Lydia Maria Child

The Hand-Book of Carving

The Hand-Book of Practical Cookery, for Ladies and Professional Cooks, by Pierre Blot

The Health Reformer's Cook Book, by Mrs. Lucretia E. Jackson

The House Servant's Directory, by Robert Roberts

The Housekeeper's Manual

How to Mix Drinks, by Jerry Thomas

The Hygienic Cook Book, by John Harvey Kellogg

Jewish Cookery Book, by Esther Levy

The Kansas Home Cook-Book, by the Ladies of Leavenworth

Mackenzie's Five Thousand Receipts in All the Useful and Domestic Arts, by Colin Mackenzie

Miss Beecher's Domestic Receipt Book, by Catharine Beecher

Miss Leslie's New Cookery Book, by Eliza Leslie

Modern Cookery, In All Its Branches, by Eliza Acton and Sarah J. Hale

Modern Domestic Cookery, and *Useful Receipt Book*, by W.A. Henderson

The Modern Family Receipt Book, by Mrs. Mary Holland

Mrs. Hale's New Cook Book, by Mrs. Sarah J. Hale

Mrs. Owen's Illinois Cook Book, by Mrs. T.J.V. Owens

Mrs. Porter's New Southern Cookery Book, by Mrs. M.E. Porter

My Mother's Cook Book, by Ladies of St. Louis

The National Cook Book, by Eliza Leslie

New American Cookery, by An American Lady

The New Art of Cookery, by Richard Briggs

The New England Cook Book

The New England Economical Housekeeper, and Family Receipt Book, by Esther A. Howland

The New Housekeeper's Manual, by Catherine E. Beecher and Harriet Beecher Stowe

The New Hydropathic Cook Book, by Russell Thacher Trall

The New Whole Art of Confectionary, by W. Young

Nouvelle Cuisiniere Canadienne

One Thousand Valuable Secrets in the Elegant and Useful Arts

The Pantropheon, by Alexis Soyer

The People's Manual, by Perrin Bliss

The Philosophy of Eating, by Albert Bellows

The Physiology of Taste, by Jean A. Brillat-Savarin

The Picayune's Creole Cookbook, by The Picayune

The Practical Distiller, by John Wyeth

Presbyterian Cook Book

Science in the Kitchen, by Thomas Hopkins and Mrs. L.A. Hopkins

Seventy-Five Receipts for Pastry, Cakes, and Sweetmeats, by Eliza Leslie

The Times' Recipes, by The New York Times

Total Abstinence Cookery

A Treatise on Bread, by Sylvester Graham

Vegetable Diet, by William Alcott

The Virginia Housewife, by Mary Randolph

What to Do with the Cold Mutton

What to Eat and How to Cook It, by Joseph Cowan

The Young Housekeeper, by William Alcott

The COMPLETE COOK

PLAIN AND PRACTICAL DIRECTIONS FOR COOKING AND HOUSEKEEPING

J.M. SANDERSON

Andrews McMeel Publishing, LLC
Kansas City · Sydney · London

The Complete Cook copyright © 2013 by American Antiquarian Society. All rights reserved. Printed in the United States of America. No part of this book may be used or reproduced in any manner whatsoever without written permission except in the case of reprints in the context of reviews.

Andrews McMeel Publishing, LLC
an Andrews McMeel Universal company
1130 Walnut Street, Kansas City, Missouri 64106

www.andrewsmcmeel.com

ISBN: 978-1-4494-5503-3

ATTENTION: SCHOOLS AND BUSINESSES
Andrews McMeel books are available at quantity discounts with bulk purchase for educational, business, or sales promotional use. For information, please e-mail the Andrews McMeel Publishing Special Sales Department: specialsales@amuniversal.com

THE COMPLETE COOK.

PLAIN AND PRACTICAL

DIRECTIONS

FOR

COOKING AND HOUSEKEEPING;

WITH UPWARDS OF

SEVEN HUNDRED RECEIPTS:

CONSISTING OF

DIRECTIONS FOR THE CHOICE OF MEAT AND POULTRY;

PREPARATIONS FOR COOKING, MAKING
OF BROTHS AND SOUPS;

BOILING, ROASTING, BAKING, AND FRYING
OF MEATS, FISH, &c.

SEASONINGS, COLOURINGS, COOKING VEGETABLES;

PREPARING SALADS, CLARIFYING;

MAKING OF PASTRY, PUDDINGS, GRUELS, GRAVIES, GARNISHES, &c.

AND, WITH

GENERAL DIRECTIONS FOR MAKING WINES.

WITH ADDITIONS AND ALTERATIONS,
BY J. M. SANDERSON,
Of the Franklin House.

PHILADELPHIA:
LEA AND BLANCHARD.
1843.

Entered, according to the Act of Congress, in the year 1843, by
LEA AND BLANCHARD,
in the clerk's office of the district court of the United States in and for the Eastern District of Pennsylvania.

J. FAGAN, STEREOTYPER.
J. AND W. KITE, PRINTERS.

PREFACE
TO
THE ENGLISH EDITION.

The following work has been written, not only with the view of furnishing a complete Cookery Book, but also for the purpose of instructing, in a simple manner, inexperienced mistresses and servants, in the elementary principles of the culinary science; not losing sight of endeavouring to inculcate the relative duties of the employer and the employed. Almost the only cookery book in our language, in which reasons are given for the doctrine laid down, is " *The Cook's Oracle*," by the late Dr. Kitchiner. The Doctor's work, though exceedingly valuable, is a book fitted more for the improvement of the initiated, than for the instruction of those who possess no knowledge of the subject. There are many other books of cookery to which exceptions might be taken, but we have no wish to enhance our own work by depreciating the labours of others. We have done our best to produce a book, which all who can read may understand, and by which all may be instructed. Dr. Kitchiner says, in his " Rudiments," and says truly, " I have taken much more pains than any of my predecessors to teach the *young cook* how to perform, in the best manner, the common business of her profession." In our "*rudiments*," we have endeavoured to teach that which a woman should know before she can be called a " young cook," as well as that which a young cook has to learn.

To conclude; ours is a book intended for the use of persons who keep servants, and those who keep none. If we give expensive receipts, we also show, that good, substantial dishes, and the most delicate, may be prepared at as little, or even less, expense than the ordinary, or common preparations of food. In our receipts, in particular, we have written, necessarily written, many things which have been written before, but we feel assured that, taken as a whole, our work will not be found devoid of originality.

For the art of baking, and all the little knick-knacks of fancy bread, such as biscuits, sweet cakes, &c., and for confectionary, we refer our readers to two little works, by the Editor of " The Cook," called " The Baker," and " The Confectioner,"* which form part of the series of " Industrial Guides."

---

* " The Baker" and " The Confectioner" will shortly be published by Lea & Blanchard, at 25 cents, in one volume.

PREFACE

TO

THE AMERICAN EDITION.

It is said that "Good wine needs no bush," and according to the same rule a good book should require no apology, (as a preface generally appears to be). In this instance, as we are not the author, we intend to devote the small space allowed us, to the praise of this our adopted work; for, of all the English books on this subject, none, according to our ideas, possess half the claims to public approval as this one does. The author, whoever he is, is certainly a proficient in his business; and, although making no pretensions to a literary character, has laid down his rules and precepts in a clear and concise manner.

Very few additions or alterations have been made in this work; in fact none, excepting where circumstances rendered it necessary; it being considered best to send it forth to the American world with all its beauties untouched; at the same time we wish it to be understood that we do so, not because the subject is a barren one; on the contrary, were we to *condense* all the *necessary* information we have on this science, we should swell our small book to the dignity of a three-volumed work; but, by so doing, we should place it beyond the reach of that class to whom its precepts will prove most valuable. We hav therefore concluded, after due reflection, to leave such labours alone until we have more time and experience.

The American stomach has too long suffered from the vile concoctions inflicted on it by untutored cooks, guided by senseless and impracticable cook-books; and it is to be hoped, that as this subject is now becoming more important in these days of dyspepsia, indigestion, &c., a really good book will be well patronised, and not only read, but strictly followed; and let it not be said hereafter that "the American kitchen is the worst in the world."

As we have made but few alterations or improvements, we do not consider it at all necessary to offer to the public any apology for our seeming presumption in thus undertaking, at our age, to edit a work which we think requires little improvement, and consequently no great degree of talent on our part. Should we ever undertake anything original, we shall then act with more humility. All that we ask, in the present case, is the wide and extended use of the "Complete Cook."

THE COMPLETE COOK.

RELATIVE DUTIES OF MISTRESS AND MAID.

In this our little work, we more particularly address ourselves to Cook Maids in small families, where two maid servants only are kept, and where, consequently, all the business of the kitchen falls upon the cook, both as regards cleaning and cooking. In such families, it is true, the mistress in the house will take a part in the business of cooking upon herself; a most laudable custom, both as regards economy, and the real interests of the cook maid. To such mistresses, particularly the younger portion, it is hoped our little book will not be unacceptable. Cooking is neither a mean, nor a simple art. To make the *best* and the *most* of everything connected with the sustenance of a family, requires not only industry and experience, but also considerable mental capacity, or, at any rate, an aptness to learn.

One of the principal, if not the principal, requisite, in a cook, is order—that faculty by which a person is enabled to keep all things in their proper places. Without order there can be no cleanliness, another indispensable requisite in a cook: to be always cleaning, is not to be clean. There are some foolish, fussy women, who, with all the disposition on earth to be clean, not having order, dirty one thing as fast as they clean another. Nor is order an essential requisite, as regards the cleanliness of a kitchen, and of kitchen utensils, only; in dressing food, without order there can be no good cooking.

We have said, that the mistress will take a part in a small family in the business of cooking. We, perhaps, should have rather said, ought to take a part; for we are sorry to say, that there is too much reason to believe, that good housewifery is much neglected in the educating of young ladies now-a-days. If a mistress be really not acquainted with the general principles of cooking, she ought to do one of two things—either to make herself acquainted with them as an humble learner, or to keep out of the kitchen altogether; for her ignorant interference with a good cook maid will do no good, but may do a great deal of harm. And while on this subject we must give a word of friendly advice to the unfortunate cook, who may happen to fall in with an ignorant, irritable mistress. Let her take care to refrain from going into a passion with her: if the mistress scolds, let the maid be mild; and above all, let her not scold again, or answer in an angry or insulting manner. This is a hard thing to do, we are aware, particularly where a servant feels herself injured; but if she can do it, she will not only gain the victory over her mistress, but she will also feel a consciousness, happy consciousness, of having left undone those things which she ought not to have done, and of having done those things which she ought to have done. But if the tempers and habits of the mistress and maid are incompatible to that good understanding which ought always to subsist between the employer and the employed, the best course for the servant to do is, to give notice and leave. Let not this, however, be done in anger: before giving warning, let her consult her pillow.

It has been well observed, that it behoves every person to be extremely careful whom she takes into her service; to be very minute in investigating the character she receives, and equally cautious and scrupulously just in giving one to others. Were this attended to, many bad people would be incapacitated for doing mischief, by abusing the trust reposed in them. It may be fairly asserted, that the robbery, or waste, which is but a milder epithet for the unfaithfulness of a servant, will be laid to the charge of that master or mistress, who knowing, or having well-founded suspicions, of such faults, is prevailed upon by false pity, or entreaty, to slide him, or her, into another place. There are, however, some who are unfortunately capricious, and often refuse to give a character, because they are displeased that a servant leaves their service; but this is unpardonable, and an absolute robbery; servants having no inheritance, and depending on their fair name for employment. To refuse countenance to the evil, and to encourage the good servant, are actions due to society at large; and such as are honest, frugal and attentive to their duties, should be liberally rewarded, which would encourage merit, and inspire servants with zeal to acquit themselves well.

Servants should always recollect, that everything is provided for them, without care and anxiety on their part. They run no risks, are subject to no losses, and under these circumstances, honesty, industry, civility, and perseverance, are in the end sure to meet with their reward. Servants possessing these qualifications, by the blessing of God, must succeed. Servants should be kind and obliging to their fellow-servants; but if they are honest themselves, they will not connive at dishonesty in others. They who see crimes committed and do not discover them, are themselves legally and morally guilty. At the same time, however, well recollect, that tittle-tattling and tale-bearing, for the sake of getting in your mistress's good graces, at the expense of your fellow-servants, is, to the last degree, detestable. A sensible mistress will always discourage such practices.

We have known servants imagine, that because their employers are kind to them, that because they do not *command* them to do this or that, but rather *solicit* them, that, therefore, they cannot do without them, and instead of repaying their good-nature and humanity by gratitude and extra attention, give themselves airs, and become idle and neglectful. Such conduct cannot be too much condemned, and those servants, who practise it, may depend upon it, that, sooner or later, they will have cause to repent. Let it be remembered, that vice as well as virtue has its reward, though of a very different character.

DUTIES OF MISTRESS AND MAID.

We shall conclude this our friendly advice to young cooks, by an extract from the "*Cook's Best Friend*," by the late Dr. Kitchiner. Nothing can be done in perfection, which must be done in a hurry, (except catching of fleas),—" Therefore," says the Doctor, " if you wish the dinner to be sent up to please your master and mistress, and do credit to yourself, be punctual; take care, that as soon as the clock strikes the dinner bell rings. This shows the establishment is orderly, is extremely gratifying to the master and his guests, and is most praiseworthy in the attendants. But remember you cannot obtain this desirable reputation without good management in every respect; if you wish to ensure ease and independence in the latter part of your life, you must not be unwilling to pay the price for which only they can be obtained, and earn them by a diligent and faithful performance of the duties of your station in your young days, in which if you steadily persevere, you may depend upon ultimately receiving the reward your services deserve."

All duties are reciprocal; and if you hope to receive favour, endeavour to deserve it by showing yourself fond of obliging, and grateful when obliged. Such behaviour will win regard, and maintain it; enforce what is right, and excuse what is wrong.

Quiet, steady perseverance, is the only spring which you can safely depend upon infallibly to promote your progress on the road to independence.

If your employers do not immediately appear to be sensible of your endeavours to contribute your utmost to their comfort and interests, be not easily discouraged; *persevere*, and do all in your power to MAKE YOURSELF USEFUL.

Endeavour to promote the comfort of every individual in the family; let it be manifest that you are desirous to do rather more than is required of you, than less than your duty; they merit little who perform nothing more than what would be exacted. If you are desired to help in any business that may not strictly belong to your department, undertake it *cheerfully, patiently*, and *conscientiously*.

The foregoing advice has been written with an honest desire to augment the comfort of those in the kitchen, who will soon find, that the ever-cheering reflection of having done their duty to the utmost of their ability, is in itself, with a Christian spirit, a never-failing source of comfort in all circumstances and situations, and that

"Virtue is its own reward."

Having thus briefly touched upon the relative duties of mistress and maid, we shall now proceed to make some general remarks (and though general, we think them most important) as respects the business of Cooking as an art, or, more properly speaking, as a science.

INTRODUCTORY GENERAL REMARKS ON COOKERY—IMPORTANCE OF GOOD COOKERY AS REGARDS HEALTH AND TEMPERANCE.

It is an old, and somewhat vulgar saying, though very expressive, that " God sends meat, and the devil cooks." This adage shows, that cooking has always been considered of some importance in this country, even among the lowest classes of society. A great deal too little attention, however, is paid to the art of preparing food for the use of those who eat; and we think we may say, without much exaggeration, that in many families, even to this day, one-half of their meat is wasted, and the other half spoilt. But the mere waste arising from this system of cooking, or rather want of system, is not the greatest evil, though this is an enormous one; the diseases that badly dressed food occasions to the stomach are even a greater evil than the one to which we have first referred. A bad cook will turn that which was intended by the Giver of all good for the nourishment of the body into a sort of poison. The functions of the stomach, when loaded with crude, undressed, or half-dressed meat, are unable to digest it. Hence the stomach is not only injured, but a train of diseases is engendered, sufficient to render one's life miserable. From the cause alluded to arises acidity, or sourness of the stomach, which gives rise again to heart-burns, hiccups, flatulencies, or wind; which again creates pains in the stomach and head, and, indeed, in other parts of the body. Then again we have, from the same cause, the various descriptions of nightmare, horrid dreams, and restless nights. Country people, in agricultural districts in particular, think themselves, when so afflicted, bewitched, or possessed by the devil, when, in fact, if possessed at all, they are possessed by bad cookery and indigestible diet. Instead of resorting to charms, such persons ought to resort to a dose of opening medicine, and take care to eat food which is not spoilt by dressing. But the greatest of all ills by which we can be afflicted, ill-dressed, indigestible food will bring about—intellectual confusion—perhaps madness—for be assured, that a deranged *stomach* is always, more or less, accompanied with a deranged *head*.

In support of these opinions we might adduce many authorities of the highest reputation, but we shall content ourselves with the following:—" It cannot be doubted," says Dr. Cheyne, "that the clear, ready, and pleasant exercise of the intellectual faculties, and their easy and undisturbed application to any subject, is never to be obtained but by a free, regular performance of the natural functions, which the lightest (most digestible) food can only procure." Again, Dr. Cheyne says, " he that would have a clear head must have a clean stomach. It is sufficiently manifest how much uncomfortable feelings of the bowels affect the nervous system, and how immediately and completely the general disorder is relieved by an alvine evacuation." Then we have the testimony of Abernethy, who says, " we cannot reasonably expect tranquillity of the nervous system, whilst there is disorder of the digestive organs. As we can imbibe no permanent source of strength but from the digestion of our food, it becomes important on this account, that we should attend to its quantity, quality, and the periods of taking it, with a view to ensure its proper digestion." But what says Dr. Kitchiner, who was an able physician, and the most learned and scientific writer upon the culinary art? "The stomach," he asserts, "is the main-spring of our system; if it be not sufficiently wound up to warm and support the circulation, the whole business of life will, in proportion, be ineffectually performed—we can neither think with precision—walk with vigour—sit down with comfort—nor sleep with tranquillity. There would be no difficulty in proving, that it influences (much more than people imagine) all our actions."

"One of the greatest, perhaps the greatest, moral writers of our age, Dr. Samuel Johnson, was a man," says Boswell, "of very nice discrimination in the science of cookery." He often remarked, "that some people have a foolish way of not minding, or pretending not to mind, what they eat; for my part, I mind my belly very studiously and very carefully, and I look upon it, that he who does not mind his belly, will hardly mind any thing else." To this, Kitchiner adds, "the Doctor might have said, *cannot* mind any thing else." The *energy* of our brains is sadly dependent on the *behaviour* of our bowels. Those who say, 'tis no matter what we eat, or what we drink, may as well say, 'tis no matter whether we eat, or whether we drink.

Again, as to the relative importance of cookery as a science. Mr. Sylvester, in his *Domestic Economy*, says, that it is not difficult to foresee, that this department of philosophy must become the most popular of all others, because every class of human beings is interested in its result." Again, the same writer says, "if science can really contribute to the happiness of mankind, it must be in this department. The real comfort of the majority of men in this country is sought for at their own fire-sides: how desirable then it becomes to give every inducement to be at home, by directing all the means of philosophy to increase domestic happiness!"

Dr. Waterhouse, in his Lectures, thus speaks of the stomach:— "The faculty the stomach has of communicating the impressions made by the various substances that are put into it is such, that it seems more like a nervous expansion from the brain than a mere receptacle for food."

From allusions in the great Milton's writings, it is quite evident, that he appreciated the science of cookery highly. Speaking of philosophy, he says,

"'Tis a perpetual feast of nectar'd sweets,
Where no crude surfeit reigns,"

Again,

"That which is not good is not delicious
To a well-govern'd and wise appetite."

But we have better evidence than these allusions, of Milton's attachment to nicely dressed dishes. In his brother's, the judge's testimony, in support of a nuncupative will, which it was alleged he made before his death in favour of his third and last wife, a passage occurs, to the effect, that, approving of his dinner on a certain occasion, he said, "this will do; get something nice for me to eat, for when I am gone it will be all your's." We quote from memory. The celebrated Dr. Parr, the great Grecian and theologian, was much attached to good eating himself, and thought it very necessary, both for the health of the body and the mind. A few weeks before his death, for he was perfectly conscious that he had but a short time to live, he made arrangements for his funeral; and, amongst other things, he prepared a bill of fare for his funeral dinner. The dishes were all cold. He expressed his regret to a clerical friend of ours, that he could not give them a hot dinner, "but that is impossible," he said, "for there is not convenience in the house to cook for so large a number. I am much afraid," he continued, "lest you parsons should get a hot dinner for yourselves, and leave the poor laymen to the cold meat; but I should be very angry if I could know it. I always liked to take care of my own stomach, and of other people's. If that is wrong, nothing can be right."

There are people who imagine, that it is beneath the dignity of a philosopher to trouble himself about eating; such a one was that gay fribble of a marquis, who, finding Descartes enjoying himself over a good dinner, exclaimed, "Hey! what, do you philosophers eat dainties?" "Do you think," replied Descartes, "that God made good things only for fools?"

There is a point with regard to the importance of good cookery, upon which we have not touched, though one of first-rate consequence, namely, temperance, from the neglect of which so many, and such deadly, evils arise. Let a man load his stomach with crude, indigestible food, that is, ill-dressed meats or other substances, and what is the consequence? he feels ill—in fact, he is ill—his mind does not possess its proper vigour and elasticity; in one word, the whole man, mind and body, is disordered—unhinged. He seeks relief in spirits, and he obtains it, perhaps, temporarily. Hence is the beginning of dram drinking, and all its concomitant evils; which it would fill a volume to enumerate. The members of temperance societies, and the promoters of temperance in general, would do well to turn their attention to this point, and we think they will agree with us on the importance of diffusing the art of cookery—the art of preparing good and wholsome food—as widely as possible among the people.

In this country we have the best of all descriptions of butcher's meat in the world, and, with a few exceptions, the worst cooks. If the poor, half-fed meats of France, were dressed as our cooks, for the most part, dress our well-fed excellent meats, they would be absolutely uneatable. In France, the cooks, both private and public, contrive to make most excellent and easily digestible food, out of substances that we should throw away, as perfectly incapable of being rendered fit to eat, or at least palatable.

INTRODUCTORY REMARKS.

It has been proved by Dr. Prout, that sugar, butter, or oil, and white of egg, or substances partaking of their nature, form the chief alimentary food of man. The saccharine, or *sugary* principle, in its extended sense, is mostly derived from vegetables. A proper knowledge of these principles forms the basis, or foundation, of French cookery, or, indeed, every other good system of cookery. It does not follow, however, that it is necessary that a cook should understand these things philosophically, so as to be able to give a reason for them. It is sufficient for him or her to take for granted the maxims or rules that have been deduced from them, and act accordingly.

In France, most substances intended for food are exposed, by means of oil or butter, or grease, in a frying-pan, to a heat of 600° Fahrenheit, that is, nearly three times hotter than boiling water. This is done by frying, or by some other method similar to frying. They are then put into a macerating or stewing vessel, with a little water, and kept for several hours at a temperature, or heat, below the boiling point; that is to say, the liquid is never allowed to *bubble up*, nor yet scarcely to simmer. By these united processes, it has been clearly proved, that the most hard and tough substances, whether vegetable or animal, are, more or less, reduced to a state of pulp, fit for the action of the stomach, and consequently for easy digestion.

In this country, the majority of cooks, particularly in small families, toss the meat into a large quantity of water, make the water boil as speedily as possible, and as fast as possible; and foolishly imagine, that it will be sooner and better done. But what is the consequence? The outside of the meat is rendered so tough, that it will not admit the heat to penetrate the inside, which remains undone, and the result is, that both the outside and inside meat are spoilt, or at least greatly damaged, both as respects flavour and wholesomeness. Here an anecdote occurs to us, which, though it has been before related, will serve to illustrate our subject. An Irishman was ordered by his master to boil him an egg for his breakfast, and was particularly enjoined to boil it soft. After waiting for more than ten minutes, the master inquired after his egg, which, however, was not forthcoming; the servant was *seeing* about it. Another five minutes elapsed, when the impatient master was coolly told his egg was not done—"Yer honour told me to bile it soft, and sure I've biled it a quarter of an hour, and it is as hard as ever."

Our ignorant, and too often unteachable, cook maid, would laugh at the simplicity of the Irishman—not considering that the very means she uses to make meat tender and palatable, that is, fast boiling, are just as absurd as those taken by Paddy to boil an egg soft.

There is no rule, they say, without an exception; but, generally speaking, ill-dressed meats, or even solid food well-dressed, taken in large quantities, are indigestible. It is a mistake to imagine, that people who take violent exercise in the open air, are always free from indigestion, and those numerous diseases to which it gives rise. That they are not so liable as those confined to a house, or a workshop is true; and there are some stomachs that appear to be able to digest any thing; but these are exceptions to the general rule—they do not affect the truth of the rule itself.

PHILOSOPHICAL COOKERY.—COUNT ROMFORD.

The first person, perhaps, with any pretensions to learning and philosophy, who studied the dressing of meat, for food, as a science, was a gentleman of the name of Thompson, who was afterwards created Count Romford, by one of the German princes. This excellent and ingenious individual lived in the last century. He demonstrated, by experiments, the principles which in our foregoing remarks we have merely asserted. We are about to give an abstract of some of his observations and experiments on this subject, which are so simply and clearly detailed, that they are perfectly intelligible to every common intellect, and we are sure will be read with interest and advantage, not only by cooks, but also by all classes of persons interested in the health and welfare of society at large.

The process by which food is most commonly prepared for the table —BOILING—is so familiar to every one, and its effects are so uniform, and apparently so simple, that few have taken the trouble to inquire *how*, or in *what manner*, these effects are produced; and whether any and what improvements in that branch of cookery are possible. So little has this matter been made an object of inquiry, that few, very few indeed, it is believed, among the *millions of persons* who for so many ages have been *daily* employed in this process, have ever given themselves the trouble to bestow one serious thought on the subject.

The cook knows *from experience*, that if his joint of meat be kept a certain time immersed in boiling water it will be *done*, as it is called in the language of the kitchen; but if he be asked *what* is done to it? or *how*, or by what agency, the change it has undergone has been effected? if he understands the question, it is ten to one but he will be embarrassed; if he does not understand it, he will probably answer, without hesitation, that "*the meat is made tender and eatable by being boiled.*" Ask him if the boiling of the water be essential to the success of the process? he will answer, "*without doubt.*" Push him a little farther, by asking him whether, *were it possible* to keep the water *equally hot* without *boiling*, the meat would not be cooked *as soon* and *as well*, as if the water were made to boil? Here it is probable that he will make the first step towards acquiring knowledge, by learning to doubt.

When you have brought him to see the matter in its true light, and to confess, that *in this view of it*, the subject is new to him, you may venture to tell him (and to prove to him, if you happen to have a thermometer at hand,) that water which *just boils* is as hot as it can possibly be made *in an open vessel*. That all the fuel which is used in making it boil with violence is wasted, without adding in the smallest degree to the heat of the water, or expediting or shortening the process of cooking a single instant: that it is by *the heat*—its *intensity*—and the *time of its duration*, that the food is cooked; and not by *boiling* or *ebullition* or bubbling up of the water, which has *no part whatever* in that operation.

Should any doubts still remain with respect to the inefficacy and inutility of boiling, in culinary processes, where *the same degree of heat* may be had, and be *kept up* without it, let a piece of meat be cooked in Papin's digester, which, as is well known, is a boiler whose cover (which is fastened down with screws) shuts with so much nicety that no steam can escape out of it. In such a *closed* vessel, boiling (which is nothing else but the escape of steam in bubbles from the hot liquid) is absolutely impossible; yet, if the heat applied to the digester be such as would cause an equal quantity of water in an open vessel to boil, the meat will not only be *done*, but it will be found to be dressed in a shorter time, and to be much tenderer, than if it had been boiled in an open boiler. By applying a still greater degree of heat to the digester, the meat may be so much done in a very few minutes as actually to fall to pieces, and even the very bones may be made soft.

Were it a question of mere idle curiosity, whether it be the *boiling* of water, or simply the *degree of heat* that exists in boiling water by which food is cooked, it would doubtless be folly to throw away time in its investigation; but this is far from being the case, for boiling cannot be carried on without a very great expense of fuel; but any boiling hot liquid (by using proper means for confining the heat) may be kept *boiling hot* for any length of time, without any expense of fuel at all.

The waste of fuel in culinary processes, which arises from making liquids boil unnecessarily, or when nothing more would be necessary than to keep them *boiling hot*, is enormous; there is not a doubt but that much more than half the fuel used in all the kitchens, public and private, in the whole world, is wasted precisely in this manner.

But the evil does not stop here. This unscientific and slovenly manner of cooking renders the process much more laborious and troublesome than otherwise it would be; and (what by many will be considered of more importance than either the waste of fuel, or the increase of labour to the cook) the food is rendered less savoury, and very probably less nourishing, and certainly less wholesome.

It is natural to suppose that many of the finer and more volatile parts of food (those which are best calculated to act on the organs of taste) must be carried off with the steam, when the boiling is violent: but the fact does not rest on these reasonings: it is *proved* to a demonstration, not only by the agreeable fragrance of the steam that rises from vessels in which meat is boiled, but also from the strong flavour and superior quality of soups which are prepared by a long process over a very slow, gentle fire. But the volatile parts of food are not only delightful to the organs of taste—the Editor has no doubt that they are also stimulating and refreshing to the stomach.

In many countries where soups constitute the principal part of the food of the inhabitants, the process of cooking lasts from one meal time to another, and is performed almost without either trouble or expense.

As soon as the soup is served up, the ingredients for the next meal are put into the pot (which is never suffered to cool, and does not require scouring;) and this pot, which is of cast iron, or of earthenware, being well closed with its thick wooden cover, is placed *by the side of the fire,* where its contents are kept simmering for many hours, but are seldom made to boil, and never but in the gentlest manner possible.

Were the pot put in a close fire-place (which might easily be constructed, even with the rudest materials, with a few bricks or stone, or even with sods, like a camp-kitchen,) no arrangement for cooking could well be imagined more economical or more convenient.

Soups prepared in this way are uncommonly savoury, and there is little doubt that the true reason why nourishing soups and broths are not more in use among the common people in most countries, is because they do not know how good they really are, nor how to prepare them; in short because they are not acquainted with them. There is another important reason which the Editor must add—the common people for the most part cannot spare time from their labour to stay at home and attend to them.

To form a just idea of the enormous waste of fuel that arises from making water boil and *evaporate* unnecessarily in culinary processes, we have only to consider how much heat is expended in the formation of steam. Now it has been proved by the most decisive and unexceptionable experiments that have ever been made by experimental philosophers, that if it were possible that the heat which actually combines with water, in forming steam (and which gives it wings to fly up into the atmosphere,) could exist in the water, without changing it from a dense liquid to a rare elastic vapour, this water would be heated by it to the temperature of red-hot iron.

Many kinds of food are known to be most delicate and savoury when cooked in a degree of heat considerably below that of boiling water; and it is more than probable that there are others which would be improved by being exposed to a *heat greater than that of boiling water.*

In many of the seaport towns of our New England States, it has been a custom, time immemorial, among people of fashion, to dine one day in the week (Saturday) on salt fish, and a long habit of preparing the same dish has, as might have been expected, led to very considerable improvements in the art of cooking it. We have often heard foreigners who have partaken of these dinners, declare that they never tasted salt fish dressed in such perfection. The secret of this cooking is to keep the fish a great many hours in water, which is just scalding hot, but which is never made actually to boil.

The Count being desirous of finding out whether it was possible to roast meat with a much gentler heat than that usually employed, put a shoulder of mutton in a machine contrived for drying potatoes: the result, which we give in the Count's own words, was as follows:

"After trying the experiment for three hours, and finding it showed no signs of being done, it was concluded that the heat was not sufficiently intense, and, despairing of success, it was abandoned to the cookmaids.

"It being late in the evening, and the cookmaids thinking, perhaps, that the meat would be as safe in the drying machine as any where else, left it there all night; when they came in the morning to take it away, intending to cook it for their dinner, they were much surprised to find it *already cooked*, and not merely eatable, but perfectly done, and most singularly well tasted. This appeared to them the more miraculous, as the fire under the machine was quite gone out before they left the kitchen in the evening to go to bed, and as they had locked up the kitchen when they left it and taken the key.

This wonderful shoulder of mutton was immediately brought in triumph, and though we were at no great loss to account for what had happened, yet it certainly was unexpected: and when the meat was tasted we were much surprised indeed to find it very different, both in taste and flavour, from any we had ever tasted. It was perfectly tender, but though it was so much done it did not appear to be in the least sodden or insipid; on the contrary, it was uncommonly savoury and high-flavoured. It was neither boiled, nor roasted, nor baked. Its taste seemed to indicate the manner in which it had been prepared: that the gentle heat to which it had for so long a time been exposed, had by degrees loosened the cohesion of its fibres, and concocted its juices, without driving off their fine and more volatile parts, and without washing away or burning and rendering rancid its oils."

Having given an abstract of Romford's opinions and experiments on boiling water as a medium for the preparation of meat for the food of man, we shall now take an opportunity of remarking, that the same rule will not apply to the cooking of the greater part of vegetables, which must be put into the water boiling hot, and which cannot be boiled too quickly. This does not apply, however, to potatoes, which cannot be boiled too slowly. These things, however, will be treated of more particularly in the receipts, which we shall give for the cooking of different kinds of vegetables.

Seasoning is a very important element in the art of cookery. Experience is absolutely necessary to acquire this art, which to be properly done, requires great judgment and delicacy of taste. All the recommendations of Dr. Kitchiner and others to season by weight and measure, as apothecaries serve out drugs, are in the nature of the thing impracticable. "What's one man's meat is another man's poison," is a homely proverb, but a true one. So in seasoning, what one person likes, another may dislike. The writers we have alluded to ridicule the idea of directing the cook to use a pinch of that, and a dust of the other. M. Ude justly observes, "that where the quantities are indefinite, it is impossible to adjust the exact proportions of spice, or other condiments, which it will be necessary to add in order to give the proper flavour." If these remarks are correct, and who can doubt it, the general terms "handful, pinch, and dust," are the best that can be applied as directions upon such a subject.

In the use of salt in cooking, considerable judgment is required. The best rule is to employ as little as possible. It is easy to make a dish too fresh, salt; but if made too salt, it cannot be made fresh again. Sugar may be applied with advantage in various dishes, where it is not generally used in this country, and which will be enumerated hereafter, but great care must be taken, that in such preparations it should be employed to enrich, not to sweeten. The taste of sugar should not predominate, or even be recognised. We allude more particularly to soups and gravies, and in some cases in vegetables, such as green peas for instance. Meat intended to be broiled, or fried, should be well peppered, but never salted; salt renders it hard. The author of "Domestic Cookery" says, that "salt should not be put into the water in which vegetables are boiled." We disagree with this lady; indeed, she disagrees with herself; for in another part of her book she directs salt to be put into the water in which potatoes are to be boiled; and we are quite sure it is very necessary in boiling cabbage, savoys, and most other descriptions of greens.

It ought to be well understood, that pepper and all descriptions of spice require to be subjected to the action of heat to bring out their genuine flavour. Thus it will be seen, that though it is very practicable to sweeten or salt things after they are dressed, it is not so as respects flavouring them with spice. In the use of spices it is, however, very important to take care that the aroma (commonly called smell), which they give forth, should not be allowed to evaporate or escape. Druggists and medical men always keep their essential oils, tinctures, volatile spirits and volatile gums, in ground stopper bottles, which are perfectly air-tight. This puts us in mind of a foolish custom, which cannot be too much deprecated, of exposing in the open air aromatic herbs, such as marjoram, thyme, mint, and several others, which are known by the general term of sweet herbs, and which are extensively used in seasoning. These herbs ought always to be kept as much as possible excluded from the air. This may be partially effected by tying the dried herbs in paper bags, but it is much better to reduce the leaves to a coarse powder, and confine it in well-corked bottles.

RULES AND MAXIMS OF THE KITCHEN.

In our foregoing remarks we have endeavoured to explain the leading principles upon which the art of cookery is founded—principles with which the young cook should become *thoroughly acquainted.* We now proceed to lay down a series of rules or maxims, relative to the dressing of meat, and the general management of the kitchen. These rules should be well studied, and the most important of them committed to memory. By doing this a cook will save a great deal of trouble and loss of time, and she will also, by her knowledge of the general principles of the art, be enabled to vary, and probably improve the receipts, which she may have occasion to consult. In short, when she knows what must be *always* done, and what must *never* be done, she is, in a great measure, mistress of her art, inasmuch as the details will be easily acquired by practice.

RULES OF THE KITCHEN.

WHAT MUST ALWAYS BE DONE, AND WHAT MUST NEVER BE DONE.

1. Keep yourself clean and tidy; let your hands, in particular, be always clean whenever it is practicable. After a dirty job always wash them. A cleanly cook must wash her hands many times in the course of the day, and will require three or four aprons appropriated to the work upon which she is employed. Your hair must never be blowsy, nor your cap dirty.

2. Keep apart things that would injure each other, or destroy their flavour.

3. Keep every cloth, saucepan and all other utensils to their proper use, and when done with, put them in their proper places.

4. Keep every copper stewpan and saucepan bright without, and perfectly clean within, and take care that they are always well tinned. Keep all your dish-covers well dried, and polished; and to effect this, it will be necessary to wash them in scalding water as soon as removed from the table, and when these things are done let them be hung up in their proper places.

5. The gridiron, frying-pan, spit, dripping-pan, &c., must be perfectly cleaned of grease and dried before they are put in their proper places.

6. Attention should be paid to things that do not meet the sight in the way that tins and copper vessels do. Let, for instance, the pudding cloth, the dish-cloth, and the dish-tub, be always kept perfectly clean. To these may be added, the sieve, the cullender, the jelly-bag, &c., which ought always to be washed as soon after they are used as may be practicable.

7. Scour your rolling-pin and paste-board as soon after using as possible, but without soap, or any gritty substance, such as sand or brick-dust; put them away perfectly dry.

8. Scour your pickle and preserve jars after they are emptied; dry them and put them away in a dry place.

9. Wipe your bread and cheese-pan out daily with a dry cloth, and scald them once a week. Scald your salt-pan when out of use, and dry it thoroughly. Scour the lid well by which it is covered when in use.

10. Mind and put all things in their proper places, and then you will easily find them when they are wanted.

11. You must not poke things out of sight instead of cleaning them, and such things as onions, garlick, &c., must not be cut with the same knife as is used in cutting meat, bread, butter, &c. Milk must not be put in a vessel used for greasy purposes, nor must clear liquids, such as water, &c., be put into vessels, which have been used for milk, and not washed; in short, no vessel must be used for any purpose for which it is not appropriated.

12. You must not suffer any kind of food to become cold in any metal vessel, not even in well-tinned iron saucepans, &c., for they will impart a more or less unpleasant flavour to it. Above all things

you must not let liquid food, or indeed any other, remain in brass or copper vessels after it is cooked. The rust of copper or brass is absolutely poisonous, and this will be always produced by moisture and exposure to the air. The deaths of many persons have been occasioned by the cook not attending to this rule.

13. You must not throw away the fat which, when cold, accumulates on the top of liquors in which fresh or salt meat has been boiled; in short, you ought not to waste fat of any description, or any thing else, that may be turned to account; such as marrow-bones, or any other clean bones from which food may be extracted in the way of soup, broth, or stock, or in any other way: for if such food will not suit your table, it will suit the table of the poor. Remember, "Wilful waste makes woful want."

14. A very essential requisite in a cook is punctuality: therefore rise early, and get your orders from your mistress as early as possible, and make your arrangements accordingly. What can be prepared before the business of roasting and boiling commences should always be prepared.

15. Do not do your dirty work at a dresser set apart for cleanly preparations. Take care to have plenty of kitchen cloths, and mark them so as a duster may not be mistaken for a pudding-cloth, or a knife-cloth for a towel.

16. Keep your spit, if you use one, always free from rust and dust, and your vertical jack clean. Never draw up your jack with a weight upon it.

17. Never employ, even if permitted to do so, any knives, spoons, dishes, cups, or any other articles in the kitchen, which are used in the dining room. Spoons are sure to get scratched, and a knife used for preparing an onion, takes up its flavour, which two or three cleanings will not entirely take away.

18. Take great care to prevent all preparations which are delicate in their nature, such as custards, blancmange, dressed milks, &c., &c., from burning to which they are very liable. The surest way to effectually hinder this is to boil them as the carpenter heats his glue, that is, by having an outside vessel filled with water.

19. You ought not to do any thing by halves. What you do, do well. If you clean, clean thoroughly, having nothing to do with the "slut's wipe," and the "lick and a promise."

20. And *last*, though *not least*, be teachable: be always desirous to learn—never be ashamed to ask for information, lest you should appear to be ignorant; for be assured, the most ignorant are too frequently the most self-opinionated and most conceited; while those who are really well informed, think humbly of themselves, and regret that they know so little.

CHOICE AND PURCHASING OF BUTCHERS' MEAT.

Inferior joints of the best animals should always be preferred to the prime joints of the ill-fed or diseased beasts. Inferior joints of good

CHOICE OF BUTCHERS' MEAT.

meat such as stickings, legs and shins of beef, shoulders of mutton and veal, may, if well dressed, be made as nourishing and palatable as the superior joints, and may be bought much cheaper; but no cooking, however well executed, will ever make bad meat good. Ill-conditioned beasts, too, are for the most part unhealthy.

21. *Beef.*—Ox beef is considered, truly, the best. Bull beef is coarse, tough, and has a strong, disagreeable smell and taste. Next to ox beef, that of a young heifer (if spayed the better) is preferred. Some persons, indeed, think it is the best. It is the most delicate and tender of all description of beef. Cow beef, particularly a young cow that has not had more than two or three calves, is very good. The grain is closer, and the fat whiter, than ox beef. Good beef has a fine, smooth, open grain, interlarded with thin streaks of delicate fat; and is of a deep healthy looking red colour. When the fat is of a dirty yellow colour, the meat is not good: it indicates its having been fed upon artificial food, such as oil cake. Grass-fed meat, or that fed upon hay and corn meal, is the best. When beef is old, a horny streak runs between the fat and lean; the harder this is, the older the meat. The flesh is not good flavoured, and eats tough.

22. *Mutton.*—Good mutton is firm in the grain; of a bright red colour; the lean delicately interlarded with thin streaks of fat; the fat itself being of a brightish white, tinted with a delicate pink. The fat of rotten mutton, in which the sheep was afflicted with a liver disease, is always of a dead white, and the flesh is of a pale colour. Such mutton is both unwholesome and unsavoury. The best way to detect this kind of mutton, is to examine the liver before it is removed from the sheep. If the liver be without bladders, or other marks of disease, the mutton is sound. Ewe mutton is not so good as wether mutton; the flesh is generally paler, and the texture finer. The best mutton is that which is fed upon the natural grasses. This is the reason why the Welsh and mountain Scotch muttons are so firm, short, and sweet. The sheep have liberty to choose their own food. Mutton fed on rape and turnips does not eat so well, nor near so well, as the grass-fed. Ram mutton has a strong, and, in some seasons of the year, an exceedingly disagreeable flavour. It is said that wether mutton, to be eaten in perfection, should be five years old; but it is scarcely ever kept to that age. In wether mutton there is a knob of fat on the part of the leg, where in the ewe you will find a part of the udder.

23. *Venison* when young has the cleft of the haunch smooth and close, and the fat is clear, bright and thick. In old venison, the cleft is wide and tough. If, after running a long, narrow, sharp knife into the lean of venison, it comes out without smelling, the venison is sweet. Some persons like it a little gone, and others a good deal. This state of putrescency is called by gourmands *haut gout*, high tasted; we should rather say at once, stinking. Venison requires more keeping than any other sort of meat to make it tender, unless it be dressed immediately it is killed, that is, before it is cold.

24. *Veal.*—This meat, to be truly good, delicate, fine flavoured, and

tender, ought not to be more than five or six weeks old, and, of course, fed exclusively upon the milk of the mother. Writers on cookery gravely tell us, that the whiteness of veal is partly caused by the calf licking chalk. This is nonsense. The chalk is given to prevent calves from scouring, not to make their flesh white. However, whiteness is no proof of veal being good and juicy; it is caused by frequent bleeding. The flesh of the bull calf is said to be the firmest, but not so white. The fillet of the cow calf is sometimes preferred for the udder. The kidney of good veal is well covered with healthy looking fat, thick and firm. The bloody vein in the shoulder should look blue; if it be of any other colour, the meat is stale. Fresh veal is dry and white. When it is spotty and clammy it is stale. The kidney is gone when the fat or suet upon it is not firm. The kidney goes first.

25. *Lamb* that is fresh will have the veins bluish in the neck and fore-quarter. If there be a faint smell under the kidney it is not fresh. When the eyes are sunk in the head, it is a sure sign the lamb has been killed too long. Grass lamb, which is the only lamb that is in perfection, comes in in April, but it is better in May and June; that is to say, when men with hard hands can afford to eat it, and when there are green peas to eat with it. House lamb, for those who can afford to pay for it, and like to eat it, may be obtained all the year round.

26. *Pork.*—The quality of this kind of meat depends in a great measure upon its feeding. If grossly fed, it is bad, for the pig will eat any thing in the absence of delicate food. Dairy-fed pork we are told is the best: it is good, but we think not the best. To our taste, that is to be preferred in every respect which is fed not merely on dairy food, but upon good wholesome corn meal, whether of barley, oats, peas, or beans. Cookery writers tell us, that "if the rind is tough, and cannot easily be impressed by the finger, the meat is old;" and they add, that a thin rind is a merit in all pork." These directions are no guide whatever to the choice of pork: the rind may be made thin by dressing, but there are those, and no bad judges either, who prefer thick rinds. Moubray, on Poultry, &c., says, " the western pigs from Berks, Oxford, and Bucks, possess a decided superiority over the eastern of Essex, Sussex, and Norfolk; not to forget another qualification of the former, at which some readers may smile, a thickness of the skin, whence the *crackling* of the roasted pig is a fine gelatinous substance, which may be easily masticated, whilst the crackling of the thin-skinned breeds is roasted into good block tin, the reduction of which would almost require teeth of iron." So much for thin rinds. When pork is fresh, the flesh will be smooth and dry; when stale, clammy. What is called measly pork is to be avoided as a poison. It may be known by the fat being full of kernels, and by the general unwholesomeness of its appearance.

27. *Bacon* is good when the fat is almost transparent and of a delicate transparent pink tinge. The lean should adhere to the bone, be of a good colour, and tender. Yellow streaks in bacon show it is

becoming rusty; when all is yellow, all is rusty and unfit to eat. Bacon and hams are frequently spoilt in the curing. Taste a little of the lean, and you will be able to judge whether it be too salt or not.

28. *Hams* are the best part of the pig when properly cured, perfectly sweet, and not too salt. To ascertain whether a ham is tainted, run a sharp knife under the bone, and if it comes out with a pleasant smell, and clean, the ham is good.

Summary of Directions.—Choose meat that has a clear red liver, free from knots and bladders, with kidneys firm, close, and well surrounded with firm, hard fat; the skirts which line the ribs should be full and fat. Meat possessing these qualifications may be depended on as of the first quality; but if the kidney or kernels of an animal have spots resembling measles, as is too frequently the case with pork, the meat is unwholesome.

We have said thus much on the choice of meats, but persons who keep up what is called an establishment, will do best to trust to their butcher, porkman, fishmonger, and poulterer, and not to choose at all, excepting tradesmen, taking care to deal only with the most respectable in the neighbourhood.

CHOICE OF POULTRY, EGGS, AND FISH, AND SEASONS OF FISH.

Poultry of all kinds are preferred of a short thick make, broad and plump in the breast and thick in the rump and fat in the back. The spurs should be short as indicating youth, and the comb red as indicating health. The beak, bill, and claws, in a young bird will be tender, and the skin of the legs comparatively smooth; the contrary are certain indications of an old bird. But the best test of a fowl, as respects its age, is to try the two bones which run by the side of the belly to the vent; if these are gristly and easily broken at the end, the fowl is young. To judge of the age of geese or ducks, little or no dependence is to be placed upon the colour of the legs and bills—this varies according to complexion; but if the bills and feet have coarse red streaks, or a tinge of red in them, the bird is old. In young geese and ducks the above marks are not to be seen, and the webs will be smooth and thin.

29. *Rabbits*, young and in good condition, will be fat about the kidneys, and by the side of the belly. The flesh should be white, and if young, the legs will break easily.

30. *Fowls* are plentiful from August to January; chickens come in about April, tame ducks in May, continue through the summer months, and go out in October. Young geese may be dressed in the latter end of May and through the summer, but a goose is not thoroughly ripe till after stubbling, that is, about Michaelmas. Turkey poults are in season from May onwards, but turkeys are in high season about Christmas.

31. *Rabbits* and *Pigeons* may be had the year round; wild rab

bits are best in the winter season; young pigeons may be had in February, and till September; wood-pigeons in December and January.

32. *Game.* — Hares, partridges and pheasants from September through the winter: the game season closes with February. All kinds of water-fowl are most plentiful in keen, dry weather, especially in cold weather, after snow; also larks, wood-cocks, snipes, &c.

33. *Eggs.*—New eggs have always a rough fresh-looking shell, but this appearance may be effected by artificial means, and the purchaser be cheated with rotten ones, instead of getting fresh. A new-laid egg will sink in water, bad ones are more or less buoyant; but this is a tedious way of testing eggs. The best way is to form a sort of tube with the left hand, holding with the right hand the egg, close and opposite to this tube, in the light. If the egg is good the meat will look clear, and partly transparent; if bad, it will look dark with black spots in it.

34. *Fish* should be broad and thick of their kind, their eyes bright, gills red, and the scales close and shining: fish should feel firm to the touch and stiff. Stale fish have always a loose, limber feel, especially about the vent; their eyes are sunk and dim, the scales loose and flabby, and the whole has a dingy, disagreeable appearance. Lobsters and crabs are to be judged by their weight; if they feel light, they have wasted themselves by long keeping.

35. *Seasons of Fish.* —There are some kinds of fish absolutely poisonous eaten out of season; such are salmon, and skate. The following will give some idea of the seasons of fish, but they vary according to the weather. Cod comes in about October, and goes out about February; it is sometimes good for a short time about August. Salmon comes in in February, is in high season during May, June, and July, declines in August, and is quite out in September. Pickled salmon is good from May till September. Herrings are in season as long as they are full of roe; when shotten, they are worthless. Sprats are best in frosty weather. Lobsters and crabs are plentiful in the spring and early part of the summer. Haddock, flounders, muscles, come in in September or October, and are out about April or May. Jacks or pikes, eels, perch, tench, carp, and other fresh water fish, become plentiful about April or May, according to the weather. Eels are never out of season, but in cold weather are hardly to be procured. Hallibut is in season from the beginning of May until the end of September.

PREPARATIONS FOR COOKING.

36. A great deal has to be done before the cook can commence the operation of cooking. She has to truss her fowls and prepare her fish, butcher's meat, and vegetables, with other things not necessary to mention here. Never wash butcher's meat except for the purpose of cleansing it of blood, which would otherwise disfigure it when dressed. Few joints require this operation; heads, hearts and scrags

PREPARATIONS FOR COOKING. 31

always require to be well washed before they are cooked, but if they or any thing else are intended for roasting or frying, they should first be rendered perfectly dry, by rubbing with a coarse cloth, or otherwise. Salt rubbed in with warm water will speedily remove the blood and cleanse the meat. Hares must be always well washed with salt and water, or milk and water.

37. *Trussing* is little required in butcher's meat; but loins, boned and stuffed, such as those of beef, mutton and pork, must of course be trussed. This is done by spreading the stuffing and seasoning over them, then rolling them up as tightly as possible, tying up with a tape or string, and securing all by skewers. The long flap of the fillet of veal must be filled with stuffing, and then secured as above directed.

38. All kinds of poultry should be killed the first thing in the morning, when their crops are empty. They should be plucked while they are warm; be sure take out all the flues, and let the hair be singed off with white paper. It is recommended to crop fowls and pigeons immediately you have them; but there is a difference of opinion as to the time of drawing them; some say they should be drawn as soon as killed, or at least as soon as bought, which prevents the disagreeable flavour so often perceived in chickens; others say, and indeed the generality of cooks are of this opinion, that they should not be drawn till just before they are dressed, as it is apt to make them dry: we are of opinion that poultry should be drawn soon after they are killed; we do not believe that this makes them dry, though we are sure that to leave them undrawn will be apt to make them stink.

39. In drawing poultry, or removing the entrails, a very small slit may be made under the vent with a penknife, at which slip in the fore-finger, and if there is any internal fat about the vent, draw it out, as it is in the way of taking out the entrails, and, if left in, would be very strong when roasted. Next get hold of the gizzard, which may be known by its being the hardest part of the interior; draw it out carefully; it will generally bring the whole of the intestines with it, but if the liver should be left, again slip in the finger and take hold of the heart, which will bring out with it the liver, which you must not touch for fear of bursting the gall-bladder. The heart is generally left in by poulterers, but it is much better out, as it is apt to give a bloody appearance to the interior of the fowl. Trim round the vent with a pair of scissors.

40. Be careful to take away the gall-bladder from the liver without breaking it, for if one drop of the gall escapes, the whole liver is spoilt. The gizzard consists of two parts, with a stomach or bag in the middle, containing gravel and undigested food; one part of the skin by which the two parts of the gizzard are united is rather narrower than the other; slit this with a knife, and turning the gizzard inside out, remove the stomach bag and trim round the gizzard, but avoid cutting the skin by which it is joined in the middle.

41. In trussing poultry, cut off the neck about two joints from its

commencement at the shoulders, but be sure to leave half an inch, or more, of the skin longer than the part of the neck remaining, for the purpose of wrapping over on being tied.

42. The legs of fowls intended to be roasted should be taken off about one inch below the first joint; the feet and legs of young chickens are generally left on, but they must be scalded in boiling water, and the claws and outside scaly skin taken off. Thrust the liver through a slit made in the skinny part of one pinion, and the gizzard through the other; then turn the top of the pinion over the back, lay the legs close to the sides; with a wire skewer fix the middle joint of the pinion outside of the knee joint of the leg, and so through the body to the other knee and pinion; with a short skewer fix the lower joint to the lower part of the body; then the feet, or whatever part of them is left, may turn back over the belly. The skewer for this purpose must go through the sidesmen, fixing the stumps or feet between them. For a fowl that is to be boiled, a slit is made on each side of the belly, and the leg-stump tucked in.

43. To remove the crop and windpipe of those whose heads are left on, open the skin a little just in front of the throat; then pull each separately gently, first from the beak or bill, then from the stomach. Fowls whose heads are taken off may have the crop removed by putting the finger down the throat. The windpipe is easily removed in the same way.

[Trussed Fowl for roasting.]

44. Before dressing, a little flour should be dusted over fowls. Poulterers, to make the bird look plump, often break the breast bone; this is a bad practice—it lets the air into the fowl, and drys the meat; it often breaks the gall-bladder, and, of course, spoils the fowl, and it always renders the bone troublesome. The head of capon, we ought to observe, is often twisted under the wing in the same way as a pheasant's.

45. *Ducks* have the feet always left on, but the wings must be taken off at the middle joint; in doing this, leave more skin than belongs to the bone. The feet must be scalded, and the skin and claws taken away; they then must be turned over the back. In placing the skewers, keep the thigh joints outside of the pinions, and run the skewer through the leg, then through the bit of skin that hangs below the pinion, then through the body, the other pinion, skin, and the

PREPARATIONS FOR COOKING.

other leg The short skewer must be inserted just above the joint, which is twisted to turn back the feet. Tie the skin round the throat; put in the seasoning at the vent and turn the rump through a small slit in the apron.

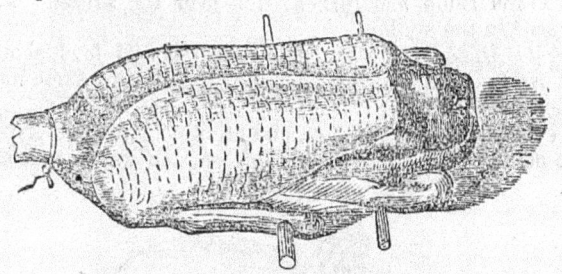

[Trussed Duck for roasting.]

46. *Geese* are trussed exactly in the same way as ducks, except the feet are cut off, and dressed with the giblets. The liver is sometimes dressed separately, and considered by some persons a great delicacy. A piece of greased white paper should be laid over the breast, and secured with a string, not skewers, before a goose is put down to roast.

47. *Turkeys* are trussed the same way as fowls, but the sinews of the leg must be drawn out before trussing. The gizzard of a turkey intended to be roasted should be scored, and both gizzard and liver covered with the caul of veal or lamb; but buttered paper does as well, and is more generally used: this is to prevent them becoming dry. The breast should be secured in the same way, with a piece of buttered paper. Nicely clean the head, and twist it under the wing.

48. *Pigeons* should be cleaned with great care. For roasting, truss with the feet on; tie the joints close down the rump, and turn the feet over the front (see engraving). Most people season them. For

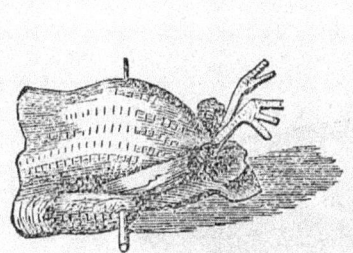

[Trussed Pigeon for roasting.]

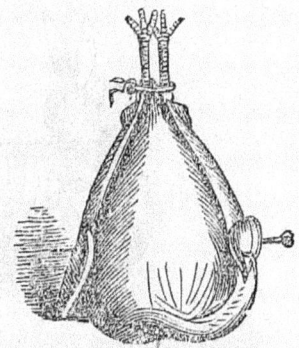

[Trussed Pheasant.]

boiling or stewing, cut off the feet, and truss just as fowls for boiling. For broiling, lay them open by cutting them down the back, and lay ing them flat. As pigeons have no gall, no extra care will be required with the liver.

49. *Pheasants*, *Partridges*, and *Guinea Fowls*, are trussed with the head tucked under the wing, and the feet on, which are twisted and tied to the rump, and turned back over the breast. The liver may be used in the stuffing.

50. *Wild Ducks*, and all other web-footed wild fowl, should have the feet left on, and be cleaned and trussed in the same manner as tame ducks.

51. *Woodcocks*, *Plovers*, &c., and all other birds that live by suction, are not drawn; the feet are left on, the knees twisted round

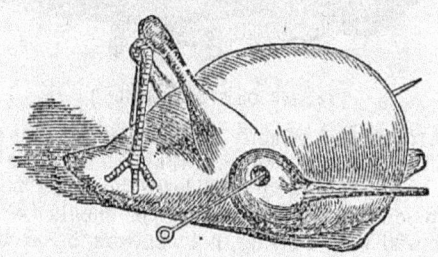

[Trussed Woodcock.]

each other, and raised over the breast, by which means each foot turns back and falls on the side of the rump.

52. *Hare*, trussed for roasting, has the legs turned back without disjointing, so that the haunches are thrown up, much in the form that a cat is often seen sitting—the end bones of the fore and hind legs meet each other, and lie side by side. Two skewers should be inserted, one where the end of the leg meets the fleshy part of the shoulder, and the other where the end of the shoulder meets the fleshy part of the leg; the head is fixed back with a skewer thrust

[Trussed Hare.]

into the mouth, through the head, and into the back between the shoulders. The belly should be slit no more than is necessary for taking out the paunch. To secure its keeping in place, a string is

PREPARATIONS FOR COOKING.

employed for bracing it; the string is laid across the back, twisted round the end of both skewers, and brought back across the back and tied. In skinning hares and rabbits, particularly hares, the ears and tails should be preserved entire, as they improve the appearance of these dishes on the table, and are much esteemed.

53. *Rabbits* for boiling are opened all the way down the belly; joint the legs at the rump so as to admit of their turning along the sides; turn the shoulders back to meet them, so that the lower joints of each lie straight along, side by side; the head should be skewered down to the right shoulder. Rabbits for roasting are trussed like hares.

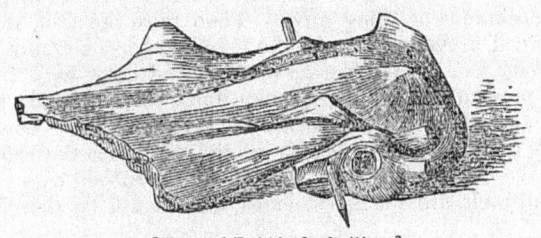

[Trussed Rabbit for boiling.]

54. *Fawns* or *Kids* are generally trussed and dressed in the same way as hares. As the flesh is of a dry nature, they should be covered with a caul or buttered paper, which should be tied on, not skewered. Fawns will not keep above a day or two at the furthest.

55. *Sucking Pigs*, the moment they are killed, should be put into cold water for a few minutes. Some persons then rub them over with powdered resin: others object to this on account of the flavour of the resin, which the pig will retain, if not well washed. Put the pig for half a minute into a pail or pan of boiling water, and take it out and pull off the hair or bristles as quickly as possible. If any should remain, put it again into hot water; when quite free from hair, wash it *thoroughly* with warm water, and then rinse it several times in cold water, that no flavour of the resin may remain. The feet should be taken off at the first joint: then make a slit down the belly and remove the entrails; once more wash the pig inside and out in cold water, and wrap it in a wet cloth till you are ready to dress it, which should be done as soon as possible. Fill the belly with seasoning, and sew it up; skewer back the legs, and the trussing is completed. The feet, heart, liver, lights, and melt, are to be dressed separately, when well cleaned. This dish is called pig's pettitoes.

56. *Fish*, in cleaning, should have every particle of the entrails very carefully removed. If the blood has settled down the back-bone, or elsewhere, it should be carefully taken away, and care should be taken not to break the gallbladder of the liver. Some fish must be slit in order to clean them; others may have their entrails drawn out at the gills, which should be always done when it is practicable. Mackerel, perch, &c. are cleaned in this way. Flat fish may be so

cleaned, but it is usual to make a slanting slit on one side, just below the gill, in order to put in the finger and remove the clotted blood from the back-bone. Fishes with scales should be scraped from the tail to the head, till all the scales are removed; others, such as soles and eels, are skinned. The cook ought not to depend upon the cleaning of fish by the fishmonger, but carefully examine them before dressing.

57. *Eels* are remarkably tenacious of life, and appear to suffer after they are cut into several pieces. In order to take the sense of feeling entirely from this fish, it is only necessary, before it is skinned, to pierce the spinal marrow, just at the back of the skull, right through, when all feeling in the eel will instantly cease, though it has the appearance of being alive. Then raise the skin, at the part cut or pierced, draw it back over the mouth and head, secure the head with a strong fork to a table, or dresser, and draw back the whole skin. To prevent the eel from slipping through your hands, rub them with salt, and you will then draw off the skin easily. Eels, except very small ones, require to be slit all the way from the vent to the gills, and the inside of the back-bone should be rubbed with salt. The liver, roe or melt, are much esteemed, and should be therefore preserved.

58. *Fish without Scales, &c.*—Cod, mackerel, whiting, and some other fish, being without scales, need nothing doing to them except drawing them and washing or wiping. Sprats, for broiling, should have a long bird-skewer run through their eyes, or a common knitting-needle. Neither sprats nor the silver-stringed herring, which is the best, should ever be drawn. They should be wiped dry and clean. Fish for frying, should not be washed if it be possible to avoid it. If they require washing, it should be done an hour or two before they are fried, and wrapped up in a coarse cloth till they are thoroughly dry.

59. *Turbot, Plaice, Flounders, &c.*, having been gutted and wiped, snould be sprinkled with salt, and hung up for several hours before dressing.

60. *Cod*, having been drawn and washed, will eat firmer if it be sprinkled with salt some time before putting it into the fish-kettle, with cold water, where it may remain an hour or two before boiling, or it may be hung up like plaice, &c.

61. *Oysters*, if fresh from the sea, that is, uncleansed by the fishmonger, should, as soon as received, be laid in a pan or tub, with the flat shell upwards, and the whole fish covered with spring water; to which put a pint of salt to every two gallons of water. In a few hours the fish will have cleansed themselves, and become fit for use. If they are required to be kept longer, the water should be taken away at night, and renewed in the morning; but they are never better than after they have been in the water from six to ten hours. There are persons who recommend that they should always be kept under water, which they say should be renewed every twelve hours. Such persons forget that oysters, in their natural state, are not under

water when the tide is out. Some writers recommend fresh water, but for what reason we know not, except to spoil the fish. Others order them to be sprinkled with flour, or oatmeal, for the purpose of making the fish white. We believe it has no such effect—much less will it feed them. Clear fresh spring water with a little salt, is the best; in this they will soon scour themselves, and become delicately white. Oysters should be opened very carefully—be turned round on the shell—the lower shell preserves the liquor best, and then served immediately; but they are better when eaten and opened at table. *Every moment the oyster is kept after it is opened, injures it in quality and flavour.* If served on the flat side of the shell, the liquor should be preserved and used for flavouring.—*N. B.* Oysters when taken fresh from the clean sea, that is, from beds devoid of mud, require no cleansing; but, on the contrary, we are assured on good authority, are much better without it. The process of cleansing deprives the fish of its flavour to a certain extent, and very much weakens the delicious liquor in the shell.

62. *Vegetables*, particularly green, in preparing for dressing, require great attention in point of cleanliness. If vegetables for boiling can be gathered perfectly clean, *immediately* before being put in the pot, they preserve their colour much better without washing. But this will seldom be the case, particularly with those purchased of the greengrocer. When they are a little stale, which is almost always the case, if not gathered in your own garden, putting them in water for a few hours will refresh them. Salt and water should be used for the purpose of bringing out the slugs, or caterpillars, in which summer cauliflowers and cabbage very often abound. Every drop of cold water, if possible, should be shaken out of them before boiling. Green peas, broad beans and French beans, ought not to be washed. Turnip greens, if quite clean and fresh, are better not washed; but if otherwise they must be washed through several waters.

63. *Asparagus, Artichokes, Spinach, &c.*—Scrape the stalks of asparagus clean, tie them up with tape, in bundles of twenty-five or thirty each; cut off the ends of the stalks to an equal length. If quite fresh they need not be washed. *Artichokes* require thorough washing, and should be soaked two hours or so in water before dressing. *Spinach* should be picked leaf by leaf; washed in three or four waters, and thoroughly drained. *Celery* should be well soaked.

64. *Potatoes* and *Jerusalem Artichokes* should be well scrubbed with a birch broom, besom, or scrubbing brush, and washed very clean just before boiling; but they should never be the least wetted till they are about to be dressed. Some persons like them best boiled in the skins; they are best peeled before boiling when they are old or specky.

65. *Carrots, Parsnips, Beetroots,* and *Turnips.*—Carrots and parsnips should be well washed and scrubbed, but not scraped, as it is apt to injure the flavour. After boiling, rub the skins with a coarse cloth. For soups, &c., they should be scraped. Beetroots should be washed and scrubbed very clean, but if the red sort be scraped, or cut

with a knife, the colour will escape. When done, carefully rub with a rough cloth. Wash and peel turnips.

Having given directions for the preparations for cooking, we now proceed to Cooking itself; and shall begin with

SOUPS AND BROTHS, &c.

In our general directions we have given pretty full instructions on the art of making broths, stews, &c., which instructions are of themselves sufficient to enable a young cook, possessed of diligence and common sense, to prepare the different varieties of these dishes, without the assistance of particular receipts. We give, however, the following.

66. *Clear Gravy Soups.*—Cut half a pound of ham into slices, and lay them at the bottom of a large stew-pan, or stock pot, with two or three pounds of veal and the same weight of lean beef; break the bones and lay them on the meat; pare two turnips and skin two large onions; wash clean, and cut into pieces two large carrots, two heads of celery; put in a large blade of mace, and three cloves; cover the stew-pan close, and set it over a clear fire; when the meat begins to stick at the bottom of the stew-pan, turn it, and when there is a nice brown glaze at the bottom of the stew-pan cover the meat with hot water; put in half a pint when it is coming to a boil; take off the scum, and put in half a pint more of cold water; then skim it again, and continue to do so till no more scum rises: now set it on one side of the fire to boil gently for four hours; strain through a clean tamis (do not squeeze it, or the soup will be thick) into a clean stone pan; let it remain till it is cold, then remove all the fat; when you bottle it, be careful not to disturb the settlings at the bottom of the pan. The broth should be of a fine amber colour, and very clear. If it is not quite as bright as you wish it, put it into a stew-pan; break two whites and the shells of eggs, mix well together and put them into the soup, set it on a quick fire, and stir it with a whisk till it boils, then set it on one side till it settles; run it through a fine napkin; then it is ready. If you skim your broth carefully as directed above, it will be clear enough; clarifying it impairs the flavour.—*Observe.* This is the basis of almost all gravy soups, which are called by the name of the vegetables that are put into them: carrots, turnips, onions, celery, and a few leaves of chervil, make what is called spring soup; to this a pint of green peas, or asparagus, or French beans cut into pieces, or a cabbage lettuce, is an improvement. With rice, Scotch barley, or vermicelli, maccaroni or celery, cut into lengths, it will be the soup usually called by those names. Or turnips scooped, round or young onions, will give you clear turnip or onion soup. The roots and vegetables used must be boiled first, or they will impregnate the soup with too strong a flavour. Seasoning for those soups is the same, viz. salt, and a very little cayenne pepper.

67. *Ox Tail Soup.*—Take three or four ox tails; divide at the joints; well wash, and soak them. Put them on the fire; to each

tail allow a quart of water; when they boil, take off all the scum. If four tails add four onions, and eight or ten corns of allspice and black pepper to each tail. Simmer it slowly till the meat on the bones is tender. Then take out the tails, scrape off all the meat and cut it small; strain the soup through a sieve. To thicken it, take two ounces of butter, and as much flour as it will take up; mix it well with the whole, and let it simmer another half hour. If not perfectly smooth, it must be strained again; then put in the meat, with a glass of wine, a table-spoonful of mushroom catsup, a little cayenne, and salt to taste; simmer it again a few minutes. Or instead of thickening the soup, the meat may be returned to the gravy and warmed again, with or without the addition of carrots and turnips.

68. *Hotch-potch.*—Take lamb or mutton chops, and stew them in good gravy, with the addition of almost every kind of vegetable. A summer hotch-potch is composed of young onions, carrots, asparagus, green peas, lettuce, turnips, spinach, and parsley; a winter one is composed of full-grown turnips cut small, old carrots cut small or grated, celery and onions sliced, dried peas—the green or blue sort are the best colours for this purpose. The peas will take much longer boiling than either meat or green vegetables. Put them in the liquor boiling, and let them boil an hour before the addition of meat, and the other vegetables. The proportion is four pounds of meat to a gallon of stock, and two quarts of vegetables. Boil the meat and vegetables between two and three hours, slow boiling, with the lid on. If you add green peas or asparagus tops among the vegetables, keep out nearly all of them till within half an hour of sending them to table; then let them boil fast till tender. Season with salt and pepper, and serve all together. Some people make it of brisket of beef, and add a bunch of sweet herbs. The beef will require stewing longer. A leg of beef, cut in pieces, and stewed six or seven hours, with carrots and the other ingredients, makes very good soup. A little small beer is an improvement to all brown soups.

69. *Fish Broth.*—Thick-skinned fish, and those which have glutinous, jelly-like substances, are the best. The liquor which eels have been boiled in is good enough of itself, as they require but little water. The liquor in which turbot or cod has been boiled, boil again, with the addition of the bones. If purposely made, small eels, or grigs, or flat fish, as flounders, soles, plaice or dabs, or the finny parts of cod, will do for the purpose. A pound of fish to three pints of water; add peppercorns, a large handful of parsley, and an onion; and boil till reduced to half. A spoonful of catsup, or vinegar, is an improvement. This broth is very nourishing and easy of digestion; but for a sick person, leave out the catsup or vinegar.

70. *Cock-a-leeky Soup.*—Take a small knuckle of veal, and a large fowl, or a scrag of mutton instead of veal. An old fowl will do. Add three or four large leeks, cut in pieces of half an inch long. Simmer in three quarts of good broth for an hour. Then add as many more leeks, and season with pepper and salt. Let it boil three-quarters of an hour longer, and serve all together. The leeks which are put

in first, is with the intention of thickening the soup; and those which are put in last, should retain their form and substance.

71. *Scotch Brose*, or *Crowdy*.—Take half a pint of oatmeal; put it before the fire, and frequently turn it till it is perfectly dry and of a light brown. Take a ladle-full of boiling water, in which fat meat has been boiled, and stir it briskly to the oatmeal, still adding more liquor till it is brought to the thickness desired, which is about that of a stiff batter; a little salt and pepper may be added, if the liquor with which it was made was not salt. Kale brose is the same thing, but with the addition of greens, cut small, and boiled in the liquor.

72. *Pease Soup.*--Put a quart of split peas to three quarts of boiling water, not more (Dr. Kitchiner says cold water,) with half a pound of bacon, not very fat, or roast beef bones, or four anchovies; or, instead of water, the liquor in which beef, mutton, pork or poultry, has been boiled; it will be very much better, but taste the liquor, as it must not be too salt. Wash two heads of celery, cut small (half a drachm of celery seed, pounded fine, and put into the soup, a quarter of an hour before it is finished, will flavour three quarts,) two onions peeled, and a sprig of savoury, or sweet marjoram, or lemon thyme. Let it simmer very gently, stirring it every quarter of an hour, to keep the peas from sticking to or burning at the bottom of the pot. Simmer till the peas are tender, which will be in about three hours. Some cooks now slice a head of celery and half an ounce of onions, and fry them in a little batter, and put them into the soup, till it is lightly browned; then work the whole through coarse hair sieve, and then through a fine sieve, or through a tamis, with the back of a wooden spoon; then put it into a clean stew-pan, with a tea-spoonful of ground black pepper; let it boil again for ten minutes, and if any fat arises skim it off. Send up on a plate some toasted bread, cut into little pieces, an inch square; or cut a slice of bread (that has been baked two days) into dice, not more than half an inch square; put half a pound of quite clean dripping, or lard, into an iron frying-pan; when it is hot fry the bread; take care to turn the bread with a slice, that it may be of a delicate brown on both sides; take it up with a fish-slice, and lay it on a sheet of paper to drain the fat; be careful that this is done nicely. Send them up in one side dish, and dried and powdered mint, or savoury, in another. The most economical method of making pease soup, is to save the bones of a joint of roast beef, and put them into the liquor in which mutton, or beef, or pork, or poultry, has been boiled, and proceed as in the first receipt. A hock or shank bone of ham, a ham bone, the root of a tongue, or a red or pickled herring, are favourite additions with some people; others send up rice or vermicelli with pease soup. Pease soup may be made savoury and agreeable to the palate, without any meat, by putting two ounces of fresh and nicely clarified beef, mutton, or pork dripping, with two ounces of oatmeal, and mix this well into a gallon of soup prepared with the peas and vegetables, according to the first receipt, or in water alone.

73. *Pease Soup and Pickled Pork*.—Take two pounds of pickled

pork, which will make very good broth for pease soup; if the pork is too salt, put it in water on the over-night. The pork should not be in salt more than two days. Put on the articles, mentioned in the first receipt, in three quarts of water; boil these gently for two hours; then put in the pork, and boil gently for an hour and a half, or two hours, according to the thickness of the pork; when done, wash the pork clean in some hot water; send it up in a dish, or cut it into little pieces, and put them into the tureen, with the toasted bread, &c., or as in the first receipt. The meat being boiled no longer than to be done enough to eat, you can get excellent soup without the expense of any other meat.

74. *Plain Pease Soup.*—To a quart of split peas, and two heads of celery, and a large onion, put three quarts of broth, or soft water; let them simmer gently over a slow fire for three hours. Stir them up every quarter of an hour, to prevent the peas sticking at the bottom of the pot, and burning.

75. *Spanish Soup.*—Take about three pounds of beef, off the leg or shin, with or without the bone—if with the bone, well crack it—a pound of knuckle of ham, or gammon. More than cover them with water, and when it boils skim it, and add a tea-spoonful of pepper. The ham will probably make it sufficiently salt—if not, add a little. Let this simmer by the side of the fire until it is three parts done, which will take two hours and a half. And then well wash some cabbage plants, or small summer cabbage; cut these into small pieces, also onions cut small; a tea-cup full of rice, with a bit of eschalot; put these in the saucepan, and let it simmer a quarter of an hour or twenty minutes, until the rice is boiled enough. Then take it from the fire; separate the meat, vegetables, and rice, from the soup, and eat the soup before the meat. Separate the meat from the bones, and mix it with the vegetables. If the plants are too strong, scald them before putting them in the saucepan. In the summer, a few young peas make a great improvement. Leeks are better than onions, as you can have more in quantity of vegetables. The Spaniards use garlic. This will dine a family of seven or eight people.

76. *Chicken Broth.*—Chicken bones, and the heads and feet, make a basin of good broth, provided the fowls have been boiled, and the liquor used instead of water. The heads and feet of four fowls may be boiled in a quart of water, with the addition of an onion and a blade of mace, a little pepper and salt. Chicken broth may be enriched by the addition of a knuckle bone of veal, a bit of beef, or three or four shank bones of mutton.

77. *Mutton Broth.*—Scrags of mutton, or sheeps' heads, make a very good family dinner. Two or three scrags of mutton, or two sheeps' heads, may be put on in a two-gallon pot; when it boils, skim it well, then add six ounces of Scotch or pearl barley, or rice; let it boil an hour or more; then add eight or ten turnips, three or four carrots, cut up, and four or five onions. Half an hour before serving, put in a few small suet dumplings, a little parsley, and a few marigold blossoms. This broth should boil two hours and a half, or three hours.

The knuckle of a shoulder of mutton answers very well in this manner. Serve the meat on separate dish, and the broth, dumplings, and vegetables, all together in a large tureen.

78. *Mutton Chop Broth.*—Cut the chops from a neck or loin of mutton; cut as much as is required into thin chops; put them in a stew-pan, with an onion or two, a little salt, and cold water enough to cover them. Skim well when it boils, and let it stew slowly three-quarters of an hour, or an hour. Turnips may be boiled in this liquor, or boiled separately, and mashed. Serve the broth and meat together. In broth intended for invalids, the vegetables and spice should be left out.

79. *Soup and Bouilli.*—For the bouilli, roll five pounds of brisket of beef tight with a tape, put it into a stew-pan; four pounds of the leg of beef; about seven or eight quarts of water; boil these up quick; scum it; add one large onion, six or seven cloves, some whole pepper, two or three carrots, a turnip or two, a leek, two heads of celery; stew them very gently, closely covered, for six or seven hours; about an hour before dinner, strain the soup through a piece of flannel (put the rough side upwards,) or a hair sieve; have ready boiled carrots and turnips sliced, spinach, a little chervil, and sorrel, two heads of endive, one or two of celery, cut in pieces. Put the soup into a tureen. The carrots and turnips in separate dishes; add a little salt and cayenne to the soup. Take the tape from the bouilli very carefully, and serve in a dish. A leg or shin of beef, with a piece of fat beef, will answer the purpose.

80. *A Cheap Soup.*—Two pounds of lean beef, six onions, six potatoes (parboiled,) one carrot, one turnip, half a pint of split peas, four quarts of water, some whole pepper, a head of celery, a red herring; when boiled, rub through a coarse sieve, add spinach and celery boiled, dried mint, and fried bread.

81. *Veal Soup.*—Cut the meat off in thin slices; put the meat in a large jug or jar; put to it a bunch of sweet herbs, half an ounce of almonds, blanched, and beat fine; pour on it four quarts of boiling water; cover it close, and let it stand all night by the fire; the next day, put it into an earthen vessel; let it stew very slowly till it is reduced to two quarts; take off the scum as it rises while boiling, and let it stand to settle; then pour it clear off, and put it into a clean saucepan; mix with three ounces of either boiled rice or vermicelli.

82. *Calf's Head Soup.*—Take a calf's head, wash it clean, stew it with a bunch of sweet herbs, an onion stuck with cloves, mace, pearl barley, and Jamaica pepper; when it is very tender, put to it some stewed celery; season it with pepper; and serve it with the head in the middle.

83. *Giblet Soup.*—The most economical way is to take a pound or two of beef skirts, or of knuckle of veal; cut it into pieces two or three inches square; a set of goose giblets, or four sets of ducks', or the head, neck, and feet, of a turkey or two, or of six or eight fowls; all of these are good, either separate or together. Clean them well, split the heads, cut the gizzards across, crack the pinions and feet

bones. Put all together into a stew-pan, with an ounce of butter; the red part of two or three carrots cut up, two or three onions sliced, and a clove or two of eschalots. Shake it over a clear slow fire a few minutes, to draw the gravy, then add water or broth enough to cover the whole; let it simmer two hours or more, then season with salt and pepper, and a large spoonful of catsup, and serve all together. It may be thickened with rice or barley, which should be added as soon as it boils.—A more expensive way: Prepare the giblets as above and set them on with good gravy, enough to cover them; tie in a muslin bag an onion or two, a small bundle of sweet herbs, a few leaves of sweet basil, and twenty corns of allspice, the same of black pepper. Let it simmer till the giblets are tender, then take them out and cover up close while you thicken the gravy; remove also the bag of spice and herbs. Make some force meat balls as follows: when the livers are done enough to chop fine, take them out or part of them, pound them fine with half their weight in butter, and the yolks of three hard-boiled eggs; season with salt, cayenne, nutmeg, sage, and onions, scalded and chopped very fine, and also a leaf or two of sweet basil. Mix with half a tea-cup full of bread crumbs, wet with the yolk of an egg, and make up into little balls with a little flour. Having removed the giblets, thicken the soup with butter and flour, and when it boils add the balls; let them simmer a quarter of an hour, then add a glass of wine, a large table-spoonful of catsup, and the juice of half a Seville orange or lemon. Put in the giblets to warm through, and it is ready.

84. *Kitchiner's cheap Soup.*—Wash in cold water four ounces of Scotch barley, and put into five quarts of water, with four ounces of sliced onions; boil gently one hour, and pour it into a pan; then put into a saucepan from one to two ounces of fresh beef or mutton dripping. Dripping for this purpose should be taken out of the pan as fast as it drips from the meat; if suffered to remain in the pan it is apt to become rancid. If no dripping is at hand, melted suet will do, or two or three ounces of fat bacon minced fine. When melted in the saucepan, stir into it four ounces of oatmeal, and rub them together until they become a soft paste. Then add, by degrees, a spoonful at a time, the barley broth, stirring it well together till it boils. For seasoning, put in a tea-cup or basin a drachm of celery or cress seed, or half a drachm of each, and a quarter of a drachm of cayenne, finely powdered, or a drachm and a half of black pepper finely powdered, or half allspice; mix them smooth with a little of the soup; then stir it into the rest; simmer it gently another quarter of an hour, season with salt, and it is ready. The flavour may be varied by any variety of herbs, or thickening with garlic or eschalot instead of celery; a larger portion of onions, or carrots and turnips, or rice, or paste, instead of oatmeal or barley.

85. *Soup Maigre.*—Divide two or three heads of celery, two large carrots, three or four moderate-sized turnips, some onions, two young lettuces, a handful of spinach leaves, and a little sorrel. Cut the worst half of the vegetables in small pieces, and put them into the

stew-pan with three ounces of butter; let them fry till the vegetables are brown and the butter absorbed; put a gallon of boiling water into the pan; when it boils fast, skim it well, stir in a little flour, and add some stale crust of bread; put in two dozen of black peppers, and the same of allspice, with two or three blades of mace; let it simmer for an hour and a half, then set it aside for a quarter of an hour, then strain it off very gently, so as not to disturb the settlings at the bottom of the stew-pan, which clean. When the soup has stood two hours, pour it back again, avoiding to disturb any sediment, if any should escape from the first draining. Cut up the remainder of the vegetables and boil them in water five minutes, then drain them, and when the soup again boils, add them to it, and let it simmer till they are tender, which will be about three-quarters of an hour; season with salt, cayenne, and a table-spoonful of catsup. If green peas are in season, the liquor in which they have been boiled, added to the soup, is a great improvement.

86. *Mock Turtle.*—Have the head and broth ready for the soup the day before it is to be eaten; it will take eight hours to prepare it properly. Get the calf's head with the skin on, the fresher the better, take out the brains and wash the head several times in cold water, let it soak in spring water for an hour, then lay it in the stew-pan, cover it with cold water, and half a gallon over; as it becomes warm a great deal of scum will rise, which must be immediately removed; let it boil gently for one hour, then take it up. When almost cold cut the head into pieces about an inch and a half long and an inch and a quarter broad; the tongue into mouthfuls, or rather make a side dish of the tongue and brains. When the head is taken out, put in about five pounds of knuckle of veal, and as much beef; add to the stock all the trimmings and bones of the head; skim it well, then cover it close, let it boil five hours; reserve two quarts of this to make gravy sauce, then strain it off and let it stand till the next morning; then take off the fat, put a large stew-pan on the fire, with half a pound of good fresh butter, twelve ounces of onions sliced, four ounces of green sage chopped; let these fry one hour; rub in half a pound of flour by degrees, add your broth till it is the thickness of cream; season it with a quarter of an ounce of ground allspice and half an ounce of black pepper, ground very fine, salt to your taste, add the rind of one lemon peeled very thin; let it simmer very gently for one hour and a half, then strain it through a hair sieve, do not rub your soup to get it through the sieve or it will make it grouty; if it do not run through easily, knock a wooden spoon against the side of the sieve; put it into a clean stew-pan with the head, and season by adding, to each gallon of soup, half a pint of wine, Madeira, or claret if you wish it dark; two table-spoonfuls of lemon juice, the same of catsup, one of essence of anchovy, a tea-spoonful of curry powder, or a quarter of a drachm of cayenne, the peel of a lemon pared very thin. Let it simmer gently till the meat is tender; this may take from half an hour to an hour; take care that it is not over-done; stir it frequently to prevent the meat sticking to the bottom of the stew-pan;

when the meat is quite done, take out the lemon peel, and the soup is ready. Serve with force meat stuffing, or balls.

87. *Carrot Soup.*—Wash and scrape six large carrots, peel off the red outside (which is the only part used for this soup), put it into a gallon stew-pan, with one head of celery, and an onion cut into thin pieces; take two quarts of veal, beef, or mutton broth, put the broth to the roots, cover the stew-pan close, and set it on a slow stove for two hours and a half, when the carrots will be soft enough; put in a tea-cup full of bread crumbs, boil for two or three minutes, rub it through a tamis, or hair sieve, with a wooden spoon, add broth, and make it nearly as thick as pease soup; season it with a little salt, and send it up with some toasted bread, cut into pieces half an inch square. The celery and onions should be sliced and fried in butter, or nicely clarified dripping, and then put in the stew-pan and the broth added to it. Or thus: Put some beef bones with four quarts of liquor in which a leg of mutton or beef has been boiled, two large onions, a turnip, pepper and salt, into a stew-pan, and stew for three hours; have ready six large carrots scraped, and cut thin; strain the soup on them, stew them till soft enough to pulp through a hair sieve, or a coarse cloth; then boil the pulp with the soup, which is to be as thick as pease soup. Make the soup the day before it is to be used; add cayenne. Pulp only the red part of the carrot, and not the yellow. The soup is better made with a shin of beef.

88. *Curry or Mulligatawny Soup.*—Cut four pounds of a breast of veal into pieces about two inches long and one inch broad; put the trimmings into a stew-pan with two quarts of water, with twelve corns of black pepper, and the same of allspice; when it boils skim it clean, and let it boil an hour and a half; then strain it off; while it is boiling, fry of a nice brown in butter the bits of veal, and four onions; when they are done put the broth to them, put it on the fire; when it boils skim it clean, let it simmer half an hour, then mix two spoonfuls of curry, and the same of flour, with a little cold water, and a tea-spoonful of salt; add these to the soup, and simmer it till the veal is quite tender, and it is ready; or bone a couple of fowls or rabbits, and stew them the same as veal, and you may put in a bruised eschalot, and some mace and ginger, instead of black pepper and allspice. The fowls and rabbits should be cut into joints, and fried of a nice brown in some batter.

89. *Eel Soup.*—To make a tureen full, take two middling sized onions, cut them in half, and cross your knife over them two or three times; put two ounces of butter into a stew-pan; when it is melted, put in the onions, stir them in the pan till they are of a light brown; cut into pieces three pounds of unskinned eels, put them into your stew-pan, and shake them over the fire for five minutes; then add three quarts of boiling water, and when they boil, take the scum off very clean, and then put in a quarter of an ounce of the green leaves (not dried) of winter savoury, the same of lemon-thyme, and twice the quantity of parsley, two drachms of allspice, the same of black pepper; cover it close, and let it boil gently for two hours, skim it

clean and strain it off. To thicken it, put three ounces of butter into a clean stew-pan; when it is melted stir in as much flour as will make it of a thick paste, then add the liquid by degrees, let it simmer for ten minutes, and pass it through a sieve, then put your soup on in a clean stew-pan, and have ready some little square pieces of fried fish of nice light brown—either eels, soles, plaice, or skate, will do, the fried fish should be added about ten minutes before the soup is served up. Force meat balls are sometimes added. Excellent fish-soup may be made of cod's head, or skate, or flounders, boiled in no more water than will cover them, and the liquor thickened with oatmeal, &c.

90. *Gourd Soup* should be made of full-grown gourds, but not those that have hard skins; slice three or four, and put them into a stew-pan with two or three onions and a good bit of butter, set them over a slow fire till quite tender, be careful not to let them burn; then add two ounces of crust of bread, and two quarts of good consommé, season with salt and cayenne pepper; boil ten minutes or a quarter of an hour, skim off all the fat, and pass it through a tamis when quite hot. Serve up with fried bread.

91. *Game Soup.*—In the game season it is easy to make very good soup at a little expense, by taking all the meat off the breasts of any cold birds that have been left on the preceding day, and pound it in a mortar; beat to pieces the legs and bones, and boil in some broth for an hour; boil six turnips, and mash them and strain them through a tamis cloth, with the meat that has been pounded in a mortar; strain your broth and put a little of it at a time into the tamis to help you to strain all of it through. Put your soup kettle near the fire, but do not let it boil. When ready to dish your dinner, have six yolks of eggs mixed with half a pint of cream, then strain it through a sieve; put your soup on the fire, and as it is coming to boil, put in the eggs, and stir it well with a wooden spoon. Do not let it boil, or it will curdle.

92. *Turnip and Parsnip Soups* are made the same as carrot soup.

93. *Celery Soup.*—Split six heads of celery into slips about two inches long; wash them well, lay them on a hair sieve to drain, and put them into three quarts of gravy soup in a gallon soup pot; set it by the side of the fire to stew very gently till the celery is tender—this will take about an hour; if any scum rises, take it off. Season it with a little salt. When celery cannot be procured, half a drachm of the seed pounded fine may be considered as the essence of celery, which may be had very cheap, and can be bought at any season; put this in about a quarter of an hour before the soup is done, and a little sugar will give as much flavour to half a gallon of soup as two heads of celery—or add a little essence of celery.

94. *Lamb Stew.*—Take a lamb's head and lights, and wash them; remove all the bones and skin from the nose, put them in the pot with some beef stock made with three quarts of water and two pounds of shin of beef, strained; boil very slowly for an hour, wash and string two or three good handfuls of spinach, put it in twenty minutes before

SOUPS AND BROTHS, &C. 47

serving, add one or two onions and a little parsley a short time before it comes off the fire; season with salt and pepper, and it is ready. Serve all together in a tureen.

95. *Hare, Rabbit, or Partridge Soup.*—When hares and rabbits and other game are too tough to eat (in the ordinary way of cooking,) they will make very good soup. Cut off the legs and shoulders of a hare, divide the body crossways, and stew very gently in three quarts of water, with one carrot, about one ounce of onions, two blades of pounded mace, four cloves, twenty-four black peppers, and a bundle of sweet herbs; stew it till the hare is tender. Most cooks add to the above two slices of ham or bacon, and a bay leaf, but the hare makes sufficiently savoury soup without this addition. The time this will take depends upon the age and time it has been kept before it is dressed; as a general rule, about three hours. Make a dozen and a half of force meat balls, as big as nutmegs. When hare is tender, take the meat off the back and upper joints of the legs; cut it into mouthfuls, and put on one side; cut the rest of the meat off the legs, shoulders, &c., mince it and pound it in a mortar with an ounce of butter, and two or three table-spoonfuls of flour moistened with a little soup; rub this through a hair sieve, and put it into the soup to thicken it; let it simmer for half an hour longer, skim it well, and put it through the tamis in the pan again; put the meat in, a glass of port or claret wine, with a table-spoonful of currant jelly to each quart of soup. Season it with salt; put in the force meat balls, and when all is hot, the soup is ready.

96. *Portable Soup.*—The fresher the meat is from which this article is made the better. Shins or legs of beef answer very well, and you may add trimmings of fresh meat, poultry, or game, and the liquor in which a leg of mutton, or a knuckle of veal, has been boiled. No salt, on any account, must be used. If you have a digester, it should be used for this article, in preference to a closely covered stew-pan, but the latter will do. Just cover the meat with cold liquor, and let an hour at least be occupied in coming to boil. Skim it, and throw in cold water two or three times, for the purpose of throwing up the scum, which must be carefully removed. When thoroughly cleared of the scum, close the vessel, and let it boil for eight or ten hours. Strain through a hair sieve into an earthenware pan, and let the liquor cool. The meat will do for potting. Every particle of fat must be removed from the top, and the gravy put into a well-tinned copper stew-pan, taking care that the sediment is separated from it; put in two drachms of whole black pepper, and let it boil briskly with the lid off over a quick fire. The scum, if any, should of course be removed. When it becomes very thick, and is reduced to about a quart, put it into a smaller stew-pan, set it over a gentle fire, and let it simmer till reduced to the consistence of very thick syrup. It must now be watched every moment. Take out a few drops on a cold spoon or plate; if it soon sets into a stiff jelly, it is done enough. If not, boil it little longer till it does. Have ready some small pots with lids, such as are used for potting meat; or it may be poured out

on a large flat dish, so as to be a quarter of an inch deep; when cold, turn it out, and, with a paste cutter, divide into squares of half an ounce or an ounce each. Or pour it into the round parts of basins or cups turned upside down. Put them in a warm room, and turn them frequently for eight or ten days, then they will be thoroughly dry and hardened like glue. Put them in a tin box, or a glass case, in a dry place, and they will keep for years. If at any time the surface appears mouldy, wipe it off, or the taste will penetrate the mass. The chief use of this article is in country places, or at sea, where fresh meat cannot be obtained. A basin of broth, soup or gravy of any strength, may be had in five minutes, by dissolving one or more of these cakes in boiling water; any flavouring ingredients may be added at pleasure. See Flavouring.

97. *Green Turtle Soup.*—This recipe has been collated from the best authorities, to which is added our own experience. The day before you wish to serve up the soup it will be necessary to cut off the head of your turtle, and place it in a position to allow all the blood to be drained from it. The next morning open the turtle, being careful to do so without breaking the gall. After cutting all around the upper and lower shell, drain the water off, divide the meat in small pieces, and wash clean and carefully. Then put the shells in a large pot of boiling water, where you let them remain until you find they separate from the flesh readily; but no longer, as the softer parts must be boiled again. Keep the liquor and stew the bones thoroughly; after which it is to be used for moistening the broth. The flesh of the interior parts, and the four legs and head, must be cooked in the following manner. Mask the bottom of a large stew-pan with slices of ham, over which lay two or three knuckles of veal, according to the size of the turtle; and over the veal place the inside flesh of the turtle, covering the whole with the other parts of the turtle. Add to it about a gallon of the liquor in which the bones were stewed, and place on the fire until thoroughly done, which you must ascertain by sticking your knife into the fleshy part of the meat; and if no blood issue from it, add another gallon of the liquor. Then throw in a bunch of the stalks of sweet marjoram, lemon thyme, bay leaves, savoury, common thyme, and sweet basil; also a handful of parsley and green onions, and a large onion stuck with cloves, and a few grains of pepper. Let the whole stew until thoroughly done, say from three to four hours. The leaves of the herbs are to be used for making a sauce, to be described hereafter. When the larger portions of the turtle are done, place them aside to be used when wanted. When the flesh is also thoroughly done, drain on a dish, and make a white thickening very thin, and add to it through a tamis some portion of the liquor of the bones, and place on the fire until it boils; and, having arrived at the proper consistency, neither too thick nor too thin, set the stewpan on the side of the stove, and skim off all the white scum and fat that arises to the surface. Then cut the softer parts—green fat and white meat—into dice of about an inch square (without any waste,) and add to the sauce, which must be allowed to simmer gently until

sufficiently done, when it must be taken off, at the same time skimming it carefully. Then take the leaves of the sweet basil, sweet marjoram, lemon thyme, common thyme and winter savoury, together with a handful of parsley, some green onions, a large onion cut in four pieces, with a few leaves of mace ; put the whole in a stew-pan with a quarter of a pound of butter. Let this simmer on a slow fire until melted, and add a bottle of Madeira and a small lump of sugar, and boil gently for an hour. Then rub it through a tamis, and add to your sauce, which you must boil until no white scum arises; then with a skimmer drain out all the bits of turtle, and put them into a clean stew-pan, and pass the sauce through a tamis into the stew-pan containing the turtle, and proceed as follows. Take out the fleshy part of a leg of veal, say about one pound, scrape off all the meat without leaving any of the fat or sinews in it, and soak in about the same quantity (one pound) of crumbs of bread, which, when well soaked, squeeze and put into a mortar with the veal, a small quantity of calf's udder, a little butter, the yolks of four eggs hard boiled, a little cayenne pepper, salt and spices, and pound the whole very fine. Then thicken the mixture with two whole eggs, and the yolk of a third ; and, to try its consistency, put it in boiling hot water; if you find it too thin, add the yolk of another egg. When it is perfected, take one half of it, and add some chopped parsley. Cook it and roll into balls the size of the yolk of an egg ; poach them in boiling water with a little salt. The other half must be made also into balls, and place the whole on a sieve to drain. Before serving your soup, squeeze the juice of two or three lemons, with a little cayenne pepper, and pour it into the soup. The fins may be served as a side dish, with a little turtle sauce. When lemon juice is used, be careful that the lemons are good; a musty lemon will spoil all the turtle, and too much will destroy its flavour.

98. *Irish Stew.*—Take two pounds of potatoes; peel and slice, and parboil, and throw away the water; rather more than two pounds of mutton chops, either from the loin or neck; part of the fat should be taken off; beef two pounds, six large onions sliced, a slice of ham, or lean bacon, a spoonful of pepper, and two of salt. This stew may be done in a stew-pan over the fire, or in a baker's oven, or in a close covered earthen pot. First put a layer of potatoes, then a layer of meat and onions, sprinkle the seasoning, then a layer of potatoes, and again the meat and onions and seasoning; the top layer should be potatoes, and the vessel should be quite full. Then put in half a pin of good gravy, and a spoonful of mushroom catsup. Let the whol stew for an hour and a half; be very careful it does not burn.

BROTHS OR STOCKS, GLAZE AND GRAVIES.

These articles are all nearly allied to each other, differing principally in degrees of strength. In extensive establishments, a large quantity of stock, both brown and white, is constantly kept. Stocks are distinguished by the names of first stock, or long broth,—in the

French kitchen, "*le grand bouillon*"—second stock, in French, "*jus de bœuf*,"—and jelly stock, in French, "*consommé.*" In preparing a regular dinner, they will all be found exceedingly useful. The materials for the making of stocks will not cost much, if the cook does her duty. In such case, she will take great care of all the trimmings of meat, and the necks, heads, gizzards, feet, &c., of game and poultry. Boiled and roast meat gravy not used ought to be carefully collected and kept. The author of "*The Housekeeper's Guide*," says, "We should recommend the cook when she sets away after the dinner the meat on clean dishes, to collect in one basin every drop of roast meat gravy; in another, every drop of boiled meat gravy; and in another, every little bit of trimming of dressed meat, and pour over it some hot liquor, in which meat has been boiled, or hot water. Next morning, when she prepares meat for dressing, let her collect all the little trimming bits, and boil them with the liquor and bits set by the day before. This may be done before the fire is wanted for other purposes. Thus she will always have gravy in store for every emergency. Then if she have white sauce to prepare, such as celery or oyster sauce, parsley and butter, or caper sauce, the cold boiled meat gravy (which she will most likely find a stiff jelly) will form an excellent basis for it, much more rich and relishing than water. If she wants good brown gravy for roast meat, or fried, the cold roast meat gravy will enrich and colour the stock or store gravy, with the addition of any flavouring that may be required. Good managers, who attend to this every day, do not know what it is to be distressed for gravy, or running to the butcher's for gravy beef." The cook, we must add, should be careful to have her broth or stock clear, and devoid of fat, which, eaten by itself, that is, unincorporated with farinaceous or vegetable substances, is very indigestible, yielding little or no nourishment, but when so incorporated, fat becomes very nutritious and wholesome—more so indeed, according to some writers, than lean meat.

99. *First Stock*, or *Beef Broth, &c.*—Wash a leg or shin of beef very clean; let the butcher crack the bone in two or three places, and take out the marrow; add meat trimmings, and heads, necks, gizzards, feet, &c., of game and poultry; cover them with cold water; watch and stir up well, and the moment the simmering commences skim it very clear of all the scum. Then add some cold water, which will make the remaining scum rise, and skim it again. No fat should enter into the composition of broth of this description, nor indeed of any other, unless incorporated with meal by way of thickening. Stock should be quite clear and limpid. When the surface of the broth is quite clear, put in carrots, turnips, celery, and onions, according to the quantity. Some persons direct one moderate sized carrot, a head of celery, two turnips, and two onions. But this is a very poor criterion as to the quantity which ought to be used of these vegetables, which differ so much in size. No taste of sweet herbs, spice, &c., should be given to the stock. After the vegetables are added, cover it close, and set it by the side of the fire, and let it sim-

BROTHS OR STOCKS, GLAZE, &C.

mer very gently, not wasting the broth, for four or five hours, or more, according to the weight of the meat. Strain through a sieve into a clean, dry stone pan, and put it in a cold place, for use. This is the basis for all sorts of soup and sauce, whether brown or white. The meat may be used for immediate food, or for making potted beef —that is, if it be not overdone to rags.

100. The following method has been adopted in the kitchen of the reviser for several years past, and is inserted as being more concise than the English plan: — Put in a large boiler, of the capacity of six or seven gallons, two large skins of beef; a small piece of the rump of about five pounds; five gallons of water, and two handsf.[1] of salt; place the pot on the fire, and before it commences to boil, and whilst boiling, skim it carefully and frequently, adding a little cold water to bring up the scum completely. When you find no more scum rising to the top, add three large carrots, three turnips, and three onions with six cloves stuck in them (that is, two cloves in each onion), and let it boil for four or five hours. Before using it, skim all the fat off the top, and strain it through a double sieve. If the beef is to be used, let it be taken out of the pot when cooked, and pour over it a little of the top of the broth, to keep it moist until it may be wanted, when you can serve it with such sauce as you may fancy. For a family it will be necessary to make the broth about once a week, but great care should be taken to keep a portion always on hand.

101. *Second Stock* may be made from the meat left after straining the first stock off, by covering it with water, and by letting it go on boiling for four or five hours. This stock will produce good glaze, or portable soup (see 316).

102. *Glaze* is a strong gravy boiled as quick as possible till it thickens, as directed in braising (see 316).

103. *Beef Gravy*, sometimes called second stock, or in French *jus de bœuf*, is thus made:—Take a slice of good lean ham, or lean bacon, four or five pounds of gravy beef, cut into eight or ten pieces, a carrot, an onion with two cloves stuck in it, and a head of celery. Cover the bottom of a clean well-tinned stew-pan with these things, putting in the ham first, and then put a pint of stock, or water; cover close; set over a moderate fire till the water is so reduced as to just save the ingredients from burning, then turn it all about and let it brown slightly and equally all over. You must put in three quarts of boiling water just at the moment the meat has obtained its proper colour; if it is suffered to burn, the gravy will have a bad taste, and if the water is put in too soon the gravy will want flavour. When it boils up, skim carefully and clean the sides of the stew-pan with a cloth. The gravy ought to be delicately clean and clear. Set it by the side of a fire, and stew gently for about four hours; strain through a tamis sieve, skim it carefully, and put it in a cold place. If well managed, that is, not boiled too fast, it will yield two quarts of good gravy.

104. *Gravy for Roast Meat.*—Take the trimmings off the joint you are about to cook, which will make half a pint of plain gravy. Colour by adding a few drops of burnt sugar. If you do not wish to

52 THE COMPLETE COOK.

make gravy in this way, about half an hour before the meat is done mix a salt-spoonful of salt with a full quarter of a pint of boiling water: drop this by degrees on the brown parts of the meat, set a dish under to catch it, and set it by; the meat will soon brown again. When the gravy you have made is cold take the fat from the surface, and when the meat is done, warm up the gravy and put it in the dish. Or you may make good browning for roast meat by saving the brown bits of boiling or roast meat: cut them small, put them into a basin and cover them with boiling water, and put them away; next put them into a saucepan and boil two or three minutes, then strain it through a sieve, and put by for use. When you want gravy for use put two table-spoonsful in a quarter of a pint of boiling water, with a little salt. If for roasted veal, put three table-spoonsful into half a pint of thin melted butter. The gravy which remains in the dish after the family has dined should be put by to enrich hashes or little made dishes.

105. *Gravy for Boiled Meat* is nothing more than a tea-cup full of the liquor in which the meat has been boiled, carefully skimmed and free from fat.

106. *Gravy for Roast Veal.* — Make in the same way as for any other roast meat, and make a tea-cup full of thick melted butter, or melt the butter in the gravy. The same gravy for target or loin of lamb.

107. *Rich brown Gravy for Poultry, Ragout, or Game.*—If your stock or store gravy is poor, to enrich it add one pound of meat to one pint of your store gravy; cut the meat clear from the bones, chop it up as fine as mince meat, chop also one ounce of ham, or gammon, unless you have by you the gravy that has settled in the dish from a ham. Lay at the bottom of the stew-pan one ounce of butter, an onion sliced, and the chopped meat; cover it close, and set it on a clear, slow fire; move it about to prevent it sticking. When the gravy draws, and the meat is rather brown, add by degrees the liquor; when it boils, put in the bones of the meat, chickens' head and feet; and when it boils again carefully skim it. Add a crust of bread toasted brown, a sprig of winter savoury, or lemon thyme and parsley, a dozen berries of allspice, a strip of lemon peel, and a dozen black peppercorns; cover it close and keep it boiling gently till it is reduced to half; when cold, take off all the fat and thicken it with the following thickening: Melt a piece of butter in a saucepan; take out all the buttermilk that may be at the top, then sprinkle flour into it, shaking it all the time: make it a thick paste, and stir this into your gravy boiling.

SAUCES.

These are a very numerous class of condiments, particularly in French cookery. Foreigners say that the English have only one sauce (melted butter) for vegetables, fish, flesh, and all other eatables requiring sauce — and they add, with some truth, that they seldom make it good. It certainly is a very general sauce, botn in England and the United States; and, therefore, we shall begin our recipes with

108. *Melted Butter* cannot be made good with mere flour and water. Dr. Kitchiner says, that he has tried every way of making this sauce, and gives it as his opinion that the following, if carefully observed, will be always found to give satisfaction: Cut two ounces of butter into little bits, put it into a clean stew-pan, with a large teaspoonful of flour, arrow-root, or potatoe starch, and add two tablespoonsful of milk; when thoroughly mixed, add six table-spoonsful of water, hold it over the fire, and shake it round the *same way* every minute, till it begins to simmer; then let it boil up. This is a good recipe for melted butter where it is not intended to be used with acids or wine, which will have the effect of curdling the milk. Pure water is best when the melted butter is intended for fish and puddings, to which any mixture of wine is intended. Clear stock or gravy, instead of water, is preferable when it is intended to be eaten with roast meat, or for vegetables to be eaten with roast meat. The old-fashioned method of mixing is as good as the Doctor's. It is as follows: Break up the butter on a trencher, and work the flour into it thoroughly, then add it to the cold liquid in the saucepan; or you may drop the flour, a quarter of an hour before it is set on the fire, on the top of the liquid, without stirring at all; when the flour has all sunk to the bottom, shake it round till the flour is well incorporated with the liquid; then add the butter, and melt over a clear brisk nre. Fresh, rich cream is sometimes used instead of milk, water, or gravy. You should take care that your saucepan for melted butter be always well tinned, and kept delicately clean. Some recommend a silver saucepan; but this seems to us to be a stupid piece of extravagance. Dr. Kitchiner, however, who talks a great deal about economy, gravely tells us that a pint silver saucepan will not cost more than four or five pounds! Melted butter is frequently spoilt in the making; for ordinary purposes it should be of the thickness of good cream, but when intended to be mixed with flavouring, it should be of the thickness of light batter. If by any chance it become oiled, put a spoonful of cold water to it, and stir it with a spoon, or pour it back and forwards till it is right again. By mixing such vegetables as parsley, chervil, and others, generally eaten with melted butter, and sending them to the table on a little plate, those who like their flavour may mix for themselves. In the same way, all descriptions of flavouring essences, such as catsup, anchovy, &c., &c., may be mixed at table. This plan will be found to be a great saving in butter.

109. *Sauce for Fricassee of Fowls, Rabbits, white Meat, Fish, or Vegetables.*—You have no occasion to buy meat for these sauces, as their flavour is but small. The liquor that has boiled fowls, veal, or rabbit, or a little broth that you may have by you, or the feet and necks of chickens, or raw or dressed veal, will do very well. Stew with a little water any of these, add to it an onion sliced, a bit of lemon peel, a little pounded mace or nutmeg, some white peppercorns, and a bunch of sweet herbs, until the flavour is good; then strain it,

and add a little good cream, a piece of butter, and a little flour; salt to your taste. A squeeze of lemon may be added after the sauce is taken from the fire, shaking it well. Yolk of egg is frequently used in fricassee, but if you have cream it is better, as the egg is apt to curdle.

110. *Sauce for cold Fowl, or Partridge.*—Boil two eggs hard, rub them down in a mortar with an anchovy, two dessert spoonfuls of oil, three of vinegar, an eschalot, cayenne (sometimes,) and a tea-spoonful of mustard. All should be pounded before the oil is added; then strain it; eschalot vinegar instead of eschalots eats well; if so, omit one spoonful of the common vinegar: salt to your taste.

111. *A very rich Mushroom Sauce for Fowls or Rabbits.*—Pick, rub and wash a pint of young mushrooms, and sprinkle with salt to take off the skin. Put them into a saucepan with a little salt, a blade of mace, a little nutmeg, a pint of cream, and a piece of butter rolled in flour: boil them up and stir till done, then pour it into the dish with the chickens; garnish with lemon. If you cannot get fresh mushrooms, use pickled ones, done white, with a little mushroom powder with the cream.

112. *Sauce for boiled Carp, or Boiled Turkey.*—Make some melted butter with a little water and a tea-spoonful of flour, and add a quarter of a pint of cream, half an anchovy not washed, chopped fine; set it over the fire, and as it boils up, add a large spoonful of Indian soy: if that does not give it a fine colour, put a little more; add a little salt, and half a lemon; stir it well to prevent it curdling.

113. *Green Sauce for green Geese or Ducklings.*—A glass of white wine, some scalded gooseberries, a pint of sorrel juice, some white sugar, and a bit of butter. Boil them up, and serve in a boat.

114. *Egg Sauce.*—Boil the eggs hard, chop them fine, then put them into melted butter.

115. *Onion Sauce.*—Take the skins off ripe onions, remove the rooty fibres and the tops, let them lie in salt and water an hour, then put them into a saucepan of boiling water, and boil them till they are tender. You should allow them plenty of water. When tender, skin them, cut them exceedingly small, or rub them through a colander; season them with pepper and salt, and mix with an equal quantity of thick melted butter. This sauce is usually eaten with shoulder or leg of mutton. If you wish it very mild, use the large silvery onions, and boil them in several waters. Onion sauce is also eaten with rabbits, boiled ducks, tripe, and sometimes with a scrag of mutton or veal.

116. *Apple Sauce.*—Take four or five juicy apples, two table-spoonfuls of cold water or cider; instead of putting the lid on, place the parings over the apples, and put them by a gentle fire. When they sink they are done; remove the saucepan from the fire, and beat up the apples; take the parings from the top first, add a bit of butter, a tea-spoonful of fine powdered sugar, and a dust of nutmeg.

117. *Gooseberry Sauce.*—Scald half a pint of green gooseberries; do them till they are tender, but not broken; drain them on a sieve;

SAUCES.

when the liquor is cold, take half a pint of it, and make a thick batter of it, stir in the gooseberries with a little grated ginger and lemon peel. This sauce is sometimes used for mackerel.

118. *Wow wow Sauce*, for stewed beef or bouilli. Quarter and slice two or three pickled cucumbers or walnuts, or part of each, chop fine a handful of parsley, make some melted butter in half a pint of broth in which the beef is boiled, add a tea-spoonful of made mustard and a table-spoonful of vinegar, and the same of port wine and mushroom catsup: let it simmer till thick, then stir in the parsley and pickles to get warm; pour the whole over the beef, or put in a sauce tureen. The flavour may be varied by a tea-spoonful or two of any kind of the vinegars.

119. *Curry Sauce* is made by putting a little powdered curry into some melted butter, or curry vinegar.

120. *Parsley and Butter.*—Wash and pick leaf by leaf some parsley; put a tea-spoonful of salt into half a pint of boiling water, boil the parsley about ten minutes; drain it on a sieve, mince it quite fine, and then bruise it to a pulp: put it into a sauce boat, and mix with it by degrees about half a pint of melted butter. Never pour parsley and butter over boiled things, but send up in a boat.

121. *Fennel and Butter for Mackerel* is prepared in the same way as parsley and butter.

122. *Plum Pudding Sauce.*—A glass of sherry, half a glass of brandy, cherry bounce or Curaçoa, or essence of punch, and two tea-spoonfuls of pounded lump sugar (a very little grated lemon peel is sometimes added,) in a quarter of a pint of thick melted butter: grate nutmeg on the top.

123. *Anchovy Sauce.*—Pound three anchovies in a mortar with a bit of butter; rub it through a double hair sieve with the back of a wooden spoon, and stir it into about half a pint of melted butter, or stir in a table-spoonful of essence of anchovy. Many cooks add cayenne and lemon juice.

124. *Caper Sauce.*—Take a table-spoonful of capers, and two tea-spoonfuls of vinegar; mince one-third of them very fine, and divide the others in half; put them in a quarter of a pint of melted butter, or good thickened gravy; stir the same way as you do melted butter, or it will oil. Sometimes half a Seville orange or lemon or parsley, chervil, or tarragon, are added.

125. *Mock Caper Sauce.*—Take French beans, gherkins, green peas, or nasturtiums, all pickled; cut them into bits the size of capers; put them into half a pint of melted butter; add two tea-spoonfuls of lemon juice or vinegar.

126. *Shrimp Sauce.*—Shell a pint of shrimps, and stir into half a pint of melted butter; a little cream makes a delicate addition. It is used with salmon, turbot, and soles.

127. *Oyster Sauce.*—Two dozen oysters will make half a pint of sauce, not more. Open the oysters, save all the liquor, perfectly free from bits of shell, scald the oysters in the liquor till they look plump, then take out the fish and add to the liquor two ounces of butter rolled

in flour, and two table-spoonfuls of cream; boil it up. Take off the beards or fringy part of the oysters; if they are large, cut them in two; stir them in the butter, and set them by the fire for a minute or two, but do not let them boil, as it hardens them.

128. *Lobster Sauce.*—Choose a hen lobster, pick out all the spawn and red coral that runs down the back, pound it to a paste with a lump of butter, pull the meat of the back and claws to pieces with two forks, stir the lobster into some boiling hot melted butter; keep it on the fire till the lobster is warmed through, and well mixed. You may add, if liked, catsup, lemon juice, cayenne, anchovy; but the simple flavour of the lobster is best. A little cream is an improvement.

129. *Liver Sauce.*—Scald the liver, clear away all the fibres and specky parts, pound it in a mortar, with a bit of butter, then boil it up with melted butter; season it with cayenne, and a squeeze of lemon juice. You may add catsup or anchovy.

130. *Bread Sauce* is either made with gravy or milk. Stew the heads, necks, and feet of the poultry for which it is intended, with an onion, a little allspice, and a few peppercorns; when reduced to half a pint, strain it and boil up again; put in a small tea-cup full of bread crumbs, let it boil till quite stiff, hold it over the fire and shake it till it boils thoroughly, then put it on the hob till time to serve; stir in a bit of salt, one ounce of butter, and two table-spoonfuls of cream.

131. *Sauce for Tripe, Calf's-head, or Cow-heel.*—Garlic vinegar according to taste, table-spoonful of brown sugar, mustard and black pepper a tea-spoonful of each, stirred into oiled melted butter. (See 466.)

132. *Celery Sauce.*—Take fresh celery; take off all the outside leaves, leave none but what are quite crisp, and which may be known by their breaking short without any strings, cut up in pieces about an inch long, take liquor that has boiled veal, chickens, or lamb, when fast boiling.

133. *Tarragon or Burnet* makes rich pleasant sauce, chiefly used for steaks; sent to table in a sauce tureen.

134. *Sorrel Sauce for Lamb or Veal, and Sweet-breads.*—Two quarts of sorrel leaves will not make more than a sauce tureen of sauce; pick and wash them clean, put them into a stew-pan with one ounce of butter, cover close and set over a slow fire for a quarter of an hour; then rub them through a coarse hair sieve, season them with salt, pepper, nutmeg, and a small lump of sugar, squeeze in the juice of a lemon, and make the whole thoroughly hot.

135. *Poor Man's Sauce.*—A handful of young parsley leaves, chopped fine, a dozen of young green onions, chopped fine, put to them salt and pepper, two table-spoonfuls of salad oil, and four of vinegar; a little scraped horse-radish, pickled French beans, or gherkins, may be added. This sauce is taken with cold meats.

136. *Truffle Sauce.*—Truffles are only good while in season, that is, in a green state. Add two ounces of butter to eighteen truffles sliced, simmer them together till they are tender; then add as much

good gravy, brown or white, as to bring it to a proper thickness, season it with salt, and squeeze in the juice of half a lemon.

137. *Sharp Sauce for Venison.*—Best white wine vinegar half a pint, loaf sugar pounded a quarter of a pound; simmer it gently; skim, and strain it through a tamis.

138. *Sweet Sauce for Venison.*—Currant jelly, either black or red, melted and served hot; others like it sent to table as jelly.

139. *Wine Sauce for Venison, Hare, or Haunch of Mutton.*—Take equal parts of rich mutton gravy, without any flavourings, and port wine. Simmer them together to half a pint, add a table-spoonful of currant jelly, let it just boil up.

140. *Sauce for a Pig.*—Three quarters of a pint of good beef gravy, six or eight leaves of sage, chopped very fine, a blade of mace, a tea-cup full of bread crumbs, and eight white peppercorns; let them boil six or eight minutes, then stir into the sauce the brains, gravy, and whatever sticks about the dish on which you have split the pig, one ounce of butter rolled in flour, two table-spoonfuls of cream, and one or two of catsup, if liked; simmer a minute or two, and serve in a sauce tureen.

141. *Turtle Sauce.*—To a pint of rich beef gravy, thickened, put a wine glass of Madeira, six leaves of basil, the juice and peel of half a lemon, a few grains of cayenne or curry powder, an eschalot sliced, a table spoonful of essence of anchovy; simmer together five minutes, then strain, and add a dozen turtle force meat balls. This sauce is used for calf's head, or hashed or stewed veal, or for any other rich dish in imitation of turtle.

142. *A Sauce for all sorts of Fish.*—Half a pint of port or claret, half a pint of rich gravy, a little nutmeg, three anchovies, two table-spoonfuls of catsup, and salt; simmer all together till the anchovies are done, then add three ounces of butter thickened with flour, arrow-root, or potatoe mucilage; when it boils, add some scraped horse-radish, a dozen or two of oysters, a lobster cut in bits, a few small mushrooms, and half a pint of picked shrimps or crawfish. This sauce is intended to pour over the fish—boiled carp, tench, pike, whiting, boiled cod, and haddock.

143. *Pudding Sauce.*—Half a glass of brandy, one glass of white wine, a little grated rind of lemon, half an ounce of grated loaf sugar, and a little powdered cinnamon, mixed with melted butter. It is a good way to keep a bottle of these ingredients to mix with melted butter when wanted. In a bottle containing one pint of brandy and two pints of sherry, steep the kernels of apricots, nectarines, and peaches, with an ounce of shaved lemon rind, half an ounce of mace, and a quarter of a pound of loaf sugar; pour off clear to mix with butter. Two table-spoonfuls will flavour a boat of sauce; the mace and lemon peel may be steeped in half a pint of brandy, or a pint of sherry, for fourteen days; strain, and add a quarter of a pint of capillaire.

144. *Custard Sauce.*—For rice or other plain puddings, or with fruit pies, stir a pint of sweet cream in a double saucepan till it boils; beat the yolks of two or three eggs, with a spoonful of cold cream,

and an ounce of powdered sugar; pour the boiling cream to them, and pour backwards and forwards two or three times to prevent curdling; then set the inner saucepan over the boiling water, and stir it continually one way till it thickens. Serve in a china basin with grated nutmeg, or pounded cinnamon strewed over the top.

145. *Roe Sauce.* — Boil the soft roes of mackerel, clear away all the skin, and bruise them with the back of a wooden spoon; beat up the yolk of an egg with a little salt and pepper, a little fennel and parsley scalded and chopped fine, rub the whole together, and stir into melted butter. Some people prefer a spoonful of catsup, essence of anchovy, or walnut pickle.

BOILING.

As this is the most common mode of preparing food for human sustenance, it is therefore the more necessary that its principles should be well understood; for though the operations of boiling may appear to be very simple, yet a great deal of skill and judgment is required to carry them into effect properly. We repeat, that the young cook ought to read attentively our observations upon this subject, in the "Introductory Remarks." Instead of using the word *boiling*, we ought rather to have said, the mode of preparing meats for food by means of hot water; for we are quite convinced, that all meats are more or less injured by being subjected to a boiling heat; that is, a heat of $212°$ of Fahrenheit. We have dressed salt cod fish in water never exceeding $145°$ of heat, and it was much more tender, and better flavoured, than when dressed in boiling water: we ought to add, that the fish is required to remain in this partially hot water four or five hours, in which time it becomes divested of the salt, and eats, comparatively speaking, quite fresh.

146. Take care that your vessel is large enough for the water to cover the meat, and to surround it. Do not suffer the steam to escape; and to effect this, see that the lid of the vessel fits it as closely as possible; by this means the water may be kept at a proper heat, that is to say, nearly simmering, but not bubbling, whereby fuel will be saved, and the meat much better dressed. In short, one of the greatest errors that can be committed in boiling meat, is to suffer the water to boil violently. It has the effect of hardening the outside of the joints, or, in other words, making it tough, while the inside will be raw, or only partially done.

147. Always prefer soft water to hard, whenever the former is to be procured. River, or clean rain water, should be used in preference to hard spring water; but your water must always be as pure and as bright as possible.

148. In making up a fire for cooking, regard must be had as to whether it is intended for boiling or roasting, or for both. A moderate fire is best for boiling, but a brisk and somewhat fierce fire is required for roasting. If you are going to roast and boil at the same fire, you must take care that your boiling vessels are sufficiently far removed

from it. With a good kitchen range, or steam cooking apparatus, all this may be done without difficulty or trouble.

149. All fresh meats are directed by the generality of culinary writers to be put into the pot, or saucepan, when the water is warm, not hot; but salt meat, for the most part, should be put in when the water is perfectly cold; by this means the superfluous salt will be extracted from it. The pot should not, with fresh meat, be allowed to boil, or rather to arrive at the boiling point, under forty or fifty minutes; more time should be taken with salt meat. The usual direction is, as above, to put fresh meat into warm water — but we are convinced, that the better plan is always to use cold. Meat, thoroughly cooked, will take twenty minutes boiling to each pound. Salt, a little more.

150. When the scum rises, let it be carefully removed; and if the heat of the water is checked with a small portion of cold water, it will throw up an additional scum, which must, of course, be also carefully taken away. The scum rises just as the water is beginning to boil. The nice clear appearance of the meat, when done, in a great measure depends upon attending to the above directions.

151. When the liquor in your vessel once boils, after all the scum has been cleared away, let it continue to simmer till the meat is done. From fifteen to twenty minutes is generally directed to be allowed for each pound of meat, but twenty is better. Never stick your fork into meat, whether boiling or roasting, upon any account; the effect will be to let out the gravy. Bacon is an exception.

152. Meats of any description, just killed, and still warm, whether to be roasted or boiled, will do as soon, and eat as tender, as meat which has hung the usual time; but if once suffered to become cold after slaughtering, it will require more dressing, and after all will not eat so tenderly, unless hung a proper time.

153. Meat which has been frozen must be immersed in cold water two or three hours, or till the frost is taken out of it, before it is dressed, or it will never be well done. In cold weather meat requires more dressing than in warm.

154. Salt meat will require more boiling than fresh, and thick parts, whether salt or fresh, rather more than thin ones.

155. In boiling bacon, if very salt, it is a good plan to take away a part or the whole of the water, when it is on the point of boiling, and filling up the pot with cold water. This process renders it more mild. Bacon or ham is done when the skin is easily removed, or the fork leaves it readily.

156. Hams, beef, tongues, and even pork, which have been kept long in pickle, should be soaked before they are boiled — if hard, in warm water. A ham weighing twenty pounds, or upwards, will take from five to six hours to dress it well (the water should not boil); and a large dry tongue should be boiled, or rather simmered, for four hours or more. The following is a good plan to dress a ham: Put a certain quantity of suet into the pan which is to be used for the cooking of the ham; then put in the ham and cover it with paper, over

which lay a cover of coarse paste, or the paper may be used without the paste, or the paste without the paper; place the pan in the oven, where let it remain till the ham is done. The gravy coming from the meat will be a jelly, which, mixed with fresh stock or broth for gravies, &c. will greatly improve it.

157. Meat boiled by steam requires no water unless soup is wanted. Meat boiled in the ordinary way should not be permitted to touch the bottom of the pot. This object may be effected by placing a fish-drain in the pot, or by putting a plate upside down in it, or laying some skewers across it a little way from the bottom.

158. There is method of boiling meat without allowing it to touch or come in contact with the water. This plan, which is little followed in America, has been strongly recommended. To effect this object, fowls filled with oysters may be boiled in a bladder, or in a close jar, by which means they are deliciously stewed, and the flavour and animal juices are all preserved. Meat of any description may be dressed in a similar manner, that is, by putting it into a close jar and immersed in water, which is kept boiling till the meat is done. The Scotch dress their haggis in this way, and the custom was followed by the ancient Romans. Similar modes of dressing meat are used by savages in different parts of the world.

159. Any thing that is to be warmed and sent to the table a second time, should be put into a basin or jar, placed in hot water, which is not permitted to come to the boiling point. If allowed to boil, the meat will harden, or the sauce will be reduced and become thick; by avoiding these chances the flavour will be preserved, and the viands may be warmed up more than once without injury. The steam apparatus now employed in most kitchens, is admirably adapted to this purpose, since the heat can be regulated by the required temperature.

160. The heads, brains, and so forth, of animals, every thing in fact, which in the cleaning process requires soaking, should be soaked in warm, not hot water, as the hot will fix the blood, and injure both the appearance and flavour of the viand. All cooks must be particular in keeping their saucepans well skimmed; nothing will more completely spoil a dish of any kind than the neglect of this essential point. In order to take off the fat from the braise, or any other gravy, plunge the basin containing it into cold water; the fat will immediately coagulate, and may be removed.

161. It is much better to dress meat immediately after it is killed, that is, while it is warm, than to suffer it to get cold, and not let it hang a proper length of time. Indeed, there is no doubt that meat dressed while warm is as tender, or nearly as tender, as when it has been hung for some days. If, therefore, you cannot procure well-hung meat, and can get that which has been just killed, you ought to prefer the latter.

162. Bacon, ham, and salt beef, may be done, if you want to use your fire for vegetables, half an hour before serving, as it will not sustain any injury by remaining that time in the hot liquor; but all other descriptions of meat would be injured by such a course of proceeding.

163. Potatoes must never be boiled with meat, or indeed with any thing else, for the meat is injured by the potatoes and the potatoes by the meat.

164. You may boil turnips, carrots, parsnips, and pease pudding, with salt meat; by so doing these vegetables will be improved, and the meat not injured; but the liquor will not keep so long, though it will be rendered better for some kinds of soup.

165. Green vegetables, such as savoys, &c., should be always put into boiling water with a handful of salt, particularly if they are harsh and strong; they are generally kept boiling till they are done. In warm countries, in Italy, for instance, they first boil them in a large quantity of water for a considerable time; but as this will neither make them sweet nor tender, they are frequently taken out of the pot, and well washed in cold spring water; they are then boiled again till they are sweet and tender. Old tough meat may be similarly treated with like effect.

166. Old potatoes must never be put into warm or hot water. On the contrary, the water in which this useful vegetable is boiled should be perfectly cold when the potatoes are first put in. New potatoes are better put in boiling water.

BOILING.—BUTCHER'S MEAT AND POULTRY.

The general directions which we have given for boiling in the preceding pages, if they have been well studied by the young cook, as we trust they have, render it useless for us to go into the question at any length; we shall, therefore, content ourselves with a few special directions relative to the dressing of the different things designated at the head of this section. It will not be necessary to give a great multiplicity of receipts; for if the general principles of boiling are well understood, and we have spared neither time nor space to make them so, the cook will find no difficulty in preparing any particular dish without especial directions from us, or any other writer. The receipts which follow are selected according to the best of our judgment. We do not pretend to say that they are original; upon such a subject it is impossible to be original, with the exception, perhaps, of a few instances. Dr. Kitchiner apologises in his "Cook's Oracle," for his "receipts differing a little from those in former cookery books." Very different is this open and candid proceeding from that of a voluminous writer of great pretensions, who claims the following mode of dressing rice, which is as old as the introduction of that article into this country, as *original!* "Tie some rice in a cloth, leaving plenty of room for it to swell; boil it in water for an hour or two, and eat it with butter and sugar, or milk."

167. *Boiled Beef.*—Fresh boiled beef is called *beef bouilli* by some, but in the French kitchen the term means fresh beef dressed, without absolutely boiling, it being suffered only to simmer till it is done. Indeed, it may be laid down as a general rule, that whether you are dressing beef bouilli, or any other meat, it should never be suffered

to go into a *boiling gallop*, except for a minute or two, for the purpose of throwing up the scum. After the scum is all cleared away, let it simmer till it is done. But you must be careful not to let your meat boil too quickly; for this purpose it should be put over a moderate fire, and the water made gradually hot, or the meat will be hardened, and shrink up as if it were scorched; but by keeping the meat a certain time heating, without boiling, the fibres of the meat dilate, and it not only yields the scum more freely, but the meat is rendered more tender. The advantage of dressing fresh meat in the way practised by the French with regard to fresh beef is twofold. In the first place, meat dressed in this manner affords much more nourishment than it does cooked in the common way, is easy of digestion, and will yield soup of a most excellent quality. (See *Soup* and *Bouilli*, and 99.)

168. *Boiled Salt Beef.*—A piece of beef of fifteen pounds will take three hours, or more, simmering after it has boiled, and it ought to be full forty minutes on the fire before it does boil; skim carefully; put a tea-cup full of the liquor, and garnish with sliced carrots. Vegetables, carrots, turnips, kale, parsnips; sauce, melted butter. Pease pudding is sometimes boiled with salt beef, and the liquor, if not too salt, will make good pease soup. An aitch, or H bone of beef, a round, or ribs salted and rolled, and indeed all other beef, are boiled in the same way. Briskets and other inferior joints require, perhaps, more attention than superior ones; they should in fact rather be stewed than boiled, and in a small quantity of water, by which means, if good meat, they will be delicious eating.

169. *Mutton.*—A leg will take from two to three hours boiling. Accompaniments—parsley and butter, caper sauce, eschalot, onion, turnips, carrots, spinach, &c., and to boiled mutton in general.

170. *Neck of Mutton.*—As the scrag end takes much longer to boil, some people cut it off and boil it half or three-quarters of an hour before the rest, as it is apt to be bloody, however well washed; you had better skim it well. When it is time to put the best end in, add cold water to check the heat, allowing an hour and a half or three-quarters, after the second boiling up. Cut off some of the fat before dressing, or at least peel off the skin when taken up. For accompaniments, see 169.

171. *Shoulder, boiled.*—The whole is sometimes boiled, and sometimes cut in half, taking the knuckle part, and leaving the oyster for roasting; it will take not less than two hours slow boiling, though it may not weigh above five pounds. Boil it either plain or in broth. Accompaniments, 169.

172. *Breast, boiled,* will require from two and a half, to three hours. Accompaniments, 169.

173. *Sheeps' Heads, plain boiled.*—Boil them two hours; before boiling, take out the brains, wash them clean and free from all skin; chop about a dozen sage leaves very small, tie them in a small bag, and let them boil half an hour, then beat them up with pepper and salt, and

half an ounce of butter; pour it over the head, or serve in a boat or tureen; skin the tongue before serving. Accompaniments, 169.

174. *Leg of Lamb, boiled.*—From an hour and a quarter to an hour and a half. Accompaniments—caper sauce, melted butter, turnips, spinach, carrots, &c.

175. *Neck, boiled.*—One hour; if very large, an hour and a quarter.

176. *Lamb's Head and Pluck.*—Parboil the lights and a small bit of the liver till it will chop fine, and boil the head in the same liquor; it will take nearly an hour to boil; scald the brains, tied up in a small bag, with five or six sage leaves, chopped very fine; they will take twenty minutes to do; warm the mince in a little of the liquor, seasoned with salt, pepper, and nutmeg; thicken with flour, and half an ounce of butter, and stir in the brains. Take up the head; skin the tongue; pour over the mince; sippets of toasted bread and slices of lemon. The liver, heart, and sweetbread, to be fried, and laid round the dish with slices of bacon; or served in a separate dish, which is preferable, as the liver requires a little brown gravy. Vegetables, turnips, carrots, &c.

Browned.—After boiling, wash the head with the yolk of an egg; sprinkle with bread crumbs and chopped parsley, and brown it in a dutch oven, the mince to be poured round it. Some people like the flavour of catsup in the mince; others like a little sliced lemon peel, and a spoonful or two of cream.

177. *Boiled Veal.*—A knuckle, whether of leg or shoulder, will take full two hours. A scrag of neck or breast, an hour and three-quarters to two hours. Sauce, melted butter, parsley and butter, celery, &c.

178. *Calf's Head, boiled.*—Let it be cut in half by the butcher, and all the inside bones removed; take out the brains, wash the head well in several waters, with a little salt, to draw out the blood; boil it slowly in plenty of water two hours or two hours and a quarter. Sauce. Well clean the brains, and boil them in a cloth half an hour, with about a dozen sage leaves chopped fine, or parsley, or part of each; when done, beat them up in a small saucepan, with a little salt and pepper, one ounce of butter, and a little lemon juice; have them ready quite hot to pour over the tongue, when skinned. Some people mix the brains with parsley and butter, and pour over the whole head. However it is dressed, it is usually garnished with sliced lemon.

179. *Tripe*, when raw, will take four or five hours simmering. If previously well boiled, twenty minutes to three-quarters of an hour. It may be in milk, or milk and water, or equal parts of milk and its own liquor. Boil with the tripe eight or ten large onions. To keep the tripe warm, serve it in the liquor, and beat up the onions with pepper, salt, and butter; or the tripe may be served without liquor, and the onion sauce poured over. If onions are not approved, serve parsley and butter, or caper sauce. Tripe may be cut in pieces the size of a hand, dipped in batter and fried, with rashers of bacon

laid round the dish.—N. B. Mustard is *always* an accompaniment of tripe, and generally vinegar also.

In some of the English towns, particularly at Birmingham, famous for tripe, the belly or paunch of the animal, after being well cleaned, (in doing which thoroughly great attention and care must be observed,) is sent to the oven in a deep earthenware pot, or jar, closely covered over the top, and baked, or rather stewed, in just a sufficient quantity of water, for four or five hours, or till it is well done. It is sold while yet hot, in the public-houses or tripe shops, at so much a "large or small *cut*," with a proportionate quantity of "broth," that is, the liquor in which it has been stewed; nothing else is eaten with it, except mustard and salt. In Birmingham it is usually eaten for supper, and of course by candle-light, and at no other meal; a relation of ours, however, was so fond of it, that he used to have the dining-room darkened, and the candles lit, in order that he might partake of it for his dinner, under the same apparent circumstances as at supper. We have heard of whist devotees who could not play the game with any gusto by daylight, and who resorted to the same expedient to imitate night as our tripe gourmand. Tripe cooked in the Birmingham fashion is delicious—far, very far, superior to that gotten in London; this may be partly accounted for by the fact that all meat is greatly deteriorated by being twice subjected to heat.

180. *Cow-heel* in the hands of a skilful cook, will furnish several good meals; when boiled tender, cut it into handsome pieces, egg and bread-crumb them, and fry them a light brown; lay them round a dish, and put in the middle of it sliced onions fried, or the accompaniments ordered for tripe.

181. *Pig's Pettitoes* consist of the feet and internal parts of a sucking pig. Set on with a quantity of water, or broth; a button onion or two may be added, if approved—also, four or five leaves of sage chopped small. When the heart, liver, and lights, are tender, take them out and chop fine; let the feet simmer the while; they will take from half to three-quarters of an hour to do. Season the mince with salt, nutmeg, and a little pepper, half an ounce of butter, a table-spoonful or two of thick cream, and a tea-spoonful of arrow-root, flour, or potatoe starch; return it to the saucepan, in which the feet are; let it boil up, shaking it one way. Split the feet, lay them round in the mince. Serve with toasted sippets. Garnish. Mashed potatoes.

182. *Salt Pork* requires long boiling, never less than twenty minutes to a pound, and a thick joint considerably more. A leg of ten pounds will take four hours simmering, a spring two hours, a porker's head the same. Be very careful that it does not stick to the pot. No sauce is required, except a quarter of a pint of the liquor in which it was boiled, to draw the gravy, and plenty of good fresh mustard. A chine is usually served quite dry. The vegetable accompaniments are pease pudding, turnips, carrots, and parsnips.

183. *Pickled Pork*, which is usually bought pickled, requires to be well washed before boiling, and must boil very slowly. It is seldom eaten alone, but as an accompaniment to fowls, or other white meat.

184. *Bacon, Ham, Tongues.*—First, well wash and scrape clean. If very salt, it may soak in cold water a few hours; allow plenty of water, fresh rain or river water is best; put it in when the chill is off, and let it be a good while coming to the boil, then keep it very gently simmering. If time allows, throw away nearly or quite all the liquor of bacon as soon as it boils up, and renew it with fresh cold water; reckon the time from the second boiling. A pound of streaky bacon will require three-quarters of an hour to boil; a quarter of an hour for every additional pound. If good bacon it will swell in boiling, and when done the rind will pull off easily. Take it up on a common dish to remove the rind, and sprinkle it over with bread raspings, sifted through a flour dredge, or grater. A ham of twelve or fourteen pounds will require four or five hours simmering, or four hours baking in a moderate oven. When done, remove the skin as whole as possible, and preserve it to cover over the ham and keep it moist. If to be served hot, strew raspings as above; but if intended for eating cold, omit the raspings. It will be much the more juicy for not cutting hot. Set it on a baking stand, or some other contrivance, to keep it from touching the dish; this preserves it from swamping in the fat that drips from it, keeps the fat nice and white for use, and also makes the ham keep the longer from becoming mouldy, by the outside being perfectly dry. Whether hot or cold, garnish with parsley. A neat's tongue, according to its size, age, and freshness, will require from two hours and a half to four hours slow boiling. When done, it will stick tender, and the skin will peel off easily. A dried chine, or hog's cheek, may be allowed the same boiling as bacon, viz. four pounds an hour and a half, and a quarter of an hour for every additional pound.

185. *To poach Eggs.*—The best vessel for this purpose is a frying pan; but it must be kept for that purpose only, or the grease will adhere to the water, and spoil the delicate appearance of the eggs. A wide-mouthed stew-pan will do as well. Both the vessel and water must be delicately clean. Break the eggs into separate cups; when the water boils, gently slip in the eggs, and set the vessel on the hob for a minute or so, till the white has set, then set it over the fire; let it once boil up, and the eggs are done. The white should retain its transparency, and the yellow appear brightly through it. Take up very carefully with a slice; trim off any rough edges of white, and serve on buttered toast, a piece for each egg, a little larger than the egg itself; or on a fish drainer. Garnish with sliced bacon or ham, sausages, or spinach.

186. *Turkeys, Capons, Chickens, &c.*, are all boiled exactly in the same manner, only allowing time according to their size. A chicken will take about twenty minutes—a fowl, forty—a fine five-toed fowl or a capon, about an hour—a small turkey, an hour and a half—a large one, two hours or more. Chickens or fowls should be killed at least one or two days before they are to be dressed.* Turkeys (espe-

---

* If they are dressed immediately after they are killed, *before the flesh is cold* all poultry eat equally tender.

cially large ones) should not be dressed till they have been killed three or four days at least—in cold weather, six or eight—or they will neither look white nor eat tender. Turkeys and large fowls should have the strings or sinews of the thighs drawn out. Fowls for boiling should be chosen as white as possible: those which have black legs should be roasted. The best use of the liver is to make sauce. Poultry must be well washed in warm water; if very dirty from the singeing, &c., rub them with a little white soap, but thoroughly rinse it off before you put them into the pot. Make a good and clear fire; set on a clean pot, with pure and clean water, enough to cover the turkey, &c.; the slower it boils, the whiter and plumper it will be. When there rises any scum, remove it; the common method of some (who are more nice than wise) is to wrap them up in a cloth, to prevent the scum attaching to them; which if it do by your neglecting to skim the pot, there is no getting it off afterwards, and the poulterer is blamed for the fault of the cook. If there be water enough, and it is attentively skimmed, the fowl will both look and eat much better this way than when it has been covered up in the cleanest cloth; and the colour and flavour of your poultry will be preserved in the most delicate perfection.

FISH.

187. *Salmon to boil.*—The water should be blood-warm: allow plenty to cover the fish, with a good handful of salt, and a quarter of a pint of vinegar; this makes the fish boil firm. Remove the scum as fast as it rises. Keep it at a very gentle boil from half an hour to an hour, according to the thickness of the fish. When the eyes start, and the fins draw out easily, it is done. Lay the fish-drainer across the kettle a minute or two before shifting the fish. Sauce, lobster, shrimp, anchovy, or parsley and butter. Melted butter is the universal sauce for fish, whether boiled, fried, or baked. Whatever other sauce is served, plain melted butter must never be omitted: we shall therefore only refer to the number of other sauces suitable for particular kinds of fish. Observe, also, potatoes, either boiled or mashed, are the only vegetables eaten with fish, excepting parsnips with salt fish.

188. *Broiled Salmon.*—This is a good method of dressing a small quantity of salmon for one or two persons. It may be cut in slices the whole round of the fish, each taking in two divisions of the bone; or the fish may be split, and the bone removed, and the sides of the fish divided into cutlets of three or four inches each: the former method is preferable, if done neatly with a sharp knife. Rub it thoroughly dry with a clean rough cloth; then do each piece over with salad oil or butter. Have a nice clean gridiron over a very clear fire, and at some distance from it. When the bars are hot through wipe them, and rub with lard or suet to prevent sticking; lay on the salmon, and sprinkle with salt. When one side is brown, carefully turn and brown the other. They do equally well or better in a tin,

or flat dish, in an oven, with a little bit of butter, or sweet oil; or they may be done in buttered paper on the gridiron. Sauce, lobster or shrimp.

189. *Baked Salmon.* — If a small fish, turn the tail to the mouth, and skewer it; force meat may be put in the belly, or, if part of a large fish is to be baked, cut it in slices, egg it over, and dip it in the force meat. Stick bits of butter about the salmon (a few oysters laid round are an improvement). It will require occasional basting with the butter. When one side becomes brown, let it be carefully turned, and when the second side is brown, it is done. Take it up carefully, with all that lies about it in the baking dish. For sauce, melted butter, with two table-spoonsful of port wine, one of catsup, and the juice of a lemon, poured over the fish; or anchovy sauce in a boat.

190. *Pickled Salmon.* — Do not scrape off the scales, but clean the fish carefully, and cut into pieces about eight inches long. Make a strong brine of salt and water; to two quarts, put two pounds of salt, and a quarter of a pint of vinegar; in all, make just enough to cover the fish; boil it slowly, and barely as much as you would for eating hot. Drain off all the liquor; and, when cold, lay the pieces in a kit or small tub. Pack it as close as possible, and fill up with equal parts of best vinegar and the liquor in which the fish was boiled. Let it remain so a day or two, then again fill up. Serve with a garnish of fresh fennel. The same method of pickling will apply to sturgeon, mackerel, herrings, and sprats. The three latter are sometimes baked in vinegar, flavoured with allspice and bay leaves, and eat very well; but will not keep more than a few days.

191. *Turbot, Halibut, and Brill, boiled.* — Score the skin across the thick part of the back, to prevent its breaking on the breast, which it would be liable to do when the fish swells in boiling. Put the fish in the kettle in cold water, with a large handful of salt; as it comes to boil, skim it well, and set it aside to simmer as slowly as possible for a quarter of an hour or twenty minutes. If it boil fast it will break. It may be garnished with fried smelts or gudgeons, laid all round like spokes of a wheel. Sauce, lobster or shrimp.

192. *Soles* and *Dutch Plaice* may be boiled exactly in the same way as turbot, and with the same garnish and sauce, or with parsley, fennel, or chervil sauce. If you have not a turbot kettle, these flat fish boil very well in a large frying pan, provided it admits depth of water to cover them.

193. *Soles, fried.* — Having cleaned, wipe them thoroughly dry, and keep them in a coarse cloth an hour or two before using. In case any moisture should remain, flour them all over, and again wipe it off. They may be fried either with or without bread crumbs or oatmeal. If bread crumbs are to be used, beat up an egg very finely; wash over the fish with a paste-brush; then sprinkle over it bread crumbs or oatmeal, so that every part may be covered, and one part not be thicker than another. Lift up the fish by a fork stuck in the head, and shake off any loose crumbs that may adhere. Have plenty of fat in your pan, over a brisk fire, and let it quite boil before you

put the fish in. The fat may be salad oil, butter, lard or dripping. If sweet and clean, the least expensive answers as well as the best, but let there be enough to cover the fish. Give the fish a gentle shove with a slice, that it may not stick to the pan. In about four or five minutes one side will be brown; turn it carefully, and do the other; which, being already warm, will not take so long. The best way to turn a large sole, is to stick a fork in the head, and raise the tail with a slice, otherwise it is liable to be broken with its own weight. If the soles are very large, it is a good way to cut them across in four or five pieces, by which means the thick parts can have more time allowed them, without overdoing the thin. The very same rules will apply to the frying of Dutch plaice, flounders, eels, jack perch, roach, and other fresh-water fish. Jack and eels to be cut in pieces three or four inches long. Sauce, anchovy, parsley and butter, or melted butter flavoured with mushroom catsup. Garnish, sprigs of parsley or lemon juice.

194. *Soles or Eels, stewed.*—They may be first half fried, so as to give them a little brownness; then carefully drain them from fat; season with pepper and salt, and set them on with as much good beef gravy as will cover them. Let them simmer very gently for a quarter of an hour or twenty minutes, according to their thickness, but be very careful that they be not overdone. Take up the fish very gently with a slice. Thicken the sauce with flour and butter; flavour with mushroom catsup and port wine; simmer a minute or two, then strain it over the fish. Some people do not like the addition of wine, and instead thereof mix the thickening with a tea-cup full of good cream, seasoned with cayenne and nutmeg, and with or without the addition of a spoonful of catsup.

195. *Cod.*—The head and shoulders, comprehending in weight two-thirds or three-quarters of the fish, is much better dressed separately; the tail being much thinner would be broken to pieces before the thicker parts are done. The best way of dressing the tail, is to fry it. For boiling cod, allow plenty of room and water, that the fish may be perfectly covered. Put it in blood-warm water, with a large handful of salt. Watch for its boiling, that it may be set a little aside. A small cod will require twenty minutes after it boils; a large one, half an hour. When the fins pull easily, and the eyes start, the fish is done. Slip it very carefully on the fish plate, that it may not be broken. Take out the roe and liver, which are much esteemed; they will serve to garnish the dish, together with horse-radish and slices of lemon, or fried smelts, or oysters. Sauce, oyster. The sound, a fat jelly-like substance, along the inside of the backbone, is the great delicacy of the fish. Cod is sometimes boiled in slices. Let them be soaked half an hour in salt water; then set on with cold spring water and salt, just enough to cover them. Let it boil up; then carefully skim and set aside for ten minutes. Serve with the same sauce as above. Slices of cod are much better fried as soles. Slices of crimped cod, for boiling, are put in boiling water, and when done served on a napkin.

FISH.

196. *Ling* is a large fish, somewhat resembling cod, and may be dressed in the same way, but is very inferior in quality.

197. *Haddock* is but a poor fish, make the best of it. It may be boiled, and served with egg sauce, but it is better stuffed, and baked or broiled, and served with good gravy, or melted butter, flavoured with anchovy or mushroom catsup.

198. *Whitings* may be skinned or not. Fasten the tail to the mouth; dip the eggs and bread crumbs, or oatmeal, and fry as soles; or they may be cut in three or four pieces, and fried. They do not take long to fry; not more than five minutes; but several minutes should be allowed to drain the fat from them, as the beauty of them is to be perfectly dry. Sauce, anchovy, or parsley and butter.

199. *Sturgeon.*—If for boiling take off the skin, which is very rich and oily; cut in slices; season with pepper and salt; broil over a clear fire; rub over each slice a bit of butter, and serve with no other accompaniment than lemon; or the slices may be dipped in seasoning or force meat, twisted in buttered white paper, and so broiled. For sauce, serve melted butter with catsup. Garnish with sliced emon, as the juice is generally used with the fish.

200. *Roast Sturgeon.*—A piece of sturgeon may be tied securely on a spit, and roasted. Keep it constantly basted with butter, and when nearly done dredge with bread crumbs. When the flakes begin to separate, it is done. It will take about half an hour before a brisk fire. Serve with good gravy, thickened with butter and flour, and enriched with an anchovy, a glass of sherry wine, and the juice of half a Seville orange or lemon.

201. *Stewed Sturgeon.*—Take enough gravy to cover the fish; set it on with a table-spoonful of salt, a few corns of black pepper, a bunch of sweet herbs, an onion or two, scraped horse-radish, and a glass of vinegar. Let this boil a few minutes; then set it aside to become pretty cool; then add the fish; let it come gradually to boil; and then stew gently till the fish begins to break. Take it off immediately; keep the fish warm; strain the gravy, and thicken with a good piece of butter; add a glass of port or sherry wine, a grate of nutmeg, and a little lemon juice. Simmer till it thickens, and then pour over the fish. Sauce, anchovy.

202. *Mackerel, boiled.*— Put them on with cold water and salt. When the kettle boils, set it aside, but watch it closely, and take up the moment the eyes begin to start, and the tail to split. Sauce, parsley and butter (fennel), or roe sauce, or gooseberry sauce. Garnish, fennel and slices of lemon.

203. *Broiled Mackerel.*—Cut a slit in the back that they may be thoroughly done. Lay them on a clean gridiron (having greased the bars), over a clear, but rather slow, fire. Sprinkle pepper and salt over them; when thoroughly done on both sides, take them up on a very hot dish without a fish plate. Rub a bit of butter over each fish, and put inside each a little fennel and parsley, scalded and chopped, seasoned with pepper and salt, and a bit of fresh butter. Fennel sauce, parsley and butter.

204. *Baked or Pickled Mackerel.*—Take off the heads; open the fish; take out the roes, and clean them thoroughly; rub the inside with pepper, salt, and allspice, and replace the roes. Pack the fish close in a deep baking pan; cover with equal parts of cold vinegar and water, and two bay leaves. Tie over strong white paper doubled, or still thicker. Let them bake an hour in a slow oven. They may be eaten hot, but will keep ten days or a fortnight. Cold butter, and fresh young fennel (unboiled), are eaten with them. Sprats or herrings may be done in the same way.

205. *Skate and Thornback.*—These fish (like cod) are frequently crimped, that is, slashed in slices, by which means the meat contracts, and becomes more firm as the watery particles escape. Cut them in pieces, and boil in salt and water; serve with anchovy sauce; or they may be fried with egg and bread crumbs, as soles; or stewed as soles.

206. *Smelts, Gudgeons, Sprats, or other small Fish, fried.*— Clean and dry them thoroughly in a cloth, fry them plain, or beat an egg on a plate, dip them in it, and then in very fine bread crumbs, that have been rubbed through a sieve: the smaller the fish, the finer should be the bread crumbs—biscuit powder is still better; fry them in plenty of clean lard or dripping; as soon as the lard boils and is still, put in the fish; when they are delicately browned, they are done; this will hardly take two minutes. Drain them on a hair sieve, placed before the fire, turning them till quite dry.

207. *Trout* is sometimes fried, and served with crisp parsley and plain melted butter. This answers best for small fish. They are sometimes broiled, which must be done over a slow fire, or they will break. While broiling, sprinkle salt and baste with butter; serve with anchovy sauce, to which may be added a few chopped capers and a little of the vinegar. The sauce is generally poured over the fish.

208. *Stewed Trout.*—When the fish has been properly washed, lay it in a stew-pan, with half a pint of claret or port wine, and a quart of good gravy; a large onion, a dozen berries of black pepper, the same of allspice, and a few cloves, or a bit of mace; cover the fish-kettle close, and let it stew gently for ten or twenty minutes, according to the thickness of the fish; take the fish up, lay it on a hot dish, cover it up, and thicken the liquor it was stewed in with a little flour; season it with a little pepper, salt, essence of anchovy, mushroom catsup, and a little chili vinegar; when it has boiled ten minutes, strain it through a tamis, and pour it over the fish; if there is more sauce than the dish will hold, send the rest up in a boat.

209. *Red Mullets.*—These delicate fish are sometimes fried, and served with anchovy sauce; but more frequently either stewed or baked.

210. *Eels, fried.*— Skin and gut them, and wash them in cold water; cut them in pieces four inches long; season them with pepper and salt; beat an egg well on a plate, dip them in the egg, and then in fine bread crumbs; fry them in fresh clean lard; drain them

well from the fat; garnish with crisp parsley. Sauce, plain, and melted butter sharpened with lemon juice, or parsley and butter.

211. *Boiled Eels.*—Twist them round and round, and run a wire skewer through them. Do them slowly in a small quantity of salt and water, with a spoonful of vinegar, and a handful of parsley. They may be put in cold water, and will take very few minutes after they boil. Sauce, parsley, or fennel, and butter.

212. *Pike or Jack.*—For either baking or boiling, it is usual to stuff them with pudding. To secure it, bind it round with narrow tape. The fish may be dressed at full length, or turned with its tail in its mouth. For boiling, use hard water with salt, and a tea-cup full of vinegar; put it in blood-warm, and when it boils set it aside that it may simmer slowly. It will take from ten minutes to half an hour, according to its size. Sauce, oyster. Garnish, slices of lemon, laid alternately with horse-radish. If baked, being stuffed, put it in a deep dish, with a tea-cup full of gravy, and some bits of butter stuck over it. Serve with rich thickened gravy, and anchovy sauce.

For frying, the fish is to be cut in pieces, and may be done with egg and bread crumbs, as soles. The usual sauce is melted butter and catsup, but anchovy or lobster sauce is sometimes used.

213. *Carp, fried.*—The same as soles; make sauce of the roe, and anchovy sauce with lemon juice.

214. *Carp, stewed.*—With the addition of preserving the blood, which is to be dropped into port or claret wine, well stirring the whole time, carp may be stewed in the same manner as sturgeon, the wine and blood to be added with the thickening, and the whole poured over the fish. Sippet of bread toasted, sliced lemon and barberries. The same process for lampreys.

215. *Perch, boiled.*—Put them on in as much cold spring water as will cover them, with a handful of salt. Let them boil up quickly; then set aside to simmer slowly for eight, ten, or fifteen minutes, according to their size. Sauce, parsley and butter, or fennel, or melted butter with catsup.

216. *Salt Fish.*—It should be soaked a considerable time in soft water, changing the water two or three times. The length of time required will be according to the hardness or softness of the fish. One night will do for that which has been but a fortnight or three weeks in salt; but some require two or even three nights' soaking, and to be laid through the intermediate days on a stone floor. Set it on in cold or luke-warm water, and let it be a long time coming to boil. It should be kept at a slow simmer from half an hour to an hour and a half. When done enough, lay the tin fish-drainer across the kettle; remove any straggling bones and skin; pour through a quart of boiling water to rinse it, and serve with plenty of egg sauce, red beet-root, parsnips, and mashed potatoes. Some of the parsnips and beet-roots should be served whole, or in slices for garnish, together with horse-radish, and a dish also of equal parts of red beet-root and parsnips, mashed together, with pepper, butter, and cream. Salt fish is sometimes served with the vegetables. When boiled as above, it is

broken in flakes, and stewed a few minutes in good gravy, flavoured with onions or eschalots, but not salted, and thickened with flour, butter, and cream; then beat up with it either potatoes, or parsnips and beet-root, mashed with cream and butter. Sauce, egg. Salt fish, whether cod, ling, haddock, or salmon, is often cut in slices, soaked in beer, and broiled as red herrings for a breakfast relish.

217. *Terrapins.*—This is a favourite dish for suppers and parties; and, when well cooked, they are certainly very delicious. Many persons in Philadelphia have made themselves famous for cooking this article alone. Mrs. Rubicam, who during her lifetime always stood first in that way, prepared them as follows. Put the terrapins alive in a pot of boiling water, where they must remain until they are quite dead. You then divest them of their outer skin and toe-nails; and, after washing them in warm water, boil them again until they become quite tender, adding a handful of salt to the water. Having satisfied yourself of their being perfectly tender, take off the shells and clean the terrapins very carefully, removing the sand-bag and gall without breaking them. Then cut the meat and entrails into small pieces, and put into a saucepan, adding the juice which has been given out in cutting them up, but *no water*, and season with salt, cayenne, and black pepper, to your taste; adding a quarter of a pound of good butter to each terrapin, and a handful of flour for thickening. After stirring a short time, add four or five table-spoonfuls of cream, and a half pint of good Madeira to every four terrapins, and serve hot in a deep dish. Our own cook has been in the habit of putting in a very little mace, a large table-spoonful of mustard, and *ten drops of the gall;* and, just before serving, adding the yolks of four hard boiled eggs. During the stewing, particular attention must be paid to stirring the preparation frequently; and it must be borne in mind, that terrapins cannot possibly be too hot.

218. *Oysters au gratin.*—Take the best oysters you can find, and dry them on a napkin; you then place them on a silver shell, made expressly for the purpose, or fine, large, deep oyster shells, if handier, which should be well cleaned, placing in them four or six oysters, according to their size; season with salt, pepper, nutmeg, parsley, mushrooms hashed very fine, a small quantity of bread crumbs, with which the surface of the oysters must be covered, placing on top of all a small piece of the best butter. Then put them in a hot oven, and let them remain until they acquire a golden colour. Serve them hot.

219. *Oysters, stewed.*—For this purpose the beard or fringe is generally taken off. If this is done, set on the beards with the liquor of the oysters, and a little white gravy, rich but unseasoned; having boiled a few minutes, strain off the beards, put in the oysters, and thicken the gravy with flour and butter (an ounce of butter to half a pint of stew,) a little salt, pepper, and nutmeg, or mace, a spoonful of catsup, and three of cream; some prefer a little essence of anchovy to catsup, others the juice of a lemon, others a glass of white wine; the flavour may be varied according to taste. Simmer till the stew is

thick, and warmed through, but avoid letting them boil. Lay toasted sippets at the bottom of the dish and round the edges.

220. A more simple, and, as we think, a better method is to put, say two hundred oysters in a saucepan with nothing but their own juice; place them on a brisk fire, and let them remain, stirring them occasionally, until they begin to boil, then remove them, and pass the juice through a tin colander, leaving the oysters to drain. Then mix well together three-quarters of a pound of good butter, and a handful of flour. When this is done, strain the juice of the oysters through a sieve into the saucepan containing the butter and flour, and put it on the fire again, and add pepper and salt to your taste, stirring the whole frequently and briskly. When it begins to boil again, add the oysters, and the following articles, well beaten together, viz., the yolks of three eggs, two table-spoonfuls of milk, and the juice of half a lemon; whilst adding these, stir the whole briskly, and serve immediately.

221. *Oysters, fried.*—Large oysters are the best for this purpose. Simmer for a minute or two in their own liquor; drain perfectly dry; dip in yolks of eggs, and then in bread crumbs, seasoned with nutmeg, cayenne, and salt; fry them of a light brown. They are chiefly used as garnish for fish, or for rump steaks; but if intended to be eaten alone, make a little thick melted butter, moistened with the liquor of the oysters, and serve as sauce.

222. *Broiled Oysters.*—The oysters should be the largest and finest you can get. Prepare your gridiron, which should be a double one made of wire, by rubbing with butter, and having placed your oysters so that they will all receive the heat equally, set them over a brisk fire, and broil both sides without burning them. Let them be served hot, with a small lump of fresh butter, pepper and salt, added to them. Some establishments serve them egged and breaded; either way, however, they are good.

ROASTING.

223. Mind that your spit is clean, and take care that it passes through the meat as little as possible. Before it is spitted, see that the meat is jointed properly, particularly necks and loins. When on the spit it must be evenly balanced, that its motion may be regular, and all parts equally done; for this purpose, take care to be provided with balancing skewers and cookholds; a cradle spit is the best.

224. The bottle or vertical jack is an excellent instrument for roasting, better than spits for joints under forty pounds; but if you have neither of these things, as is often the case in small families, a woollen string twisted round a door key makes a good substitute. In this case a strong skewer should be passed through each end of the joint, in order that it may be conveniently turned bottom upwards, which will insure an equality of roasting and an equal distribution of the gravy. A Dutch oven is a convenient utensil for roasting small joints; but by far the best and most economical thing of the kind is, improperly, called the American oven, by which you may roast meat before   sitting-room fire, without any extra fuel, and without the

6 *

slightest inconvenience to the persons occupying the apartment. This contrivance will save, in the course of a year, all the expense, and more, of its original cost, in bakings, with this additional consideration, that meat so dressed will be equal to roasted meat. Meat cooked in a common oven, to say nothing of the abstracting of the dripping by the generality of bakers, is greatly inferior, both in flavour and tenderness, to that dressed in the American oven, where the air is not confined. It is not, however, meat alone that may be dressed in the American oven. All sorts of cakes may be made in it, and indeed, all the operations of baking and roasting may be performed by it, on a limited scale, but sufficiently large for a small family in contracted circumstances; in short, with the addition of the recent improvement, a sort of oval iron covering, we have baked bread before a parlour fire as perfectly as it could be produced by the regular process of baking; in one word, no family, whether in poor or middling circumstances, ought to be without the American oven, which may be had for a few shillings.

225. The fire for roasting should be made up in time, but it is better not to be very hot at first. The fire should, in point of size, be suited to the dinner to be dressed, and a few inches longer at each end than the article to be roasted, or the ends will not be done.

226. Never put meat down to a fierce fire, or one thoroughly burnt up, if you can possibly avoid it; but if not, you must take care and place it a considerable distance from the grate; indeed, meat should always be done slowly at first; it is impossible to roast a joint of very considerable size well under some hours. It is said that George III., who lived principally upon plain roasted and boiled joints, employed cooks who occupied four, five, or even six hours in roasting a single joint; but the result amply repaid the loss of labour and time; the meat was full of gravy, perfectly tender, and of a delicious flavour.

227. In placing paper over the fat to preserve it, never use pins or skewers; they operate as so many taps, to carry off the gravy; besides, the paper frequently starts from the skewers, and is, consequently, liable to take fire, to the great injury of both the flavour and appearance of the meat. For these reasons, always fasten on your paper with tape, twine, or any other suitable string.

228. The fire should be proportioned to the quantity of the meat intended to be roasted, as we have intimated above. For large joints make up a good strong fire, equal in every part of the grate, and well backed by cinders or small coals. Take care that the fire is bright and clear in the front. The larger the joint to be roasted, *the farther it must be kept from the fire till nearly done—mind that*. When you have to roast a thin and tender thing, let your fire be little and brisk.

229. When your fire is moderately good, your meat, unless very small, ought not to be put down nearer than from ten to fifteen inches off the grate; in some instances a greater distance would be preferable, but it is impossible to lay down any definite rule on this subject.

230. Slow roasting, like slow boiling, is the best, and the more

slow, in reason, the better. The time usually directed to be allowed for roasting meat, where the fire is good, the meat screen sufficiently large, and the meat not frosted, is rather more than a quarter of an hour to a pound, but we take this to be too short time; however, the cook must judge for herself; much will depend upon the temperature of the atmosphere, &c., and more upon the degree of basting it has undergone. The more the meat is basted the less time it will take to do, for the meat is rendered soft and mellow outside, and consequently, admits the heat to act upon the inside. On the contrary, meat rendered hard on the outside by having too hot a fire, or neglecting to baste, the fire is prevented from operating upon the interior. When the meat is half done the fire should be well stirred for browning, that is, it must be made to burn brightly and clearly. When the steam begins to rise, depend upon it the meat is thoroughly done, that is, well saturated with heat, and all that goes off from the meat in evaporation is an absolute waste of its most savoury and nourishing particles.

231. A good cook will be particular to place her dripping pan so as to catch the dripping, but not the loose hot coals which may chance to fall from the fire. Your dripping pan should be large, not less than twenty-eight inches long and twenty inches broad, and should have a well-covered well on the side from the fire, to collect the dripping; "this," says Dr. Kitchiner, "will preserve it in the most delicate state."

232. Roasting and boiling, as being the most common operations in cooking, are generally considered the most easy; this is a great error: roasting, in particular, requires unremitting attention to perform it well, much more so than stewing, or the preparing many made dishes. A celebrated French author, in the *Almanack des Gourmands*, says, that "the art of roasting victuals to the precise degree, is one of the most difficult things in this world, and *you may find half a thousand good cooks sooner than one perfect roaster; five minutes on the spit, more or less, decide the goodness of this mode of cookery.*"

ROASTING, BROILING, AND FRYING.

Before entering into any detail as to the best method of preparing the different dishes under this head, we must recommend the young cook to again carefully read our preliminary observations on roasting. We may here too be allowed to enter our most decided protest against baking meat, generally speaking — whether in the common brick oven, or in the iron ovens attached to kitchen ranges, particularly in the latter, unless they have a draught of air through them, when they will dress, or rather roast meat very well. Meat cannot be subjected to the influence of fire without injury, unless it is open to the air, by which the exhalations are carried off, and the natural flavour of the meat is preserved. Under the idea of saving fuel, persons are induced to use stoves in their kitchen instead of ranges. They should consider, however, that baking not only injures the meat, but absolutely spoils the dripping, which from roasted meat is much more valuable than the extra cost of coals. For a small family, we recommend the bottle jack—and for large establishments, a kitchen range, a smoke jack, and the usual quantity of plating for stewing, or boiling. In the following receipts we have generally indicated the time which a joint will take roasting, but a good cook will never wholly depend upon time, either in roasting or boiling; she ought to exercise her own judgment, as to whether a thing is done or not. When roast meat streams towards the fire, it is a sure sign that the meat is nearly done. On no account, whatever, should gravy be poured over any thing that is roasted. It makes the meat insipid, and washes off the frothing, or dredging.

233. *Sirloin of Beef, roasted.* — Sirloin or ribs, of about fifteen pounds, will require to be before a large sound fire about three and a half or four hours; take care to spit it evenly, that it may not be heavier on one side than the other; put a little clean dripping in the dripping pan (tie a piece of paper over it to preserve the fat), baste it well as soon as it is put down, and every quarter of an hour all the time it is roasting, till the last half hour; then take off the paper, and make some gravy for it; stir the fire and make it clear; to *brown* and *froth* it, sprinkle a little salt over it, baste it with butter, and dredge it with flour; let it go a few minutes longer, till the froth rises; take it up. Garnish it with a hillock of horse-radish, scraped as fine as possible with a very sharp knife. A Yorkshire pudding is an excellent accompaniment. The inside of the sirloin should never be cut hot, but reserved entire for the hash, or a mock hare.

234. *Rump and Round.*—Rump and rounds of beef are sometimes roasted; they require thorough doing, and much basting to keep the outside from being dry. It should be before the fire from three hours, and upwards, according to size. Gravy and garnish as above.

235. *Mock Hare.* — The inside lean of a sirloin of beef may be dressed so as to resemble hare, and is by many people greatly preferred to it. Make a good stuffing. If possible, get the inside meat of the whole length of sirloin, or even of two, lay the stuffing on half the length, turn the other end over and sew up the two sides with a strong twine, that will easily draw out when done; roast it nicely, taking care to baste it well, and serve with sauces and garnishes the same as hare; or, it may be partly roasted and then stewed, in rich thickened gravy with force meat balls, and sauce.

236. *Ribs of Beef, boned.* — Take out the ribs, &c. and roll it as round as possible; bind with tape; roast with or without veal stuffing, laid over before rolling. Thoroughly soak it, and brown it before a quick fire. Roast beef accompaniments, and, if liked, wow-wow sauce.

237. *Roasting Mutton.* — A saddle of mutton of ten or twelve pounds will take from two hours and a half to three hours roasting. Mutton should be put before a brisk fire; a saddle of mutton requires to be protected from the heat by covering it with paper, which should

be taken off about a quarter of an hour before it is done; when of a pale-brown colour, baste it; flour it lightly to froth. The *leg of mutton*, the *shoulder*, the *loin*, the *neck*, the *breast*, and the *haunch*, require the same treatment as the saddle, with the exception of papering, which, however, may be sometimes required. The haunch should be served with plain but rich mutton sauce, and with sweet sauce; of course separately.

238. *Mutton, Venison fashion.* — Hang till fit for dressing a good neck of mutton; two days before dressing it, rub it well twice each day with powdered allspice, and black pepper; roast it in paste, as ordered for the haunch of venison.

239. *Roasting Veal.*—This meat requires particular care to roast it a nice brown; the fire should be the same as for beef; a sound large fire for a large joint, and a brisker for a smaller: soak thoroughly, and then bring it nearer the fire to brown; baste on first putting down, and occasionally afterwards. When done and dished, pour over it melted butter, with or without a little brown gravy. Veal joints, not stuffed, may be served with force meat balls, or rolled into sausages as garnish to the dish; or fried pork sausages. Bacon or ham, and greens, are generally eaten with veal.

240. *Fillet of Veal* of from twelve to sixteen pounds will require from four or five hours at a good fire; make some stuffing or force meat, and put it under the flap, that there may be some left to eat cold, or to season a *hash ;* brown it, and pour good melted butter over it; garnish with thin slices of lemon and cakes or balls of stuffing. A *loin* is the best part of the calf, and will take about three hours roasting; paper the kidney fat and back. A *shoulder* from three hours to three hours and a half; stuff it with the force meat ordered for the fillet of veal, or balls made of 271. *Neck,* best end, will take two hours; same accompaniments as the fillet. The scrag part is best in a pie or broth. *Breast* from an hour and a half to two hours. Let the caul remain till it is almost done, then take it off to brown it; baste, flour and froth it.

241. *Veal Sweetbread.*—Trim a fine sweetbread (it cannot be too fresh), parboil it for five minutes, and throw it into a basin of cold water. Roast it plain, or beat up the yolk of an egg, and prepare some bread crumbs. When the sweetbread is cold, dry it thoroughly in a cloth; run a lark-spit or a skewer through it, and tie it on the ordinary spit; egg it with a paste-brush; powder it well with bread crumbs, and roast it. For sauce, fried bread crumbs round it, and melted butter, with a little mushroom catsup, or serve them on buttered toast, garnished with egg sauce, or with gravy. Instead of spitting them, you may put them into a tin dutch oven or fry them.

242. *Roasting Lamb.* — To the usual accompaniments of roasted meat, lamb requires green mint sauce or salad, or both. Some cooks, about five minutes before it is done, sprinkle it with a little fresh-gathered and finely minced parsley, or crisped parsley. Lamb and all young meats ought to be thoroughly done; therefore, do not take either lamb or veal off the spit till you see it drop white gravy.

When green mint cannot be got, mint vinegar is an acceptable substitute for it, and crisp parsley, on a side plate, is an admirable accompaniment. *Hind-quarter* of eight pounds will take from an hour and three-quarters to two hours; baste, and froth it. A quarter of a porkling is sometimes skinned, cut, and dressed lamb fashion, and sent up as a substitute for it. The leg and the loin of lamb, when little, should be roasted together, the former being lean, the latter fat, and the gravy is better preserved. *Fore-quarter* of ten pounds, about two hours. It is a pretty general custom, when you take off the shoulder from the ribs, to squeeze a Seville orange, or lemon, over them, and sprinkle them with a little pepper and salt; this may be done by the cook before it comes to table. Some people are not remarkably expert at dividing these joints nicely. *Leg* of five pounds, from an hour to an hour and a half. *Shoulder*, with a quick fire, an hour. *Ribs*, almost an hour to an hour and a quarter; joint them nicely, crack the ribs across, and divide them from the brisket after it is roasted. *Loin*, an hour and quarter. *Neck*, an hour. *Breast* three-quarters of an hour.

243. *Roasting Pork.* — If this meat be not well done, thoroughly well done, it is disgusting to the sight and poisonous to the stomach. "In the gravy of pork, if there is the least tint of redness," says Dr. Kitchiner, "it is enough to appal the sharpest appetite. Other meats under-done are unpleasant, but pork is absolutely uneatable." A *Leg* of eight pounds will require about three hours; score the skin across in narrow stripes (some score it in diamonds) about a quarter of an inch apart; stuff the knuckle with sage and onion minced fine, and a little grated bread, seasoned with pepper, salt, and the yolk of an egg. See 252 and 270. Do not put it too near the fire; rub a little sweet oil on the skin with a paste-brush, or a goose-feather; this makes the crackling crisper and browner than basting it with dripping, and it will be a better colour than all the art of cookery can make it in any other way; and this is the best way of preventing the skin from blistering, which is principally occasioned by its being put too near the fire.

244. *Leg of Pork roasted without the skin; or Mock Goose.* — Parboil a leg of pork, take off the skin, and then put it down to roast; baste it with butter, and make a savoury powder of finely minced or dried or powdered sage, ground black pepper, salt, and some bread crumbs rubbed together through a colander; you may add to this a little very finely minced onion; sprinkle it with this when it is almost roasted; put a half pint of made gravy into the dish, and goose stuffing under the knuckle skin, or garnish the dish with balls of it, fried or broiled.

245. *Spare rib:* when you put it down to roast, dust on some flour, and baste it with a little butter; dry a dozen sage leaves, rub them through a hair sieve, put them into the top of a pepper box, and about a quarter of an hour before the meat is done baste it with butter; dust the pulverised sage, or savoury powder, in, or sprinkle it with duck stuffing; some people prefer it plain.

ROASTING.

246. *Loin of Pork*, of five pounds, must be kept at a good distance from the fire, on account of the crackling, and will take about two hours—if very fat, half an hour longer: stuff it with duck stuffing (252 and 270;) score the skin in stripes about a quarter of an inch apart, and rub it with salad oil. You may sprinkle over it some of the savoury powder recommended for the mock goose (244.)

247. *Sucking Pig* should be about three weeks old, and it ought to be dressed as quickly as possible after it is killed; if not quite fresh, the crackling can never be made crisp. It requires constant attention and great care in roasting. As the ends require more fire than the middle, an instrument called the pig-iron has been contrived to hang before the latter part. A common flat iron will answer the purpose, or the fire may be kept fiercest at the ends. A good stuffing may be made as follows:—Take five or six ounces of the crumb of stale bread; crumble and rub through a colander; mince very fine a handful of sage, and a large onion; mix with an egg, pepper, salt, and a piece of butter about the size of an egg; fill the belly, and sew it up; put it to the fire, and baste it with butter tied up in a rag, by applying it to the back of the pig. Kitchiner recommends basting it with olive oil till it is done. It should never be left. It should be placed before a clear brisk fire, at some distance; and great care should be taken that the crackling should be nicely crisped, and delicately browned. It will require from an hour and a half to two hours, according to the size of the pig. When first put to the fire, it should be rubbed all over with fresh butter, or salad oil; ten minutes after this, and when the skin looks dry, dredge it well with flour all over. Let this remain on an hour, and then rub it off with a soft cloth. A sucking pig being very troublesome to roast, is frequently sent to the oven. A clever baker will do it so as to be almost equal to roasted; he will require a quarter of a pound of butter, and should be told to baste it well. (See 284.) Before you take the pig from the fire, cut off the head, and part that and the body down the middle; chop the brains very fine with some boiled sage leaves, and mix them with good veal or beef gravy, or what runs from the pig when you cut the head off. Send up a tureen full of gravy besides. Currant sauce is still a favourite with some of the old school. Lay your pig back to back in the dish, with one half of the head on each side, and the ears at each end, which you must take care to make nice and crisp, or you will get scolded, and deservedly. When you cut off the pettitoes, leave the skin long, round the end of the legs.

248. *Turkey, Turkey Poults, and other Poultry.*—A fowl and a turkey require the same management at the fire, only the latter will take longer time. Let them be carefully picked, break the breastbone (to make them look plump,) and thoroughly singe them with sheet of clean writing paper. Prepare a nice brisk fire for them. Make stuffing according to 269; stuff them under the breast where the craw was taken out; and make some into balls, and boil or fry them, and lay them round the dish; they are handy to help, and you can reserve some of the inside stuffing to eat with the cold turkey, or

to enrich a hash. Score the gizzard; dip it in the yolk of an egg, or melted butter, and sprinkle it with salt and a few grains of cayenne; put it under one pinion, and the liver under the other; cover the liver with buttered paper, to prevent it getting hardened or burnt. When you first put your turkey down to roast, dredge it with flour, then put about an ounce of butter into a basting ladle, and as it melts baste the bird. Keep it at a distance from the fire for the first half hour that it may warm gradually, then put it nearer, and when it is plumped up, and the steam draws towards the fire, it is nearly done enough; then dredge it lightly with flour, and put a bit of butter into your basting ladle, and as it melts baste the turkey with it; this will raise a finer froth than can be produced by using the fat out of the pan. A very large turkey will require about three hours to roast it thoroughly; a middling sized one, of eight or ten pounds, about two hours; a small one may be done in an hour and a half. Turkey poults are of various sizes, and will take about an hour and a half. Fried pork sausages are a very savoury accompaniment to either roasted or boiled turkey. Sausage meat is sometimes used as a stuffing, instead of the ordinary force meat. If you wish a turkey, especially a very large one, to be tender, never dress it till at least four or five days (in cold weather, eight or ten) after it has been killed, unless it be dressed immediately after killing, before the flesh is cold; be very careful not to let it freeze. Hen turkeys are preferable to cocks for whiteness and tenderness, and the small tender ones, with black legs, are most esteemed. Send up with them oyster, egg, and plenty of gravy sauce.

249. *Capons* or *Fowls* must be killed a couple of days in moderate, and more in cold, weather, before they are dressed, unless dressed immediately they are killed, or they will eat tough: a good criterion of the ripeness of poultry for the spit, is the ease with which you can pull out the feathers; when a fowl is plucked, leave a few to help you to ascertain this. They are managed exactly in the same manner, and sent up with the same sauces, as a turkey, only they require proportionably less time at the fire—a full-grown five-toed fowl about an hour and a quarter; a moderate sized one, an hour; a chicken, from thirty to forty minutes. Have also pork sausages fried, as they are in general a favourite accompaniment, or turkey stuffing; see Force meats, 278; put in plenty of it, so as to plump out the fowl, which must be tied closely (both at the neck and rump,) to keep in the stuffing; some cooks put the liver of the fowl into this force meat, and others mince it and pound it, and rub up with flour and melted butter. When the bird is stuffed and trussed, score the gizzard nicely; dip it into melted butter; let it drain, and then season it with cayenne and salt; put it under one pinion, and the liver under the other; to prevent their getting hardened or scorched, cover them with double paper buttered. Take care that your roasted poultry be well browned; it is as indispensable that roasted poultry should have a rich brown complexion, as that boiled poultry should have a delicate white one.

For sauces, see 111; or liver and parsley, and those ordered in the last receipt.

250. *Goose.*—When a goose is well picked, singed and cleaned, make the stuffing with about two ounces of onion, and half as much green sage; chop them very fine, adding four ounces of stale bread crumbs, a bit of butter about as big as a walnut, and a very little pepper and salt (to this some cooks add half the liver, parboiling it first,) the yolk of an egg or two, and, incorporating the whole together, stuff the goose; do not quite fill it, but leave a little room for the stuffing to swell. From an hour and a half to an hour and three-quarters will roast a fine full-grown goose. Send up gravy and apple sauce with it. Geese are called green till they are about four months old.

251. *Canvass Back Ducks, or Red Neck Ducks.*—Let your duck be young and fat, if possible; having picked it well, draw it and singe carefully, without washing it, so as to preserve the blood, and consequently, all its flavour. You then truss it, leaving its head on for the purpose of distinguishing it from common game, and place it on the spit before a brisk fire, for at least fifteen minutes. Then serve it hot, in its own gravy, which is formed by the blood, &c., on a large chafing dish. The best birds are found on the Potomac river; they have the head purple, and the breast silver colour, and it is considered superior in quality and flavour to any other species of wild duck. The season is only during the cold weather.

252. *Duck.*—Mind your duck is well cleaned, and wiped out with a clean cloth; for the stuffing, take an ounce of onion and half an ounce of green sage; chop them very fine, and mix them with two ounces of bread crumbs, a bit of butter about as big as a walnut, a very little black pepper and salt, and the yolk of an egg to bind it; mix these thoroughly together, and put into the duck. From half to three-quarters of an hour will be enough to roast it, according to the size; contrive to have the feet delicately crisp, as some people are very fond of them;—to do this nicely, you must have a sharp fire. Gravy sauce, and sage and onion sauce. To hash or stew ducks, the same as goose. If you think the raw onion will make too strong an impression upon the palate, parboil it. To insure ducks being tender, in moderate weather kill them a few days before you dress them.

253. *Haunch of Venison.*—To preserve the fat, make a paste of flour and water, as much as will cover the haunch; wipe it with a dry cloth in every part; rub a large sheet of paper all over with butter, and cover the venison with it; then roll out the paste about three-quarters of an inch thick. Lay this all over the fat side, cover it with three or four sheets of strong white paper, and tie it securely on with packthread; have a strong close fire, and baste your venison as soon as you lay it down to roast (to prevent the paper and string from burning;) it must be well basted all the time. A buck haunch which generally weighs from twenty to twenty-five pounds, will take about four hours and a half roasting in warm, and longer in cold, weather. A haunch of from twelve to eighteen pounds will be done in about three hours, or three hours and a half. A quarter of an hour before it is done, the string must be cut, and the paste carefully taken off; now

baste it with butter, dredge it lightly with flour, and when the froth rises, and it has got a very light-brown colour, it is done. Garnish the knuckle bone with a ruffle of cut writing paper, and send it up with good strong (but unseasoned) gravy in one boat, and currant jelly sauce in the other, or currant jelly in a side plate (not melted.) See for Sauces, 137, 138, 139. Buck venison is in greatest perfection from Midsummer to Michaelmas, and doe from November to January. *Neck* and *Shoulder* of venison are to be treated the same way as the haunch, but they will not take so much time, nor do they need the paste covering.

254. *A Fawn* should be dressed as soon after it is killed as possible; when very young, it is dressed the same as a hare; but they are better eating when the size of the house lamb, or when they are large enough to be roasted in quarters. The hind-quarter is considered the best. Fawns require a very quick fire. They are so delicate that they must be constantly basted, or be covered with sheets of fat bacon; when nearly done, remove the bacon, baste it with butter, and froth it. Serve with venison sauce.

255. *A Kid* is very good eating when a suckling, and when the dam is in fine condition. Roast, and serve it like a fawn or hare.

256. *Hare* when young is easy of digestion, and very nourishing—when old, the contrary, unless rendered so by keeping and dressing. When you receive a hare, take out the liver—if it be sweet, parboil it, and keep it for stuffing. Wipe the hare quite dry; rub the inside with pepper, and hang it in a cool place till it is fit to be dressed, that is to say, till it comes to the point of putrefaction, but not putrefied. Then paunch and skin, wash and lay it in a large pan of cold water four or five hours, changing the water two or three times; lay it in a clean cloth; dry it well, and truss. To make the stuffing, see 272. Let it be stiff; put it in the belly, and sew it up tightly. The skin must be cut to let the blood out of the neck. Some persons baste it with skimmed milk, but we decidedly prefer dripping; it ought to be constantly basted till it is nearly done; then put a little bit of butter into your basting ladle; flour and froth nicely. Serve with good gravy and currant jelly. Cold roast hare, chopped to pieces, and stewed in water for a couple of hours, will make excellent soup.

257. *Rabbit.*—Put it down to a sharp clear fire; dredge it lightly and carefully with flour; take care to have it frothy and of a fine light brown; boil the liver with parsley while the rabbit is roasting; when tender, chop them together; put half the mixture into melted butter, use the other half for garnish, divided into little hillocks. Cut off the head, divide it, and lay half on each side the dish. A fine well-grown and well-hung warren rabbit, dressed as a hare, will eat very much like it.

258. *A Pheasant* should have a smart fire, but not a fierce one; baste it, butter and froth it, and prepare sauce for it. Some persons, the pheasant being a dry bird, put a piece of beef or rump steak into the inside before roasting. It is said that a pheasant should be suspended by one of the long tail feathers till it falls. It is then ripe

and ready for the spit, and not before. If a fowl be well kept, and dressed as a pheasant, and with a pheasant, few persons will discover the pheasant from the fowl.

259. *Guinea Fowls, Partridges, Pea Fowls, Blackcock, Grouse,* and *Moorgame,* are dressed in the same way as pheasants. Partridges are sent up with rice sauce, or bread sauce, and good gravy. Blackcock, moorgame, and grouse, are sent up with currant jelly and fried bread crumbs.

260. *Wild Ducks, Widgeon,* and *Teal,* are dressed before a clear fire, and on a hot spit. Wild ducks will require fifteen or twenty minutes to do them in the *fashionable* way, but to do them *well* will require a few minutes longer. Widgeon and teal, being smaller birds, of course will require less time.

261. *Woodcocks* and *Snipes* are never drawn; they should be tied on a small bird spit, and put to roast at a clear fire; a slice of bread is put under each bird, to catch the trail, that is the excrements of the intestines; they are considered delightful eating; baste with butter, and froth with flour; lay the toast on a hot dish, and the birds on the toast; pour some good gravy into the dish, and send some up in a boat. They are generally roasted from twenty to thirty minutes—but some epicures say, that a woodcock should be just introduced to the cook, for her to show it the fire, and then send it up to table. Garnish with slices of lemon. Snipes are dressed in the same way, but require less time.

262. *Pigeons,* when stuffed, require some green parsley to be chopped very fine with the liver and a bit of butter, seasoned with a little pepper and salt; or they may be stuffed with the same as a fillet of veal. Fill the belly of each bird with either of these compositions. They will roast in about twenty or thirty minutes. Serve with parsley and butter, with a dish under them, with some in a boat. Garnish with crisp parsley, fried bread crumbs, bread sauce, or gravy.

263. *Small Birds.*—The most delicate of these are larks, which are in high season in November and December. When cleaned and prepared for roasting, brush them with the yolk of an egg, and roll in bread crumbs; spit them on a lark-spit, and tie that on a larger spit; ten or fifteen minutes at a quick fire will do them; baste them with fresh butter, and sprinkle them with bread crumbs till they are quite covered, while roasting. Sauce, grated bread fried in butter, which set to drain before the fire that it may harden; serve the crumbs under the larks when you dish them, and garnish them with slices of lemon. *Wheatears* are dressed in the same way.

264. *Reed Birds.*—Having carefully picked your birds, which should be very fat, draw them with the greatest care possible so as not to rob them of any fat, and truss them on a skewer, which you fasten to the spit, and cook them before a brisk fire; a very few minutes is requisite. In serving them, place them on buttered toast, and pour a small portion of gravy over them. Let them be hot. This is generally considered the best manner of serving reed birds, although many persons prefer them breaded and fried, or barbacued.

When they are very fat it is unnecessary to draw them. The season for this delicious bird is from the middle of September to the first or second week in October.

SEASONINGS.

The art of making seasonings, or stuffings, principally consists in so proportioning the flavours as that none may predominate, or be tasted more than another. In stuffing, care must be taken to leave room for swelling; if not, it is apt to be hard and heavy.

265. *Seasoning for Roast Pork, Ducks, or Geese.*—Two-thirds onion, one-third green sage, chopped fine, bread crumbs equal in weight to the sage and onions; season with a little pepper and salt, and incorporate it well with the yolk of an egg or two, and a bit of butter. Some omit the bread crumbs, and some again do not like the onions, while others add to them a clove of garlic.

266. *Seasoning for a Sucking Pig.*—A large teacup full of grated bread, two ounces of butter, season with nutmeg, salt, and pepper; scald two small onions, chop fine, and about thirty leaves of young sage, and egg beat fine, and mix altogether, and sew it in the belly of the pig.

267. *Seasoning for a Goose.*—Scald the liver, chop fine, crumb twice its weight in bread, chop fine four small onions, or an equal weight of chives, half the weight of green sage, half an ounce of butter, the yolk of an egg, and a table spoonful of potato starch; season highly with salt and pepper; mix well.

268. *Chesnut Seasoning for Goose.*—Fry or boil chesnuts till the outer skin comes off very easily, and the inside will pound or grate; reduce them to powder, scald the liver of the goose, and an onion or two, the juice of a lemon, season with pepper, cayenne, salt; mix well together.

STUFFINGS AND FORCE MEATS.

269. *Stuffing for Veal, Roast Turkey, Fowl, &c.*—Mince a quarter of a pound of beef marrow (beef suet will do,) the same weight of bread crumbs, two drachms of parsley leaves, a drachm and a half of sweet marjoram (or lemon thyme,) and the same of grated lemon peel, an onion, chopped very fine, a little salt and pepper, pound thoroughly together, with the yolk and white of two eggs, and secure it in the veal with a skewer, or sew it in with a needle and thread. Make some of it into balls or sausages; flour and fry or boil them, and send them up as a garnish, or in a side dish, with roast poultry, veal, or cutlets, &c. This is sufficient quantity for a turkey poult; a very large turkey will require twice as much; an ounce of dressed ham may be added to the above, or use equal parts of the above stuffing and pork sausage meat.

270. *Goose or Duck stuffing.*—Chop very fine about one ounce of green sage leaves, two ounces of onion also chopped fine (both un-

boiled,) a bit of butter about the size of a walnut, four ounces of bread crumbs, a little salt and pepper, the yolk and white of an egg; some add to this a little apple.

271. *Force meat balls* for turtle, mock turtle, or made dishes:—Pound some veal in a marble mortar, rub it through a sieve with as much of the udder as you have of veal, and about the third of the quantity of butter; put some bread crumbs in a stew-pan, moisten with milk, add a little chopped eschalot, and a little parsley; rub them well together in a mortar till they form a smooth paste; put it through a sieve, and when cold, pound and mix all together, with the yolk of three eggs boiled hard; season it with curry powder, or cayenne pepper and salt; add the yolks of two unboiled eggs, rub it well together, and make small balls; a few minutes before your soup is ready, put them in.

272. *Stuffing for Hare.*—Three ounces of fine bread crumbs, two ounces of beef suet, chopped fine, eschalot half a drachm, one drachm of parsley, a drachm of lemon thyme, marjoram, winter savoury, a drachm of grated lemon peel, and the same of pepper and salt; mix these with the white and yolk of an egg; do not make it thin, for if it is not stiff enough, it will be good for nothing; put it in the hare and sew it up. If the liver is quite sound, parboil it, mince it very fine, and put to the stuffing.

273. *Veal Force meat.*—Of undressed veal take two ounces, scrape it quite fine, and free from skin and sinews, the same quantity of beef or veal suet, and the same of bread crumbs; chop fine one drachm of lemon peel, two drachms of parsley, the same quantity of sweet herbs, and half a drachm of mace or allspice beaten to a fine powder; pound all together in a mortar, break into it the yolk and white of an egg, rub it all well together, and season with pepper and salt. This may be made more savoury by adding cold pickled tongue, eschalot, anchovy, cayenne, or curry powder.

274. *Stuffing for Pike, Carp, or Haddock.*— A dozen oysters bearded and chopped, two yolks of eggs, a small onion, or two cloves of eschalot and a few sprigs of parsley chopped fine, season with cayenne, mace, allspice, pepper, and salt; add their weight of bread crumbs, or biscuit powder, then put two ounces of butter into a stew-pan, and simmer them till they have sucked up the butter; as they begin to bind, sprinkle over them more bread crumbs or biscuit powder, till the whole forms into a ball, with which stuff the fish. Some people like the addition of ham or tongue scraped, and suet or marrow instead of butter.

Another way. Beef suet, or marrow and fat bacon, and fresh butter, two ounces of each; pound them with the meat of a lobster, ten or twelve oysters, one or two anchovies; season with thyme, parsley, knotted marjoram, savoury, chopped fine and scalded; add salt, cayenne, and nutmeg, a few drops of essence of eschalot; add the yolk of an egg, and bread crumbs. This pudding will be sufficiently done in the belly of the fish, if you do not add the eschalot in substance.

275. *Stuffing for Heart and many other purposes.*—Take half a pound of grated bread; chop fine a quarter of a pound of beef or lamb suet, or beef marrow; season with salt, pepper, and nutmeg; a handful of parsley leaves, thyme about a quarter as much, six sprigs of marjoram and vervain, winter savoury or knotted marjoram, and the juice of a quarter of a lemon. Mix well with two eggs well beaten. You may add a dozen of oysters, chopped, and the liquor, or two ounces of dressed ham, chopped. This stuffing may be used for a turkey, with an equal quantity of sausage meat parboiled; rub them well together, and keep out half a pound, to which add an egg, to make up into balls and fry, and lay round the dish as a garnish. Turkey is sometimes stuffed with chesnuts (see 267); take basil and parsley instead of onions, and add a quarter of a pound of dressed ham grated, and a little nutmeg.

276. *A very rich stuffing for Veal, Poultry, and Game.*—Take two pounds of beef suet, one pound of bread crumbs, a tea spoonful of thyme, the same quantity of marjoram, a tea-cup full of chopped parsley, chopped eschalot a table spoonful, half a lemon grated, half a nutmeg, half an ounce each of salt and pepper, and five eggs, well mixed.

277. *Veal Cake.*—Boil six eggs hard, cut the yolks in two, butter a mould; lay some of the pieces of egg at the bottom, sprinkle salt, pepper, and chopped parsley; then lay thin slices of veal and ham; sprinkle again with the seasoning, and then eggs, and so on till the dish is filled. Then add gravy, till it covers the top of the meat; spread one ounce of butter over the top, tie it over with paper, and bake one hour; then press it close together with a spoon, and let it stand till cold. Another way is to pound the meat instead of slices, two-thirds of lean veal and one-third of fat ham. When the cake is wanted, set the mould in boiling water for a minute or two, and the cake will turn out.

278. *Force meat for Veal or Fowls.*—Take equal parts of cold veal, beef suet, ham or gammon, a few parsley leaves, a small onion, the rind of lemon a little; chop all together very fine; season with pepper, salt, cayenne, mace, or nutmeg; pound the whole in a mortar, with an equal quantity of bread crumbs, and add two eggs to bind it. This is a good force meat for patties.

279. *Light force meat balls.*—Cold veal or chicken a quarter of a pound, chopped, half a pound of suet, chopped, crumbs of bread a tea-cup full. Season with sweet herbs, and spice and eschalots, and three or four eggs beat separately; mix these articles with all the yolks and as much of the whites as is necessary to bring it to a moist paste, roll them in small balls, and fry them in butter, or lard, for garnish to roast turkey, fowl, &c.

280. *Egg balls.*—Boil four eggs for ten minutes and put them into cold water; when they are cold beat the yolks in a mortar with the yolk of a raw egg, some chopped parsley, a tea-spoonful of flour, a pinch or two of salt, and a little black pepper, or cayenne; rub them well together, roll them into small balls, and boil them two minutes.

281. *Brain balls.*—Take a calf's brains, or two or three lambs', scald them for ten minutes, quite free from every bit of vein and skin, beat up with seasoning the same as egg balls, adding a tea spoonful of chopped sage; rub a tea-cup full of bread crumbs, three tea spoonfuls of flour, and a raw egg with them. Make them up into balls, rub each ball with bread, fry them with butter or lard; serve as a garnish to calf's head, or as a separate side dish.

282. *Curry balls.*—Take bread crumbs, the yolk of an egg boiled hard, and a bit of fresh butter; beat together in a mortar, and season with curry powder; make them into small balls, and boil or fry them.

BAKING MEAT, &c.

283. As baking is the only means by which the poor inhabitants of towns for the most part can enjoy a joint of meat at home,[*] we shall say a word or two upon the subject, particularly with regard to those joints which, when they are carefully baked, most resemble roasted ones. Legs and loins of pork, legs of mutton, fillets of veal, &c., may be baked with advantage, if the meat be good and tolerably fat. Besides the joints here enumerated, there are many others which may be baked, providing the meat is not poor or lean. The following are observations on baking meat by a well-experienced baker; they are particularly deserving the attention of a careful housekeeper.

284. "A pig when sent to the baker prepared for baking should have its ears and tail covered with buttered paper, properly fastened on, and a bit of butter tied up in linen to baste the back with, otherwise it will be apt to blister. With a proper share of attention from the baker, this way is thought to be equal to a roasted one.

285. "A goose prepared as for roasting, taking care to have it on a stand, and when half done, to turn the other side upwards. A duck should be treated in the same way.

286. "After a buttock of beef has been in salt about a week, well wash it, and put it in a brown earthen pan with a pint of water, cover the pan quite over and tightly with two or three thicknesses of cap or foolscap paper (never use brown paper — it contains tar, &c.). Bake for four or five hours in a moderate heated oven. A ham properly soaked may be baked in the same way.

287. "Bakers are in the habit of baking small cod fish, haddock, and mackerel, with a dust of flour and some bits of butter put on them. Eels, when large and stuffed. Herrings and sprats in a brown pan, with a little vinegar and a little spice, and tied over with paper. A hare, prepared the same as for roasting, with a few pieces of butter and a little drop of milk put into the dish, and basted several times, will be found nearly equal to roasting; or cut it up, season it properly, put it into a jar or pan, and cover it over, and bake it in a

---

[*] We hope, however, in a few years, to see the American oven supersede the custom of dressing meat in the public bake-house.

moderate oven for about three hours. In the same manner legs and shins of beef, ox cheeks, &c., prepared with a seasoning of onions, turnips, &c., may be baked: they will take about four hours; let them stand till cold to skim off the fat; then warm up altogether, or part, as you may want it.

288. "The time that each of the above articles should take, depends much upon the state of the oven; they should be sent to the baker in time, and he must be very neglectful if they are not *ready* at the time they are ordered."

289. We may be here allowed to remark, that the process of dressing meat in an oven in a covered pan is more analogous to stewing than it is to baking. It is, however, an excellent mode of cooking. The great objection to baking meat in an open pan, and among many other different descriptions of dishes, is the bad flavour which is apt to be imparted to it. There is, too, another objection to baked meat, which arises from the exclusion of the external air, or for want of a draught. The exhalations from the meat in baking, &c., not being carried off, they have a tendency to sodden it.

290. Dr. Kitchiner, no mean authority, deprecates the machines which the economical grate-makers call roasters, being in fact, as he asserts, "in plain English—ovens." The Doctor intimates, that these things are all very well for saving fuel, but affirms that the rational epicure, who has been accustomed to enjoy beef well roasted, will soon discover the difference. Notwithstanding this high authority, we have no hesitation in stating, that meat cooked in the roaster attached to Flavell's cooking apparatus, is as good as meat roasted before the fire. But we ought to observe, that Mr. Flavell's roaster has a current of air passing through it when so employed, but when used as an oven the current of air is prevented by the introduction of a damper. We can state from the experience of some years, that the apparatus alluded to is a most excellent contrivance for cooking generally.

291. "Nothing can be more preposterous," says Mr. Sylvester, in his 'Philosophy of Domestic Economy,' "and inappropriate, than the prevailing construction and management of a gentleman's kitchen. Before the discovery of the stew hearths, all the culinary processes were carried on with one immense open grate, burning as much fuel in one day as might do the same work for ten. The cook and the furniture of the kitchen get a proportion of this heat, the articles to be dressed another portion, but by far the greatest quantity goes up the chimney.

292. "The introduction of the stew hearth has in some degree reduced the magnitude of these grates; but they are yet disgraceful to science and common sense. In the present state (1819) of culinary improvement, a kitchen may be fitted up with apparatus, requiring much less labour and attention, with much less consumption of fuel; rendering the food more wholesome and agreeable, and also preventing that offensive smell which has made it so often necessary to detach the kitchen from the rest of the house."

293. The stew hearth is a most useful addition to the ordinary kitchen grate, but small families of limited means are seldom possessed of one. A stew hearth, indeed, or a substitute for one, which may be easily obtained, is indispensable in French, and indeed in good English cookery.

FRYING.

294. Frying, as is properly observed by Dr. Kitchiner, is often a convenient mode of cookery; it may be performed by a fire which will not do for roasting or boiling, and by the introduction of the pan between the meat and the fire, things get more equally dressed.

295. Be very particular that your frying pan is perfectly clean before using it. Never use any oil, butter, lard, or drippings, which are not perfectly free from salt, and perfectly sweet and fresh. As frying is, in fact, boiling in oil fat, it is of the first importance that your fat should be clean, or it will spoil the look as well as the flavour, and salt will prevent the meat from browning.

296. Good oil is, perhaps, the best to fry in, but sweet fresh lard, or clarified mutton or beef suet, will answer every purpose, nearly, if not quite as well as the best oil or butter, and, what is of greater importance, at a much less expense. Nice clean dripping is almost as good as any thing. After you have done frying preserve your fat, which, if not burnt, will do for three or four fryings; but fat in which fish has been fried will do for nothing else.

297. If your fat is not of a proper heat, your frying cannot be well done; this is, in short, the great secret in frying, which the young cook ought and must acquire. The frying pan must be always set over a sharp and clear fire, or otherwise the fat is too long before it becomes ready. When the fat has done hissing, or bubbling, that is, when it is still, you may be pretty sure that it is hot enough. It is a good way to try the heat of your fat, by throwing a little bit of bread into the pan; if it fries crisp, the fat is of the right heat—if it burns the bread, it is too hot.

298. When your things are well done, take care and drain all the fat from them *most thoroughly*, particularly those that have been fried in bread crumbs, &c.; if you do not, your cookery will be marred. Fried fish ought to be quite dry. This depends in a great measure upon the fat in which they are dressed being of a proper heat. If the fish are well done, and are well drained of the fat, they will become quite dry and crisp in a few minutes after they have been taken out of the pan. If this, however, should not be the case, and the fish on the contrary should be damp and wet, lay them on a soft cloth before the fire, turning them occasionally till they are dry. They will sometimes take ten or fifteen minutes drying.

299. In preparing bread crumbs in a considerable quantity, in order to save unbroken the crust, and preserving it fit for the table, cut your loaf into three equal parts, that is, cut off the bottom and top crusts, and use the middle part or the crumb for your frying. The

bread should be at least two days old. A good and cheap substitute for bread is oatmeal, which will cost, comparatively speaking, nothing.

It is scarcely necessary to refer the cook to our general remarks upon the above operation. Frying is preferred by many persons to broiling; and our own opinion is, that steaks, chops, &c., may be dressed with much more certainty and regularity by the former, than by the latter, method. But plenty of oil, butter, or sweet grease, must always be used, or the frying will be imperfect.

300. *Steaks.*—Cut them rather thinner than for broiling; put some butter, or, what is much cheaper and quite as good, some clarified dripping or suet, into an iron frying-pan, and when it is quite hot put in the steaks, and keep turning them until they are done enough. The sauce for steaks, chops, cutlets, &c., is made as follows:—Take the chops, steaks or cutlets, out of the frying pan; for a pound of meat, keep a table-spoonful of the fat in the pan, or put in an ounce of butter; put to it as much flour as will make it a paste; rub it well together over the fire till they are a little brown; then add as much boiling water as will reduce it to the thickness of good cream, and a table-spoonful of mushroom or walnut catsup, or pickle, or browning; let it boil together a few minutes, and pour it through a sieve to the steaks, &c. To the above is sometimes added a sliced onion, or a minced eschalot, with a table-spoonful of port wine, or a little eschalot wine. Garnish with scraped horse-radish, or pickled walnut, gherkins, &c. Some beef-eaters like chopped eschalots in one saucer, and horse-radish grated in vinegar in another. Broiled mushrooms are favourite relishes to beef-steaks.

301. *Beef-steaks and Onions.*—The steaks are fried as directed above; the common method is to fry the onions cut small, but the best plan perhaps is to use onions prepared as directed in 115.

302. *Sausages.*—Sausages are not good unless they are quite fresh. Put a bit of butter or dripping into a frying-pan, before it gets hot put in the sausages, shake the pan, and keep turning them (be careful not to break or prick them in so doing); fry them over a very slow fire till they are nicely browned on all sides; when they are done, lay them on a hair sieve, place them before the fire for a couple of minutes to drain the fat from them. The secret of frying sausages is, to let them get hot very gradually—then they will not burst, if they are not stale. You may froth them by rubbing them with cold fresh butter, and lightly dredge them with flour, and put them in a cheese-toaster for a minute. The common practice to prevent their bursting is to prick them with a fork; but this lets out the gravy.

303. *Veal Cutlets* should be about half an inch thick; trim and flatten; fry in plenty of fresh butter, or good dripping; when the fire is very fierce, you must turn them often—but when not so, do them brown on one side before you turn them. Make gravy of the trimmings, &c.; you may add some browning, mushroom or walnut catsup, or lemon, pickle, &c. Or you may dress them as follows: Cut the veal into pieces about as big as a crown piece; beat them with a

cleaver, dip in egg, beat up with a little salt, and then in fine bread crumbs; fry them a light brown in boiling lard; serve under them some good gravy or mushroom sauce, which may be made in five minutes. Garnish with slices of ham, or rashers of bacon, or pork sausages. Many persons prefer frying veal cutlets with ham or bacon rashers, which will afford sufficient fat to fry them, but will be done much sooner; remove the rashers, and keep them warm. When the veal is done, take it out, pour off any fat that may remain, and put into the pan a large tea-cup full or more of gravy or broth, and a piece of butter rolled in flour. When it boils, add herbs and crumbs of bread, pour over the veal, and lay the rashers round the edge of the dish. Garnish, sliced lemon.

304. *Sweetbreads* should always be got fresh and parboiled immediately. When cold cut them in pieces about three-quarters of an inch thick, dip them in the yolk of an egg, then in fine bread crumbs (some add spice, lemon peel, and sweet herbs;) put some clean dripping into a frying-pan; when it boils put in the sweetbreads, and fry them a fine brown. For garnish, crisp parsley; and for sauce, mushroom catsup and melted butter, or anchovy sauce, or bacon, or ham. This is called full dressing. They are dressed plain as follows: Parboil and slice them as before, dry them on a clean cloth, flour them, and fry them a delicate brown; take care to drain the fat well from them, and garnish them with slices of lemon and sprigs of chervil, parsley, or crisp parsley. For sauce, mushroom catsup, or force meat balls made as 278.

305. *Lamb or Mutton Chops* are dressed in the same way as veal cutlets, and garnished with crisp parsley, and slices of lemon. If they are bread-crumbed, and covered with buttered writing paper, and then broiled, they are called "*Maintenon cutlets.*"

306. *Pork Chops.*—Take care that they are trimmed very neatly; they should be about half an inch thick; put a frying-pan on the fire, with a bit of butter; as soon as it is hot, put in your chops, turning them often till brown all over, and done; take one upon a plate and try it; if done, season it with a little finely minced onion, powdered sage, and pepper and salt. Sauce, sage and onions, or Robert sauce.

307. *Fried Eggs.*—Well-cleansed dripping, or lard, or fresh butter, is the best fat for frying eggs. Be sure the frying-pan is quite clean; when the fat is hot, break two or three eggs into it; do not turn them, but, while they are frying, keep pouring some of the fat over them with a spoon; when the yolk just begins to look white, which it will in about a couple of minutes, they are done enough; the white must not lose its transparency, but the yolk be seen blushing through it. If they are done nicely, they will look as white and delicate as if they had been poached; take them up with a tin slice, drain the fat from them, trim neatly, and send them up with toasted bacon round them. *For Frying Fish, see section Fish,* p. 66, par. 193, &c.

BROILING.

308. Let your gridiron be quite clean, particularly between the bars, and keep it bright on the top. Before using it, you should be careful to make the bars thoroughly hot, or otherwise that part of the meat which is covered by the bars will not be equally done with the other parts of the steak or chop.

309. Chops, steaks, or slices for broiling, should be from half to three quarters of an inch in thickness; if too thick, they will be done outside before the inside—and if too thin, they will be dry and gravyless.

310. In broiling, a brisk and clear fire is indispensable, and to obtain this you should prepare your fire in time, so that it may burn clear. It is a good plan to lay over a pretty strong fire a layer of cinders, or coke; some use charcoal, but cinders or coke are equally good. If your fire is not bright you cannot give the nice brown appearance to the meat, which is not only pleasing to the eye, but is relishing to the taste.

311. The bars of the best gridirons are made concave, terminating in a trough to catch the gravy, and keep the fat from falling into the fire and making a smoke, which will spoil both the appearance and taste of the broil. Before using the gridiron the bars should be rubbed with clean mutton suet. The cook should watch the moment when the broil is done. Send it to the table immediately on a hot dish, from whence it should be transferred to the mouth all hot!—smoking hot!!! The upright gridiron, which is made of strong wire and may be now bought in the streets for a few pence, is, as Dr. Kitchiner avers, the best, as it can be used at any fire, without fear of smoke, and the trough under it preserves all the gravy. The Dutch oven, or bonnet, may be substituted for the gridiron, when the fire is not clear.

312. *Steaks and Chops.*—Meat to be broiled should be hung till it is tender; the inside of a sirloin of beef, cut into steaks, is greatly preferred by most people. But steaks are generally cut from the rump (the middle is the best), about six inches long, four inches wide, and half an inch thick. Do not beat them, it makes them dry and tasteless. Steaks should be done quickly; for this purpose, take care to have a very clear brisk fire, throw a little salt on it, make the gridiron hot, and set it slanting to prevent the fat from dropping into the fire, and making a smoke. It requires more practice and care than is generally supposed to do steaks to a nicety; and for want of these little attentions, this very common dish, which every body is supposed capable of dressing, seldom comes to table in perfection. Some like it under, some thoroughly, done. It is usual to put a table-spoonful of catsup, or a little minced eschalot, into a dish before the fire, while you are broiling; turn the steak with a pair of steak-tongs; it will be done in about ten or fifteen minutes; rub a bit of butter over it, and send it up garnished with pickles and finely scraped horse-radish. Serve with the usual sauces.

313. *Kidneys.*—Cut them through the long way, score them, sprinkle a little pepper and salt on them, and run a wire skewer through them to keep them from curling on the gridiron, so that they may be evenly broiled. Broil them over a very clear fire, turning them often till they are done; they will take about ten or twelve minutes, if the fire is brisk: or, fry them in butter, and make gravy from them in the pan (after you have taken out the kidneys), by putting in a tea spoonful of flour; as soon as it looks brown, put in as much water as will make gravy; they will take five minutes more to fry than to broil. Serve with the usual sauce. Some cooks chop a few parsley leaves very fine, and mix them with a bit of fresh butter and a little pepper and salt, and put a little of this mixture on each kidney.

314. *A Fowl or Rabbit.*—Pick and truss it the same as for boiling, cut it open down the back, wipe the inside clean with a cloth, season it with a little pepper and salt, have a clear fire and set the gridiron at a good distance over it, lay the chicken on with the inside towards the fire (you may egg it and strew some grated bread over it), and broil it till it is a fine brown; take care the fleshy side is not burnt. Lay it on a hot dish, pickled mushrooms or mushroom sauce thrown over it, or parsley and butter, or melted butter flavoured with mushroom catsup. Garnish with slices of lemon, and the liver and gizzard, slit and notched, seasoned with pepper and salt, and broiled nicely brown.

315. *Pigeons.*—Clean them well, and pepper and salt them; broil them over a clear slow fire; turn them often, and put a little butter on them; when they are done, pour over them either stewed or pickled mushrooms, or catsup and melted butter. Garnish with fried bread crumbs, or sippets. Or, when the pigeons are trussed for broiling, flat them with a cleaver, taking care not to break the skin of the backs or breast; season them with pepper and salt, a little bit of butter, and a tea spoonful of water, and tie them close at both ends; so, when they are brought to table, they bring their sauce with them Egg and dredge them well with grated bread (mixed with spice and sweet herbs), lay them on the gridiron, and turn them frequently; if your fire is not very clear, lay them on a sheet of paper well buttered, to keep them from getting smoked. They are much better broiled whole.

BRAISING, GLAZING, BLANCHING, LARDING, AND BONING.

316. A braiser, or braising pan, is a sort of oblong camp kettle, with a bordered lid, on which, and secured by the border, is put small burning coal, charcoal, or wood ashes. The lid should fit the pan as close as possible.

317. *Braising.* To braise your meat, put the meat into the braiser (a good stew-pan will answer the purpose, but not so well); then cover the meat with thick slices of fat bacon; lay round it six or eight

onions, a bunch of sweet herbs, some celery, and if it be to brown, some thick slices of carrots; meat trimmings, or fresh meat bones, a pint and a half of water, or the same quantity of stock, which will make it richer than water will; over the meat lay a sheet of white paper, season and put the pan, with the lid well fastened down and tight, over a moderately hot stove, rather slow. It will require two or three hours, according to its size or quality. The meat and gravy are then put into a colander to drain, but be sure to keep it quite hot, skim the gravy very carefully, and boil it as quick as you can till it thickens; then glaze the meat—and if it has been larded, put it into the oven for a few minutes.

318. *Glazing* consists in covering meat with a preparation called glaze, which is strong gravy boiled as quick as possible till it thickens, as directed in braising. The glaze is put on with a brush kept for the purpose. Hams, tongues, and stewed beef, may be thus glazed, if thought proper.

319. *Blanching* is performed by putting the article in cold water over the fire, and when it boils up, take it out and plunge it into cold water, and let it remain till quite cold. This will make it white and plump. Tongues, palates, &c., are said to be blanched, when after long boiling the skin can be easily peeled off.

320. *Larding* and *Forcing*. Possess yourself of larding pins of different sizes; cut slices of bacon into bits of proper length, quite smooth; pierce the skin and a very little of the meat with the larding pin, leaving the bacon in; the two ends should be of equal length outwards. Lard in rows the size you think proper. Forcing is nothing more than stuffing fowls, &c., with force meat, which is generally put in between the skin and the flesh.

321. *Boning*. To bone any bird, the cook should begin first to take out the breast-bone; she will then have sufficient space to remove the back with a sharp small knife, and then she must take out the leg bones. The skin must be preserved whole, and the meat of the leg be pushed inwards.

COLOURINGS, THICKENINGS, FLAVOURINGS, SEASON-
INGS, STOCKS, GRAVIES, SAUCES, STUFFING, FORCE-
MEAT, AND CLARIFYING.

Having laid down, as we trust, clearly and fully, under the preceding heads, all that is necessary to be known, generally speaking, with regard to ordinary dishes, we shall now proceed to treat of those preparations which are employed in the compounding of made dishes. together with those articles which the prudent, care-taking cook wil. always keep by her as stores, ready to be used when wanted. By 'made dishes' we mean not only those commonly so called, but also those in the dressing of which other articles are sometimes, or always, used by way of stuffing, seasoning, &c.—such, for instance, as geese, ducks, and roast pork. This done, we shall then give direc-

COLOURING, OR BROWNING.

tions for the choice of meat, fish, and poultry, recipes for cooking them, and the best mode of carving them, under separate heads. Recipes for cooking all other dishes, will also, of course, be given.

COLOURING, OR BROWNING.

322. The greater part of the preparations for colouring are very unwholesome, or, in other words, very indigestible. They are employed to give the appearance of richness, but they are worse than useless, being used for the silly purpose of pleasing the eye only, generally at the expense of the stomach and taste. Most of the preparations for colouring are a medley of burnt butter, spices, catsup, wine, flour, and other things not necessary to mention. A French writer says, the generality of cooks calcine bones till they are as black as a coal, and throw them hissing hot into the stew-pan, to give a brown colour to their broths and soups. These ingredients, under the appearance of a nourishing gravy, envelop our food with stimulating acid and corrosive poison. Such things as essence of anchovy are frequently adulterated with colouring matters containing red lead! The following recipes for colouring are pretty harmless, and, except for the purpose of pleasing the eye, as useless as they are innocent.

Some persons, instead of colouring or browning their soups after they are made, brown the meat of which they are intended to be made, by putting it into a stew-pan with a little butter, salt, and pepper, but without water; then covering it close, placing it over a clear fire, all the time shaking it to keep it from sticking to the pan, till the meat becomes of a light brown, when the liquor of which the soup or gravy is to be made is added.

The best colouring is, perhaps, the following: Half a pound of powdered lump sugar and a table-spoonful of water, put into a clean saucepan, or frying-pan, and set over a slow fire and stirred with a wooden spoon till it is of a fine brown colour, and begins to smoke; then add an ounce of salt, and dilute by degrees with water, till it is of the thickness of soy; boil, take off the scum, and put it into well-corked bottles; or you may, provided you do not wish to keep the above by you, colour your gravies or soups by pounding a tea-spoonful of lump sugar, and putting it into an iron spoon, which hold over a quick fire till the mixture becomes of a dark-brown colour; mix with the soup or gravy while it is hot. Some persons use butter in the first mixture instead of water.

Toasted bread, quite hard and of a deep brown, not burnt, may be put into the boiling gravy, without stirring, and then carefully strain off the gravy without any crumbs of bread in it. You may also colour with flour browned on a flat-iron over the fire. Various flavouring articles serve also the purpose of colouring.

THICKENINGS.

323. Flour, or some other farinaceous article, is, or ought to be, the basis of all thickenings; starch of potatoes, or indeed any other pure starch, is a good substitute for flour. We do not recommend preparations of Carraghan moss, ivory dust, or eggs; they are troublesome, and not at all necessary. A table-spoonful of potatoe or any other starch, such as arrow-root, mixed in two table-spoonsful of cold water, and stirred into soup, sauce, or gravy, &c. and afterwards simmered, just before serving, will thicken a pint. Flour will also answer the same purpose. In large establishments, the following thickening is generally kept ready prepared; the French call it *roux*; it is thus made: Put some fresh butter, if clarified the better, (or some use the skimmings of the pots, clean and not impregnated with vegetables,) into a stew-pan over a clear slow fire; when it is melted, add fine flour sufficient to make it the thickness of paste; stir well together when over the fire, for ten or fifteen minutes, till it is quite smooth and of a fine "yellow-boy" colour. Do all this gradually and patiently, or you will spoil your thickening by getting it burnt, or giving to it a burnt flavour, which will spoil your gravy, &c. Pour it into an earthen pan for use, it will keep for a fortnight; and if, when cold, it is thick enough to be cut with a knife, a large spoonful will be enough to thicken a quart of gravy, &c. Most made dishes, such as sauces, soups, and ragouts, are thus thickened. The broth or soup, &c., to which the thickening is put, must be added by degrees, so as to incorporate them well together. To cleanse or finish a sauce, put into a pint two table-spoonsful of broth, or warm water, and put it by the side of the fire to raise any fat, &c., which must be carefully removed as it comes to the top.

We would strongly recommend mistresses of families, particularly those residing in the country, where potatoes are cheap, to keep a good stock of potatoe starch always by them. If kept dry and from the air, it will keep almost for any length of time. Damaged potatoes will yield starch or mucilage, if raw. It may be made from the old potatoes, when by germination in the spring they have become unfit for the table, or from the refuse of a newly gathered crop in the autumn. The starch will be found extremely useful, not only in a thickening, but also for mixing with wheat flour in making bread, &c. Starch may be made, and is made, from various vegetable substances, and used as a substitute for corn flour. The following is the mode of making potatoe starch; arrow-root starch and all other starches are made by a similar process:

The potatoes must be carefully washed and peeled, and every speck removed; provide yourself with a number of deep dishes, according to the quantity of starch you wish to make; for every pound of potatoes to be prepared in each dish, put a quart of clear water; grate them into the water on a bread grater; stir it up well, and then pour it through a hair sieve, and leave it ten minutes to settle, or till the water is quite clear; then pour off the water, and put to it a quart of fresh water: stir it up, then let it settle, and repeat this till the water is quite clear. You will at last find a fine white powder at the bottom of the vessel; lay this on a piece of paper in a hair sieve to dry, either in the sun or before the fire; when thoroughly dry, it is ready for use. It is perfectly tasteless, and may be used to thicken melted butter, instead of flour. A great deal of the arrow-root sold in the shops is neither more nor less than potatoe starch. Though we strongly recommend it as effectual and economical for the above purpose, for an invalid it is very inferior in strength and nutricious qualities to the Indian arrrow-root starch.

324. *White Thickening.*—Put half a pound of good butter into a sauce-pan, and melt over a slow fire, then drain the butter and take out the buttermilk, then add to the butter enough flour to make a thin paste, and place it on the fire for fifteen minutes, taking care not to let it colour. Pour it into a pan and let it stand until wanted.

FLAVOURINGS.

325. Judiciously prepared flavourings are of the first importance in the higher branches of cookery, and indeed, they are indispensably necessary in all descriptions of made dishes. The principal agents employed for flavouring are mushrooms, onions, anchovy, lemon juice and peel, vinegar, wine, especially claret, sweet herbs, and savoury spices. A good housewife will always take care to have a stock of the principal flavourings by her ready for use, as occasion may require. They are easily prepared for keeping, and the making of essences and flavoured vinegars, &c., from the herbs, is a very agreeable employment, and one highly becoming a good wife and mistress of a family. We by no means wish to undervalue elegant accomplishments in ladies, but accomplishments after all are but ornaments, whereas good housewifery is an essential; so thought our ancestors two hundred years ago, and so continue to think all those who set a proper value on the comforts of domestic life. Markham, in his *English Housewife*, 1637, says, "to speak then of the knowledge which belongs to our British housewife, I hold the most principal to be a perfect skill in cookery. She that is utterly ignorant therein, may not, by the lawes of strict justice, challenge the freedom of marriage, because, indeed, she can performe but half her vow; she may love and obey, but she cannot cherish and keepe her husband." Having said enough, we trust, to induce young ladies, particularly in the above quotation, to take our advice into their consideration, we shall proceed to make a few observations on taste, as intimately connected with this part of our subject.

A correct taste is a qualification which every cook ought to possess, but few persons naturally do possess it, and therefore, the palate requires to be cultivated as much in the culinary art, as the eye in the art of drawing. But tastes differ in different persons, and therefore, the cook, in providing a dinner, ought, if possible, to consult the tastes of the parties who are to eat it, rather than her own. This subject, however, if pursued, will run us out to a much greater extent than our limits will allow, and, after all, wĕ should not be able to lay down any definite rules of taste. There is one direction which we shall give, and which a cook will find it worth her while to attend to, namely, *whenever she finds the palate become dull by repeatedly tasting, one of the best ways of refreshing it is to masticate an apple, or to wash her mouth well with milk.*

FLAVOURINGS, ESSENCES, POWDERS, &c.

326. *To prepare sweet Herbs for keeping.*—It is highly desirable, according to the taste and style of living of the family, that preparations of sweet herbs, either in powder, dried bunches (the powder is best,) or in the form of essences and tinctures, be always kept at hand, ready for use. The following is the best way of preparing them:—Gather your herbs, including thyme of the various sorts, marjoram and savoury, sage, mint, and balm, hyssop and pennyroyal, when they are come to full growth, just before they begin to flower; when they must be gathered perfectly free from damp, dust, dirt, and insects. Cut off the roots, and tie the herbs in small bundles. Dry as quick as possible, either in the sun, in a dutch oven before the fire, or in a dry room with a thorough draught. When quite dry, pick off the leaves, and rub them till they are reduced to a fine powder, when bottle close for use. Seeds of parsley, fennel, and celery, should be kept for the purpose of flavouring, when the green herb cannot be obtained.

327. *Savoury Soup Powder* is compounded of parsley, winter savoury, sweet marjoram, and lemon thyme, of each two ounces; sweet basil, one ounce; verbinia leaves and knotted marjoram, of each half an ounce; celery seed and bay leaves (some leave out the bay leaves,) of each two drachms. Dry in a Dutch oven, thoroughly, but not to scorch; then rub the leaves to a fine powder. The seeds will be best ground, but pounding will do; sift all through a hair sieve, and bottle for use. This is an excellent compound.

328. *Curry Powder* may be made almost, if not altogether, as good as the Indian, by taking three ounces of coriander seeds; turmeric two or three ounces; black pepper, mustard, and ginger, one ounce of each; allspice and lesser cardamons, half an ounce each, and cumin seed, a quarter of an ounce. Put the ingredients in a cool oven for the night; thoroughly pound and mix together, and close bottle for use. Do not use cayenne in a curry powder.

329. *Powder for Ragouts.*—A good powder for flavouring ragouts is compounded of salt, one ounce; mustard, lemon peel, and black pepper, ground, of each half an ounce; allspice and ginger, ground, nutmeg, grated, and cayenne pepper, of each a quarter of an ounce. Dry in a Dutch oven before a gentle fire; pound in a mortar, and sift through a hair sieve.

330. *Powder for Brown made dishes.*—Black pepper and Jamaica, ground, of each half an ounce; nutmeg, grated, half an ounce; cinna-

mon, in powder, a quarter of an ounce; cloves, one drachm; dry; finely powder and bottle.

331. *Powder for White made dishes.*—White pepper half an ounce; nutmeg a quarter of an ounce; mace one drachm; dried lemon peel, grated, one drachm.

332. *Preserved Orange and Lemon Peels.*—Shave the thin skin, without a particle of white, off your superfluous Seville orange and lemon peel; put in a mortar, with a small lump of dried sugar to each peel; beat them well till the rind and sugar be blended together in a kind of marmalade; let the mixture be pressed close in a bottle, with a tea-spoonful of brandy at top, and secure from the air with a cork or bladder. This will be found a better flavouring, and more handy than grating dry rinds.

333. *Essences,* or *Tinctures of Herbs,* &c.—Combine their essential oils with good tasteless spirits (which is better than brandy, and much cheaper) in the proportion of one drachm of essential oil to two ounces of spirits; or fill a wide-mouthed bottle with the leaves, seeds, roots, or peel, perfectly dry, then pour over them spirits of wine, vinegar, or wine; keep the mixture steeping in a warm place, not hot, for twelve or fourteen days, when strain and bottle close for use. Bottles with glass stoppers are best. These essences are very handy, and are to be had all the year round.

334. *Essence of Anchovies.*—Purchase the best anchovies, that have been in pickle about a year. Pound twelve of them in a mortar to a pulp, then put them into a well-tinned saucepan, by the side of the fire, with two table-spoonfuls of best vinegar sherry, or brandy, or mushroom catsup; stir it very often till the fish are melted, then add fifteen grains in weight of the best cayenne pepper; stir it well, then rub it through a hair sieve with a wooden spoon; bottle and cork very tight with the best cork. When the bottle is opened, cork it well again with a new cork, as the least air spoils it. That which remains in the sieve makes a pleasant relish for breakfast or lunch, with bread and butter. If a large quantity is made, press it down in small jars. Cover it with clarified butter, and keep it in a cool place.

335. *Anchovy Powder.*—Pound the anchovies in a mortar, rub them through a sieve, make them into a paste with the finest flour, dried, roll it into thin cakes; dry them before a slow fire; when quite crisp, pound or grate them to a fine powder, and put into a well-stopped bottle. It will keep good for years, and is a savoury relish sprinkled on bread and butter.

336. *Oyster Powder.*—Open the oysters carefully, so as not to cut them, except in dividing the gristle from the shells; put them into a mortar; add about two drachms of salt to a dozen oysters, pound them and rub them through the back of a hair sieve, and put them into a mortar again, with as much flour, thoroughly dried, as will make them into a paste; roll it out several times, and lastly, flour it and roll it out the thickness of half a crown, and divide it into pieces about an inch square; lay them in a dutch oven before the fire, take care they do not burn, turn them every half hour, and when they

begin to dry, crumble them; they will take about four hours to dry; then pound them fine, sift them, and put them into bottles; seal them over.

337. *Spirit of mixed Herbs.*—Take winter savoury, lemon thyme, sweet basil, and lemon rind, celery seed one drachm, steep them in a pint of spirits of wine. Then drain and bottle the liquor. The herbs, after draining, will keep two or three weeks, and may be used for flavouring.

338. *Tincture of Lemon or Seville Orange Peel.*—Half fill a wide-mouthed bottle with good spirits; shave the thin rind off the lemon, and put it into the bottle until it is full: it may be either strained off into bottles, or suffered to remain on the rind.

339. *Spirits of mixed Spice.*—Black pepper one ounce, allspice half an ounce, both finely powdered; nutmeg quarter of an ounce, grated; infuse in a pint of spirits of wine, strain, and bottle.

MADE DISHES.

There is little to be added to our general remarks on this subject, under the heads of Stewing, Hashing, Thickening, Flavouring, &c. Made dishes are almost innumerable. They are, however, nothing more than meat, poultry, or fish, stewed very gently till they are tender, with a thickening sauce of some kind or other poured over them. Their difference consists in their flavour, which may be so modified by an ingenious cook as to make them almost endless. Let our preliminary remarks on these subjects be well studied. We subjoin a few receipts.

340. *Calf's Head.*—Take the half of one, with the skin on; put it into a large stew-pan, with as much water as will cover it, a knuckle of ham, and the usual accompaniments of onions, herbs, &c., and let it simmer till the flesh may be separated from the bone with a spoon; do so, and while still hot cut it into as large a sized square as a piece will admit of; the trimming and half the liquor put by in a tureen; to the remaining half add a gill of white wine, and reduce the whole of that, by quick boiling, till it is again half consumed, when it should be poured over the large square piece, in an earthen vessel, surrounded with mushrooms, white buttoned onion, small pieces of pickled pork, half an inch in breadth, and one and a half in length, and the tongue in slices, and simmered till the whole is fit to serve up; some brown force meat balls are a pretty addition. After this comes from table, the remains should be cut up in small pieces, and mixed up with the trimmings and liquor, which (with a little more wine,) properly thickened, will make a very good mock turtle soup for a future occasion.

341. *Hashed Meat.*—Cut the meat into slices about the thickness of two shillings, trim off all the sinews, skin, and gristle, put nothing in but what is to be eaten, lay them on a plate ready; prepare your sauce to warm in it, put in the meat, and let it simmer gently till it

MADE DISHES.

is thoroughly warm; do not let it boil, as that will make the meat tough and hard.

342. *Hashed Beef or Mutton.*—One tea-spoonful of Harvey sauce, one of Tomata sauce, the same quantity of any other sauce; pepper, salt, cayenne, half a wine glass of port wine, and a couple of capsicums cut fine; mix with the remains of the gravy of the preceding day, of beef or mutton; if necessary to thicken, add one shake of the flour dredger. This is a good hash.

343. *Sandwiches* are an elegant and convenient luncheon, if nicely prepared; the bread should be neatly cut with a sharp knife; whatever is used must be carefully trimmed from every bit of skin, gristle, &c., and nothing must be introduced but what you are absolutely certain will be acceptable to the mouth.

344. *A good Scotch Haggis.*—Make the haggis-bag perfectly clean; parboil the draught, boil the liver very well, so as it will grate, dry the meat before the fire, mince the draught and pretty large piece of beef very small; grate about half of the liver, mince plenty of suet and some onions small; mix all these materials very well together, with a handful or two of the dried meal; spread them on the table, and season them properly with salt and mixed spices; take any of the scraps of beef that are left from mincing, and some of the water that boiled the draught, and make about a quart of good stock of it; then put all the haggis meat into the bag, and that broth in it; then sew up the bag, but be sure to put out all the wind before you sew it quite close. If you think the bag is thin, you may put it in a cloth. If it is a large haggis, it will take at least two hours boiling.

345. *Mr. Phillips's Irish Stew.*—Take five thick mutton chops, or two pounds off the neck or loin; two pounds of potatoes, peel them, and cut them in halves; six onions, or half a pound of onions, peel and slice them also. First, put a layer of potatoes at the bottom of your stew-pan, then a couple of chops and some of the onions; then again potatoes, and so on, till the pan is quite full; a small spoonful of white pepper, and about one and a half of salt, and three gills of broth or gravy, and two tea-spoonfuls of mushroom catsup; cover all very close in, so as to prevent the steam from getting out, and let them stew for an hour and a half on a very slow fire. A small slice of ham is a great addition to this dish. Great care should be taken not to let it burn.

346. *Mutton Chops delicately stewed, and good Mutton Broth.*—Put the chops into a stew-pan with cold water enough to cover them, and an onion; when it is coming to the boil, skim it, cover the pan close, and set it over very slow fire till the chops are tender; if they have been kept a proper time, they will take about three-quarters of an hour very gentle simmering. Send up turnips with them—they may be boiled with the chops; skim well, and then send all up in a deep dish, with the broth they were stewed in.

347. *Minced Collops.*—Take beef, and chop and mince it very small, to which add some salt and pepper; put this, in its raw state, into small jars, and pour on the top some clarified butter. When in-

tended for use, put the clarified butter into a frying-pan, and slice some onions into the pan, and fry them. Add a little water to it, and then put in the minced meat. Stew it well, and in a few minutes it will be fit to serve up.

348. *Brisket of Beef, stewed.*—This is prepared in exactly the same way as "soup and bouilli."

349. *Harricot of Beef.*—A stewed brisket cut in slices, and sent up with the same sauce of roots, &c., as we have directed for harricot of mutton, is a most excellent dish, of very moderate expense.

350. *Salt Beef, baked.*—Let a buttock of beef, which has been in salt about a week, be well washed and put into an earthen pan, with a pint of water; cover the pan tight with two or three sheets of foolscap paper; let it bake four or five hours in a moderately heated oven.

351. *Beef baked like red deer, to be eaten cold.*—Cut buttock of beef longways, beat it well with a rolling pin, and broil it; when it is cold, lard it, and macerate it in wine vinegar, salt, pepper, cloves, mace, and two or three bay leaves, for two or three days; then bake it in rye paste, let it stand till it is cold, and fill it up with butter; let it stand for a fortnight before it is eaten.

352. *Shin or Leg of Beef, stewed.*—Have the bone sawed in three or four pieces, and the marrow either taken out, or stopped with paste. Cover with cold water, and having skimmed it clean, add onions, carrot, celery, sweet herbs, and spice. Let the whole stew very gently three hours and a half or four hours. Meanwhile, cut up the red part of two or three carrots, two or three turnips, peel two dozen button onions, boil them, and drain them dry; as the onions and turnips should retain their shape, and the carrots require longer to boil, they ought to be put in a quarter of an hour earlier. Do not let them be over-done. When the meat is quite tender, take it out with a slice, and strain the soup. Thicken the soup with a small tea-cup full of flour, mixed either with a little butter, or the fat of the soup. Stir this well in till it boils, and is perfectly smooth; if not, it must be strained through a tamis, and carefully skimmed, and then returned to warm the vegetables. The meat may be served whole, or scraped from the bones, and cut in pieces. Season the soup with pepper, salt, and a wine glass each of port wine and mushroom catsup, and pour over the meat; or, if necessary, put the meat in a stew-pan to warm. Serve all together. Curry may be added, if approved—also, force meat balls.

353. *Hare.*—Instead of roasting a hare, stew it; if young, plain—if an old one, lard it. The shoulders and legs should be taken off, and the back cut in three pieces; these, with a bay leaf, half a dozen eschalots, one onion pierced with four cloves, should be laid with as much good vinegar as will cover them, for twenty-four hours in a deep dish. In the meantime, the head, the neck, ribs, liver, heart, &c., should be browned in frothed butter, well seasoned; add half a pound of lean bacon, cut in small pieces, a large bunch of herbs, a carrot, and a few allspice. Simmer these in a quart of water till it is reduced to about

MADE MEATS.

half the quantity, when it should be strained, and those parts of the hare which have been infused in the vinegar, should (with the whole contents of the dish) be added to it, and stewed till quite done. Those who like onions may brown half a dozen, stew them in part of the gravy, and dish them round the hare. Every ragoût should be dressed the day before it is wanted, that any fat which has escaped the skimming spoon may with ease be taken off when cold.

354. *Jugged Hare.*—Wash it very nicely, cut it up in pieces proper to help at table, and put them into a jugging pot, or into a stone jar, just sufficiently large to hold it well; put in some sweet herbs, a roll or two of rind of a lemon, and a fine large onion with five cloves stuck in it; and if you wish to preserve the flavour of the hare, a quarter of a pint of water; if you are for a ragoût, a quarter of a pint of claret or port wine, and the juice of a lemon. Tie the jar down closely with a bladder, so that no steam can escape; put a little hay in the bottom of the saucepan, in which place the jar; let the water boil for about three hours, according to the age and size of the hare (take care it is not over-done, which is the general fault in all made dishes,) keeping it boiling all the time, and fill up the pot as it boils away. When quite tender, strain off gravy from fat, thicken it with flour, and give it a boil up; lay the hare in a soup dish, and pour the gravy to it. You may make a pudding the same as for roast hare, and boil it in a cloth, and when you dish your hare, cut it in slices, or make force meat balls of it for garnish. For sauce, currant jelly. Or a much easier and quicker way of proceeding is the following: Prepare the hare as for jugging; put it into a stew-pan with a few sweet herbs, half a dozen cloves, the same of allspice and black pepper, two large onions, and a roll of lemon peel; cover it with water; when it boils, skim it clean, and let it simmer gently till tender (about two hours;) then take it up with a slice, set it by a fire to keep hot while you thicken the gravy; take three ounces of butter and some flour, rub together, put in the gravy, stir it well, and let it boil about ten minutes; strain it through a sieve over the hare, and it is ready.

355. *Stewed Rump Steaks.*—The steaks must be a little thicker than for broiling; let them all be the same thickness, or some will be done too little, and others too much. Put an ounce of butter into a stew-pan, with two onions; when the butter is melted, lay in the rump steaks, let them stand over a slow fire for five minutes, then turn them, and let the other side of them fry five minutes longer. Have ready boiled a pint of button onions; they will take from half an hour to an hour; put the liquor they were boiled in to the steaks; if there is not enough of it to cover them, add broth or boiling water to make up enough for that purpose, with a dozen corns of black pepper, and a little salt, and let them simmer very gently for about an hour and a half, and then strain off as much of the liquor (about a pint and a half,) as you think will make the sauce. Put two ounces of butter in a stew-pan; when it is melted, stir in as much flour as will make it into a stiff paste; some add thereto a table-spoonful of claret or port wine, the same of mushroom catsup, half a tea-spoonful of salt, and

a quarter of a tea-spoonful of ground black pepper; add the liquor by degrees, let it boil up for fifteen minutes, skim it, and strain it; serve up the steaks with the onions round the dish, and pour the gravy over it.

356. *Broiled Rump Steaks with Onion Gravy.*—Peel and slice two large onions, put them into a quart stew-pan, with two table-spoonfuls of water; cover the stew-pan close, set it on a slow fire till the water has boiled away, and the onions have got a little browned, then add half a pint of good broth, and boil the onions till they are tender; strain the broth from them, and chop them very fine, and season with mushroom catsup, pepper, and salt; put the onion into it, and let it boil gently for five minutes, pour it into the dish, and lay it over a broiled rump steak. If instead of broth you use good beef gravy, it will be superlative. Stewed cucumber is another agreeable accompaniment to rump steaks.

357. *Bubble and Squeak.*—For this, as for a hash, select those parts of the joint that have been least done; it is generally made with slices of cold boiled salted beef, sprinkled with a little pepper, and just lightly browned with a bit of butter, in a frying-pan; if it is fried too much, it will be hard. Boil a cabbage, squeeze it quite dry, and chop it small; take the beef out of the frying-pan, and lay the cabbage in it; sprinkle a little pepper and salt over it; keep the pan moving over the fire for a few minutes, lay the cabbage in the middle of the dish, and the meat round it.

358. *Hashed or minced Veal.*—To make a hash, cut the meat into into slices: to prepare minced veal, mince it as fine as possible (do not chop it); put it into a stew-pan with a few spoonfuls of veal or mutton broth, or make some with the bones and trimmings, as ordered for veal cutlets, a little lemon peel minced fine, a spoonful of milk or cream; thicken with butter and flour, and season it with salt, a table-spoonful of lemon pickle or basil wine, or a pinch of curry powder. If you have no cream, beat up the yolks of a couple of eggs with a little milk; line the dish with sippets of lightly toasted bread.

359. *To make an excellent Ragoût of cold Veal.*—Either a neck, loin, or fillet of veal will furnish this excellent ragoût with a very little expense or trouble. Cut the veal into handsome cutlets; put a piece of butter, or clean dripping, into a frying-pan; as soon as it is hot, flour and fry the veal of a light brown; take it out, and if you have no gravy ready, put a pint of boiling water into the frying-pan, give it a boil up for a minute, and strain it in a basin while you make some thickening in the following manner: Put about an ounce of butter into a stew-pan; as soon as it melts, mix it with as much flour as will dry it up; stir it over the fire for a few minutes, and gradually add to it the gravy you made in the frying-pan; let them simmer together for ten minutes; season it with pepper, salt, a little mace, and a wine-glassful of mushroom catsup or wine; strain it through a tamis to the meat, and stew very gently till the meat is thoroughly warmed. If you have any ready boiled bacon, cut it in slices, and put it to warm with the meat.

MADE MEATS.

360. *Veal Olives.*—Cut half a dozen slices off a fillet of veal, half an inch thick, and as long and square as you can; flat them with a chopper, and rub them over with an egg that has been beat on a plate; cut some fat bacon as thin as possible, the same size as the veal; lay it on the veal, and rub it with a little of the egg; make a little veal force meat, and spread it very thin over the bacon; roll up the olives tight; rub them with an egg, and then roll them in fine bread crumbs; put them on a lark-spit, and roast them at a brisk fire; they will take three-quarters of an hour. Rump steaks are sometimes dressed this way. Mushroom sauce, brown or beef gravy.

361. *Knuckle of Veal to ragoût.*—Cut the knuckle of veal into slices of about half an inch thick; pepper, salt, and flour them; fry them a light brown; put the trimmings in a stew-pan, with the bone, broke in several places; an onion shred, a head of celery, a bunch of sweet herbs, and two blades of bruised mace; pour in warm water enough to cover them about an inch; cover the pot close, and let it stew very gently for a couple of hours; strain it, and then thicken it with flour and butter; put in a spoonful of catsup, a glass of wine, and juice of half a lemon; give it a boil up, and strain into a clean stew-pan; put in the meat, make it hot, and serve up. If celery is not to be had, use a carrot instead, or flavour it with celery seed.

362. *Scotch Collops.*—The veal must be cut the same as for cutlets, in pieces about as big as a crown piece; flour them well, and fry them of a light brown, in fresh butter; lay them in a stew-pan; dredge them over with flour, and then put in as much boiling water as will cover the veal, pour this in by degrees, shaking the stew-pan, and set it on the fire; when it comes to a boil, take off the scum, put in an onion, a blade of mace, and let it simmer very gently for three-quarters of an hour; lay them on a dish, and pour the gravy through a sieve over them. Lemon juice and peel, wine, catsup, are sometimes added. Add curry powder, and you have curry collops.

363. *Slices of Ham or Bacon.*—Ham or bacon may be fried, or broiled on a gridiron over a clear fire, or toasted with a fork; take care to slice it of the same thickness in every part. If you wish it curled, cut it in slices about two inches long (if longer, the outside will be done too much before the inside is done enough); roll it up, and put a little wooden skewer through it; put it in a cheese-toaster, or dutch oven, for eight or ten minutes, turning it as it gets crisp. This is considered the handsomest way of dressing bacon; but we like it best uncurled, because it is crisper and more equally done. Slices of ham or bacon should not be more than half a quarter of an inch thick, and will eat much more mellow if soaked in hot water for a quarter of an hour, and then dried in a cloth before they are broiled. If you have any cold bacon, you may make a very nice dish of it, by cutting it into slices of about a quarter of an inch thick; grate some crusts of bread, as directed for ham, and powder them well with it on both sides; lay the rashers in a cheese-toaster—they will be brown on one side in about three minutes—turn them, and do the other. These are delicious accompaniments to poached or fried eggs. The

bacon having been boiled first, is tender and mellow. They are an excellent garnish round veal cutlets, or sweetbread, or calf's head hash, or green peas, or beans, &c.

364. *A Devil.*—The gizzard and rump, or legs, &c., of a dressed turkey, capon, or goose, or mutton or veal kidney, scored, peppered, salted, and broiled, sent up for a relish, being made very hot, has obtained the name of a "Devil."

365. *Marrow Bones.*—Saw the bones even, so that they will stand steady; put a piece of paste into the ends; set them upright in a saucepan, and boil till they are done enough; a beef marrow bone will require from an hour and a half to two hours; serve fresh toasted bread with them.

366. *Ragoût of Duck, or any other kind of Poultry or Game.*— Partly roast, then divide into joints, or pieces of a suitable size for helping at table. Set it on in a stew-pan, with a pint and a half of broth, or, if you have no broth, water, with any little trimmings of meat to enrich it; a large onion stuck with cloves, a dozen berries each of allspice and black pepper, and the rind of half a lemon shaved thin. When it boils skim it very clean, and then let it simmer gently, with the lid close, for an hour and a half. Then strain off the liquor, and take out the limbs, which keep hot in a basin or deep dish. Rinse the stew-pan, or use a clean one, in which put two ounces of butter, and as much flour or other thickening as will bring it to a stiff paste add to it the gravy by degrees. Let it boil up, then add a glass of port wine, a little lemon juice, and a tea-spoonful of salt; simmer a few minutes. Put the meat in a deep dish, strain the gravy over, and garnish with sippets of toasted bread. The flavour may be varied at pleasure, by adding catsup, curry powder, or any of the flavouring tinctures, or vinegar.

ARTIFICIAL PREPARATIONS OF MEAT, FISH. &c., FOR DRESSING, SALTING, DRYING, &c.

By the phrase "artificial preparations of meat," we allude to those things which, before dressing, have to undergo the processes of salting, drying, smoking, pickling, &c. Before these meats can be cooked they must be prepared, and we, therefore, think it right (if for nothing else but the sake of order), to deviate from the line of proceeding of our predecessors, and to give directions for such preparations previous to the recipes for cooking them. It is impossible, fo. instance, to dress salt meat before it is salted.

SALTING.

367. There are many methods recommended for carrying this operation into effect. The following in our opinion are the best:— Before salting, particularly in the summer, all the kernels, pipes, and veins, should be taken out of the meat, or all your salting will be in vain. The meat will not keep. The salt should be rubbed thoroughly

SALTING.

and equally into every part of the meat, and great care should be taken to fill the holes with salt, where the kernels have been taken out, and where the butcher's skewers have been stuck. It is also necessary, directly meat comes into the house for salting, to wipe away any slime or blood that may appear. In very hot weather meat will not hang a single day without being liable to fly-blows; if once tainted, it will not take the salt. In winter it is best to let it hang for two or three days, but take care that it does not get frost-bitten. The salt should be heated in very cold weather before it is applied to the meat.

368. It is a good plan to slightly sprinkle meat with salt a day or two before finally salting; this will draw out the blood. But the first brine should be thrown away, as it is apt to injure butcher's meat, and always has a tendency to make bacon rusty. The meat should be wiped thoroughly clean after the preparatory salting.

369. Different quantities of salt are recommended; a pound of salt is sufficient for a middling sized joint; for a round of beef of twenty-five pounds, a pound and a half should be rubbed in all at once, though others rub in a little at a time for two or three days; but at any rate it requires to be turned and rubbed every day with the brine. The less salt used the better, providing you use enough to preserve the meat. Too much salt extracts the juices of the meat and makes it tough. Coarse sugar or treacle and bay salt are used by some in the following proportions: Two ounces of bay salt, two ounces of sugar, add three-quarters of a pound of common salt. A little saltpetre rubbed in will make the meat red, but is apt to harden it.

370. Meat should not be kept in salt any longer than is necessary to thoroughly cure it. In the course of four or five days it will be ready for dressing; but if intended to be eaten cold, two or three days more will make it keep longer and improve its flavour. Some people let meat lie in salt for a fortnight, and perhaps this is necessary for large hams and thick pieces of beef, but much depends upon the quantity of brine. If this be sufficient to cover the one-half of the meat, every time it is turned, less time will be required.

371. *Hasty salting* is sometimes necessary. When this is the case, rub half the quantity of salt to be used into the meat, which put in a warm place till the time of dressing. Before putting it into the pot, flour a coarse cloth and pack the meat in it; put it into the water when boiling. After it has boiled half of the usual time, that is, when it is half done, take it up, rub in the remainder of the salt and again pack it in a floured cloth: it should boil a little longer than when salted in the usual manner. Some persons simply boil it in very salt water, but the above plan is the best.

372. *Flavoured salt meat* may be made by pounding some sweet herbs, onions, &c., with salt, and it may be rendered still more relishing by the addition of a little zest, or savoury spice.

373. *Pickling meat* is effected as follows: there are other plans, but we prefer the method given in the Encyclopædia Britannica:—Six pounds of salt, one pound of sugar, and four ounces of saltpetre,

boiled in four gallons of water, skimmed and allowed to cool, forms a very strong pickle, which will preserve any meat completely immersed in it. To effect this complete immersion, which is essential, either a flat stone or heavy board must be laid on the meat. The same pickle may be used repeatedly, provided it be boiled up occasionally with additional salt to restore its strength, diminished by the combination of part of the salt with the meat, and by the detection of the pickle by the juices of the meat extracted. By boiling, the albumen (which would cause the pickle to spoil) is coagulated, and rises in the form of scum, which must be carefully removed. Albumen is so called because it resembles in appearance the white of an egg, and of whose nature it also partakes. It is a constituent in all meat. Pickled meat gains in weight; salted in the common way, that is, not immersed or covered with brine, it loses about one and a half in sixteen.

374. *Jerked beef* is made by cutting it into thin pieces, or slices, and dipping them into sea or salt water, and then drying them quickly in the sun. In the West Indies, where they can scarcely cure meat in the ordinary way on account of the excessive heat, they adopt the above method of preserving beef.

375. *Curing bacon* is effected by various methods: some use common salt only, which answers the purpose very well, but others consider a mixture of salt and sugar or molasses to be preferable. The proportions are, common salt, bay salt, and coarse sugar, or molasses, two pounds each, saltpetre six ounces. The quantity used must depend upon the size of the hog to be cured. The blood should be thoroughly drawn out of the meat by common salt before finally dressed for curing, and the dirty brine thrown away. Finely powder and dry the salt, and let it be well rubbed in; the heavier the hand employed, the sooner the bacon will be cured. The flitches must be always kept with the rind downwards. The top flitch must be put every day for a month at the bottom—thus changing them all round. Some use bay salt only, others rub in a little saltpetre, for the purpose of reddening the lean of the bacon (see Drying, No. 381.)

376. *Hams.*—The modes of curing hams are various in different parts of the country, and by different people. We give the following: For three hams about twenty pounds each, take common salt and coarse sugar two pounds each, bay salt and saltpetre six ounces each, black pepper four ounces, juniper berries two ounces; mix together, and grind or pound, and dry before the fire; rub this mixture, while warm, into the hams, and then add as much common salt as will entirely cover them. In two or three days pour over the hams a pound of molasses; baste them with the pickle every day for a month, putting each day the top ham to the bottom; drain and smoke (see Drying and Smoking;) or, take two quarts of water, two pounds of salt, four ounces of saltpetre, one pound of bay salt, two pounds of molasses; boil all together, and when cold pour the mixture over the ham, but do not rub them. To give a smoky flavour, some persons recommend a pint of tar water to be poured into the brine! This

pickle is sufficient for two moderately sized hams, they will require to be about three weeks in pickle, when they must be drained, and sewed up separately in coarse hessens wrappers, and hung to dry in a kitchen of moderate temperature, or laid upon a bacon rack.

377. *Yorkshire hams* are completely covered with the following pickle, in quantities according to the meat to be cured: Common salt, a peck; bay salt, five pounds; saltpetre and sal prunel, of each two ounces, all pounded together. Having thoroughly cleansed your hands, rub thoroughly in this mixture, and lay the rest over them; after lying three days, take out the meat and boil the pickle in two gallons of water; put in as much common salt as will make the pickle bear an egg; skim and strain: when cold, pour it over the meat, and let it lie a fortnight. Yorkshire hams are not smoked.

378. *Tongues, chines, chops, &c.*—The pickle first given in 376 will answer for tongues, &c. A neat's tongue will take a fortnight to pickle, a calf's or hog's tongue eight or ten days, a small chine ten days, or not more than a fortnight; a large one, nearly three weeks.

379. *Mutton hams.*—The following is a good pickle for mutton hams and tongues of all kinds. Take equal parts of common salt, bay salt, and coarse sugar; to every pound of this mixture add of saltpetre and sal prunel one ounce each, and of black pepper, allspice, juniper berries, and coriander seed, half an ounce each; bruise or grind altogether, and dry before the fire; apply this mixture hot.

380. *Hung* or *Dutch beef.*—Hang a fine tender round of beef, or the silver part only, for three or four days, or as long as the weather will allow; then rub it well with the coarsest sugar (about a pound will do,) two or three times a day, for three or four days. The sugar having thoroughly penetrated the meat, wipe it dry, and apply the following mixture: Four ounces each of common salt and bay salt, two ounces each of saltpetre and sal prunel, one ounce each of black pepper and allspice. Rub them well in every day for a fortnight; then roll up the beef tight, and bind or sew it in a coarse cloth, and smoke it. (See 381, &c.) Boil a part as it may be wanted, press it with a heavy weight till cold, when it may be grated for sandwiches. It will keep a long time.

DRYING, SMOKING, &c.

381. Drying may be effected by simply draining your salted or pickled meat, and hanging it within the warmth of a fire in a dry kitchen, but smoked dried meat is preferred by most persons, and certainly deserves the preference. The fuel employed for this purpose must be wood; sawdust (not deal or fir sawdust) is generally employed. Care must be taken not to melt or scorch the meat; if dried in a common kitchen chimney, it must be hung high enough. The fire must be kept in a smothering state, which may be easily done with sawdust, and in a place set apart for smoking; it is or ought to be kept burning slowly night and day. The best way is to send your meat to persons who make a business of smoking—(not tobacco.) Do

not dry your meat in a bakehouse, or strew it with bran when drained for drying; both will render the meat liable to be infested with those voracious little wretches called weevils. Drying meat by a malthouse kiln generally causes it to rust. After smoking, the wrappers should be removed and replaced with clean ones. It is not a bad plan to whitewash hams two or three times, when they are required to keep a long time.

382. *Dried* or *kippered salmon* is prepared by cleaning (without washing,) and scaling the fish; split and remove the bone; pickle for two or three days with equal parts of salt and sugar, and a little black pepper and saltpetre; keep it well pressed down; when cured, stretch each fish with a piece of stick, and dry it either with smoke or otherwise.

383. *Herrings, &c.* must be wiped clean; salted as above; in twenty-four hours take them out of the salt, run a stick through the eyes, and hang them in rows over an old cask half filled with dry sawdust, in the midst of which thrust a red-hot iron.

384. *Haddock, cod,* and *ling, &c.* are usually split down the middle for salting let them lie two or three days in equal parts of salt and sugar; then stretch on sticks, and dry in the sun or artificially.

CURING, &c. WITH PYROLIGNEOUS ACID.

385. Mr. Lockett, according to Dr. Wilkinson, in the Philosophical Magazine, 1821, was the first person who applied pyroligneous acid in the curing of meat. Mr. S. ascertained, that if a ham had the reduced quantity of salt usually employed for smoke-dried hams, and was then exposed, putrefaction soon took place where pyroligneous acid was not used; even one-half of this reduced portion of salt is sufficient when it is used, being applied cold, and the ham is then effectually cured without any loss of weight, and retaining more animal juices. In fact, pyroligneous acid, or acid of burnt wood, communicates the same quality to the meat as the process of smoking.

386. In using this acid for curing hams, mix about two tablespoonfuls in the pickle for a ham of ten or twelve pounds, and when taken out of the pickle, previous to being hung up, paint the ham over with the acid by means of a brush; a little more acid is required for neats' tongues. Dried salmons brushed twice with the acid, will be more effectually cured than by smoking them for two months.

387. This acid will preserve meat for many weeks without salt. Mr. Lockett kept some beef-steaks perfectly sweet above six weeks. He covered the bottom of the plate with the acid, and turned the steaks every day.

388. Hams and beef cured in this way, require no previous soaking in water to being boiled, and when boiled, they swell in size and are extremely succulent; the flavour is increased, and the meat rendered more nutritious. Two table-spoonfuls of acid added to the pickle for Westphalia ham is required, and when the ham is removed

from the pickle, it must be well washed in cold spring water and dried, and then some of the acid applied over it by means of a brush, and this repeated two or three times at about a week's interval.

389. To cure herrings, cod, haddock, and other fish, with pyroligneous acid, salt them a little for a day or two—not more—less may do; then dry them well with a coarse cloth, then dip them into the acid, and dry in the air; when dry, repeat the process a few times, suspending them like the manufacturer of candles. The red colour in dried salmons and herrings is generally attributed to nitre (saltpetre;) very frequently tobacco dissolved in a fluid not very agreeable (urine) is employed for the purpose of reddening, in Holland. Pyroligneous acid will not answer for pickling, being too strong when diluted with water it loses its virtue. The vinegar of the shops may be advantageously improved by the addition of this acid.

KEEPING FRESH MEAT.

390. All kinds of meat should be hung till they are tender, but not till they are putrescent; or, at any rate, not a moment longer than when you can perceive a slight degree of putrescency in them. Some things, such as venison, hares, &c., require to be hung longer than others, and some persons require meat to be high, or partly putrescent, before it is dressed, and these we fear must have their palates pleased whatever may be the consequence to their stomachs. Dr. Kitchiner says, " Although we strongly recommend that animal food should be hung up in the open air, till its fibres have lost some degree of their toughness, yet let us be clearly understood also to warn you, that if kept till it loses its natural sweetness, it is as detrimental to health as it is disagreeable to the smell and taste." Meat should be hung in a draught of air, and in the shade, particularly in the summer months; and it should be dried twice a day to keep it from being rendered musty by the damp. The time meat should be hung to be tender depends upon the dampness or dryness of the air, and the degree of heat. In damp warm weather it is exceedingly liable to become putrescent; in cold dry weather, not.

391. If you find that your meat will not keep till it is wanted, it is a good plan to slightly roast it, or boil it, which will enable you to keep it a day, or even two or three days longer; but we repeat it must be very slightly roasted or boiled, or it will eat like meat done a second time.

392. Boerhave says, that the best method of keeping flesh in summer, is to steep it in Rhenish wine, with a little sea salt, by which means it may be preserved a whole season.

393. According to Dr. Franklin, as quoted by Dr. Kitchiner, game or poultry killed by electricity becomes tender in the twinkling of an eye; and if it be dressed, will be delicately tender. We have no doubt, indeed it is an established fact, that if they are killed by the operation of cold lead, the twisting of the neck, or any other of the ordinary modes of destroying animal life, the same result will take

place, provided they are dressed before they are cold, that is, before the sinews and muscles have become set; once set, they must be suffered to relax by keeping, before the animal, whether game or poultry, or any other creature, is fit for dressing. Take a fowl, kill it, put it into an oven, or amongst hot ashes, while it is still warm with life, without picking off the feathers or taking out the entrails, and it will be delicately tender eating, and perfectly sweet. The feathers will be burnt away, and the entrails are taken out in the shape of a ball; the gypsies understand this mode of cooking. A military friend of ours partook of part of a calf roasted alive in the burning of the buildings of a farm-yard, in an enemy's country; he was not particularly hungry, but he says he never ate meat more delicious and tender. We mention these things merely to illustrate a principle, not as an example to be followed. In this country it is impracticable to dress butcher's meat while still warm with life; in hot countries it is nearly always done.

394. For keeping meat from becoming putrescent, recipes, of which the following is the substance, were published some years ago, and sold at the enormous price of seven shillings and sixpence: Take a quart of the best vinegar, two ounces of lump sugar, two ounces of salt; boil these ingredients together for a few minutes, and when cold, anoint with a brush the meat to be preserved. For fish, the mixture is directed to be applied inside; for poultry, inside and out. Of course both fish and poultry are to be cleansed.

395. Pyroligneous acid, either with or without the sugar and salt, would be much more effectual; besides, it possesses, to a certain extent, the property of not only preventing putrescency, but of curing it when commenced.

ON THE USE OF ACIDS IN DRESSING FOOD.

On perusing our work previous to going to press, we do not think that we have dealt sufficiently on the use of vinegar in dressing food. Of pyroligneous acid in the preservation and curing of meats, we have treated pretty largely. In all stews, and most made dishes, the flavour is much improved, and we think the food rendered more digestible, by the moderate use of vinegar: we recommend, however, none but the best vinegar, which ought to be applied to the meat previous to its being put in the stew-pan. We will give for example the following receipt for

396. *Brazilian Stew.*—Take shin or leg of beef; cut it into slices or pieces of two or three ounces each; dip it in good vinegar, and, with or without onions, or any other flavouring or vegetable substances, put it in a stew-pan, and *without water;* let it stand on a stew-hearth, or by a slow fire, for two three, or four hours, when it will be thoroughly done, will have yielded plenty of gravy, and be as "tender as a chicken." Great care must be taken that the heat is sufficiently moderate. This is the usual mode of dressing all descriptions of meat in the Brazils. We have recommended leg or shin of

beef, because it in fact makes the richest and most nutritious stew, and may be had at a low price; but any other meat or fish may be so dressed. The only objection to it is, that it is too rich; but this may be remedied by eating less of it, and a greater quantity of potatoes or other vegetables. A pound and a half of leg of beef, without bone, so dressed, and plenty of potatoes, will dine four people luxuriously.

397. *Alamode Beef* of the shops, which, when well dressed, is very delicious, is made by thickening the gravy of beef that has been very slowly stewed as above with vinegar, and flavoured with bay leaves, allspice, &c., according to taste. The following process will be found a good one: cut your beef, mouse buttock, or sticking pieces, or legs (legs are the best), &c., into pieces of two or three ounces each; put into a deep stew-pan some beef dripping, to keep the meat from sticking to the bottom; mince onions, which mix with the beef, previously dipped in vinegar, and put the mixture into a deep stew-pan. When quite hot, flour the meat with a dredger, and continue to do so till you have stirred in enough to thicken it; then cover it with boiling water, which should be put in by degrees, stirring it together with a wooden spoon. Flavour with black pepper, allspice, bay leaves, champignons, truffles, mushrooms, &c., according to taste; but allspice, black pepper, and salt, will answer every useful purpose. Let it stew as slowly as possible for four or five hours. We can testify from experience that our Brazilian stew and beef alamode are cheap and delicious dishes.

COOKING VEGETABLES.

This branch of cookery, though apparently very simple, requires the utmost attention, and no little judgment.

398. You should always boil vegetables in soft water, if you can procure it; if not, put a tea-spoonful or more of carbonate of soda in it to render it so.

399. Take care to wash and cleanse all vegetables from dust and other impurities, before putting them into the pot or pan; they should be thoroughly cleansed; for which purpose it will be necessary to open the leaves of greens, or otherwise you may send to the table some fine, fat, overfed caterpillars, and thus spoil the whole dish.

400. Upon the whole, it is best to boil vegetables in a saucepan by themselves. The quicker they boil, the greener they will be. When they sink, they are generally done enough, if the water has been kept constantly boiling. When done, take them up *immediately*, and thoroughly drain. If vegetables are a minute too long over the fire, they lose all their beauty and flavour. If not thoroughly boiled tender, they are tremendously indigestible; and much more troublesome during their residence in the stomach, than underdone meats.

401. Vegetables are in greatest perfection, when in greatest plenty, and they are only in greatest plenty when in full season. All vegetables are best when they are so cheap as to enable the artisan to eat them. Very early peas, or very early potatoes—that is, peas or po-

tatoes raised by artificial means—may be valued as great rarities, but for nothing else. We may assert the same thing of nearly all other vegetables. Sea kale and early rhubarb are, perhaps, exceptions. All vegetables should be ripe; that is, ripe as vegetables; otherwise, like fruits, they are bad tasted and unwholesome. To eat peas or potatoes in perfection, you must eat them not much before Midsummer.

402. With regard to the quality of vegetables, the middle size are to be preferred to the very large. Green vegetables, such as savoys, cabbages, cauliflowers, &c., should be eaten fresh, before the *life* is out of them. When once dead, they are good for nothing but the dunghill. This description of vegetables will live a long time after they are cut, but the fresher they are the better. Any one may easily see if they have been kept too long. There are two ways of sending peas to market; the one is, by packing them in sacks, where they frequently become heated, and, of course, in a great measure spoilt. The other is, by sending them in sieves, which is by far the best way, but, being somewhat more expensive, sieve peas fetch a higher price than sack peas.

403. Greens, roots, salads, &c. &c., when they have lost their freshness by long keeping, may be refreshed a little by putting them in cold spring water for an hour or two before they are dressed; but this process will not make them equal to those which are gathered just before they are boiled.

404. The following remarks, by a writer in the *Edin. Encyclo.* on this subject, are very just, and well worth the perusal:—" Most vegetables, being more or less succulent, require their full proportion of fluids for retaining that state of crispness and plumpness which they have when growing. On being cut or gathered, the exhalation from their surface continues, while, from the open vessels of the cut surface, there is often great exudation or evaporation, and thus their natural moisture is diminished, the tender leaves become flaccid, and the thicker masses, or roots, lose their plumpness. This is not only less pleasant to the eye, but is a real injury to the nutritious powers of the vegetable; for in this flaccid and shrivelled state its fibres are less divided in chewing, and the water which exists in vegetable substances in the form of their respective natural juices, is directly nutritious. The first care, therefore, in the preservation of succulent vegetables is, to prevent them from losing their natural moisture."

405. To preserve colour, or give colour, in cookery, many good dishes are spoilt. This is a great folly. Taste, nourishment, and digestibility, ought to be the only considerations in the dressing of food.

406. When vegetables are quite fresh gathered, they require much less boiling than those that have been kept. According to Kitchiner, fresh vegetables are done in one-third less time than stal

407. Strong-scented vegetables, we need scarcely say, ough' to be kept apart. If onions, leeks, and celery, are laid amongst such del cate things as cauliflowers, they will spoil in a very short time

DRESSING VEGETABLES.

408 Succulent vegetables, such as cabbages, and all sorts of greens, are best preserved in a cool, damp, and shady place. Potatoes, turnips, carrots, and similar roots, intended to be stored up, should never, on any account, be cleaned from the earth adhering to them, till they are to be dressed. Never buy washed potatoes, &c. from your shopkeeper; have them with the soil about them, and wash them just before they are boiled.

409. As the action of frost destroys the life of vegetables, and causes them speedily to rot, and as the air also injures them, all roots should be protected by laying them in heaps, burying them in sand or earth, and covering them with straw or mats. There are, however, some sorts of winter greens, such as savoys, &c., which are made much better and more tender by frost.

PARTICULAR DIRECTIONS FOR DRESSING VEGETABLES.

410. *Cauliflowers.*—Take off the outer leaves; round such as are young, leave just one leaf; put them with some salt into boiling water; boil according to size, from fifteen to twenty minutes; try the stalk with a fork; when the stalk feels tender, and the fork is easily withdrawn, the flower is done; take up instantly, with a wire ladle. Both brocoli and cauliflower, unless boiled till they are tender, are neither pleasant to the taste, nor wholesome to the body; but overboiling will break and spoil them. Sauce, melted butter.

411. *Brocoli.*—Choose close firm heads, nearly of a size. Put them into boiling water with salt; allow them plenty of room in boiling, or they will break; and boil them fast, or they will lose their colour. They will take from ten minutes to half an hour, according to the size of the heads. When the stalks are tender, which you can know by putting a fork up the middle of the stalk, they are done. Take them up with a wire ladle, that the water may run off without bruising the heads. Serve on a buttered toast. Sauce, melted butter.

412. *Cabbage.*—Large full-grown cabbage and savoys will take half an hour or more in boiling. Strip all the outside leaves till you come to the white quick grown ones; then shave the stocks of the leaves that are left on, and score the stalk a little way up. Drain them carefully when boiled, and serve them on a drainer.

413. *Young Coleworts and Sprouts*—Do not be too saving in trimming sprouts, as harsh or bad leaves will spoil a whole dish. They will take from ten minutes to a quarter of an hour in boiling. Be careful in draining, so as not to spoil the shape of the heads.

Cold cabbage may be fried and served with fried beef. It will require a little bit of butter, a little good gravy, and a little pepper and salt. Shake it about well, and let it remain no longer in the pan than is necessary to make it hot through.

414. *Red Cabbage.*—This is sometimes stewed, for eating with bouilli beef. Take a small red firm cabbage; wash, pick, and cut it

in slices half an inch thick; then pick it to pieces leaf by leaf. Make half a pint of melted butter, in a saucepan large enough to contain the whole. Shake the cabbage from the water that hangs about it, and put it to the melted butter, with a tea-cup full of good gravy, an onion, sliced, and pepper, salt, and cayenne. Let it stew half an hour or more, keeping the saucepan close shut. When quite tender, add a glass of vinegar; let it just boil up; then serve.

415. *Spinach.* — Pick leaf by leaf, wash it in three waters, put a little salt in the boiling water, boil it very quickly, and keep it under the water; seven or eight minutes will be sufficient to boil it; strain it on the back of a sieve, and press it as dry as possible between two plates; spread it on a dish, and score it crossways, in squares of an inch and a half, or two inches. Spinach is often served with poached eggs and buttered toast, or slices of fried bread. It is sometimes stewed in the following manner:—When it has boiled five minutes, strain and press it, and put it in a small stew-pan, the bottom just covered with rich boiling gravy; add a bit of butter, a little pepper, salt and nutmeg, and two table-spoonsful of cream; stew it five minutes.

416. *Vegetable Marrow* or *Gourd.* — Gather the fruit when the size of an egg; put it into boiling water, with a little salt; boil it until it is tender, which will be in about half an hour; cut it in slices half an inch thick; lay it on buttered toast; sprinkle it with pepper and salt; pour melted butter over it. If the fruit has seeds in it, the seedy part must be scooped out, but they are not so good in this state. The fruit may be cut in slices raw, and fried in butter, and served with melted butter and vinegar.

417. *Turnips.* — Put them into boiling water, with a little salt; when tender, take them up and drain the water from them; they will take from half an hour to an hour boiling. If for mashing, boil them a little longer. If they are lumpy or stringy, rub them through a colander, then put them into the saucepan, with an ounce of butter, a spoonful of cream, a little pepper and salt; stir them well till the butter is melted, and the whole well mixed.

418. *Green Peas.* — Peas do not require much water to boil them in. Before you put the peas into the boiling water, throw in a lump of sugar and a little salt; boil a few tops of mint with them. If they are young and fresh, they will not take more than ten minutes to a quarter of an hour; if not very young, they will require from twenty minutes to half an hour. Chop up the mint to garnish; stir a lump of butter with them in the dish, and a little pepper and salt.

419. *To stew Peas.* — Young peas are best for this purpose; but stewing is the best way of preparing old ones. To a quart of peas allow a quart of gravy; put them in when the gravy boils, with three lumps of sugar, and a little pepper and salt; stew till the peas are quite tender, then thicken with a piece of butter rolled in flour. They may be stewed without gravy; thus, to a quart of peas allow a lettuce, two or three tops of mint, and an onion, cut up and washed; the water that hangs round the lettuce will be sufficient; add pepper,

salt, and sugar, as above; stew very gently for two hours; then beat up an egg, and stir in with an ounce of butter.

420. *Carrots.*—Wash them well before you put them into the pot. They are best boiled with meat which they do not injure. If they are young they will boil in twenty minutes or half an hour; large old ones will take two hours to boil them tender; do not quarter carrots to boil—it renders them tasteless. If they are young, leave on a little of the top, and rub them with a coarse cloth; old ones are best rubbed after they are boiled; the skin comes from them more easily. Never scrape carrots—if they are rough, brush them. Sauce, melted butter.

421. *Windsor Beans.*—Young beans are best when the eyes are of a green colour; when the eyes are dark, they are old and eat strong; young beans will boil from twenty minutes to half an hour. Put them into plenty of boiling water, and a spoonful of salt; if you boil them after they become tender, the skins will shrivel; boil a large bunch of parsley with them; chop some for parsley and butter. Stir a lump of butter with them, and put a little parsley in the dish for garnish.

422. *French* or *Kidney Beans.*—The smooth or dwarf beans come in earliest, but the scarlet runners are considered the best; choose them young and nearly of a size, top and tail them, slit them down the middle and cut across. If they are old, take the skin from each side; put them in boiling water with some salt; boil them fast from ten minutes to a quarter of an hour; stir with them a lump of butter. Sauce, melted butter.

423. *Harricot Beans* are the seeds of French beans, full grown; they are sometimes called colly beans. Stew them in gravy, thickened with flour and cream, or they may be fried in butter; stir in a lump of butter when in the dish, a little pepper, salt, and nutmeg, then put in some gravy.

424. *Jerusalem Artichokes.*—Scrub them clean, and put them into the pot with cold water; throw in a handful of salt, do not let them be covered with water, and leave off the lid; they take about the same time boiling as potatoes. When they are tender they are done; drain them and peel them. Keep them as hot as possible; they may be kept hot by putting them in a dish over another dish in which is hot water. Sauce, melted butter and vinegar, or good thick gravy.

425. *Asparagus.*—Scrape the stalks clean; tie them in bundles with bass, put them in boiling water with a little salt in it; a tin saucepan is best. If they are fresh, they will be done in ten or twelve minutes; if they are not fresh, they will take a little longer. Take up the moment they are tender, otherwise the heads will be broken, the flavour spoilt, and the colour spoilt; take them up very carefully with a slice, cut the bass, just dip some toasted bread in the liquor in which the asparagus has been boiled, put it on a drainer with a little melted butter, and the heads of the asparagus should be laid inwards round the dish; or they may be laid on a buttered toast.

426. *Artichokes.*—Soak in cold water; put them into plenty of

boiling water, throw in a handful of salt. They require an hour and a half or two hours in boiling. Try them by pulling a leaf; if it draw out easily, they are done; drain them on a sieve, or serve on a vegetable drainer. Sauce, melted butter and vinegar.

427. *Red Beet-root.*—Boil them whole, put them in boiling water; they require from an hour and a half to three hours in boiling. If for garnish, leave them whole till wanted for use, then scrape and cut up into slices. If for salads, scrape and cut in slices hot, and pour cold vinegar over them.

For stewing, boil them an hour or more, then skin and slice them; season them with pepper and salt, and stew till tender, with young onions, in good gravy: when nearly done, stir in a bit of butter rolled in flour and cream: this is a pleasant and nourishing dish. They may be baked dry in the same manner as potatoes, and eaten with cold butter, salt, and pepper.

428. *White Beet-root.*—This useful and wholesome plant affords two very pleasing varieties. The leaves stripped from their large fibrous stalks resemble spinach. Put in boiling water and boil them very fast; they take but a few minutes; drain, and press them very dry. Sauce, melted butter. The stalks tie in bundles, dress as asparagus. Sauce, melted butter and vinegar.

429. *Herbs to fry to eat with liver, or with rashers and eggs.*—Clean and drain four handfuls of young spinach, and two of young lettuce leaves, two handfuls of parsley and one of young onions chopped small; set them over the fire in a stew-pan; put one ounce of butter and some pepper and salt; close the pan up and shake it well, and when it boils, set it on the hob or stove to simmer slowly till the herbs are tender. Serve them on a dish with the liver, or rashers and eggs; lay them on the herbs.

430. *Kale, Sea and Scotch.*—This last kale is a favourite sort of greens for winter and spring; the heads should not be gathered before November. These will take a quarter of an hour or twenty minutes fast boiling; put them into boiling water. The sprouts, which in spring are very abundant, will boil in a few minutes. Sauce, melted butter.

Sea Kale is boiled tied up in bunches, like asparagus. It is eaten with rich gravy, or thick melted butter, and may be served on toasted bread.

431. *Celery* makes an excellent addition to salads; it also gives an agreeable flavour to soups and sauce, and is sometimes stewed as an accompaniment to boiled or stewed meat. Wash six or eight heads, and take off the outer leaves; cut the heads up in bits three or four inches long. Stew them till tender in half a pint of veal broth, or white gravy; then add two spoonsful of cream and an ounce of butter rolled in flour, season with pepper, salt, and nutmeg, and simmer the whole together. The leaves will do to flavour soup that is to be strained.

432. *Mushrooms.*—The large flap mushrooms are excellent broiled. Have a very clear fire; make the bars of the gridiron very clean, and

rub them with mutton suet to prevent them from sticking; a few minutes will broil them. When they steam out, sprinkle them with pepper and salt; have ready a very hot dish, and when they are taken up, lay a bit or two of butter under and over each. To stew them, put them in a small saucepan with pepper and salt, a bit of butter and a spoonful or two of gravy of roast meat or cream; shake them about, and when they boil they are done.

433. *Morels* resemble mushrooms in their growth and many other respects, and are usually dressed in the same manner. It is not possible, however, to make catsup from them, which shows that they do not possess the same qualities as mushrooms. For a stew or *ragoût* of morels, take off their stalks; split them, if large, into two or three pieces; wash them and put them into a basin of warm water, and cleanse them from the sand, &c.; then blanch, drain and put them into a stew-pan, with a piece of butter and some lemon juice. Moisten, after a few turns in the stew-pan, with either brown or white sauce. There are various other modes of dressing them, but as morels are not much eaten in this country, the above may suffice. Morels are of a higher and finer flavour in Eastern countries than here.

434. *Truffles.*—These are a very curious description of vegetables; they grow under ground, no part of the plants ever being seen on the surface. It is like the mushroom kind, a species of fungus, and is propagated by seed which is nurtured by the decaying of the old plant. They are found about ten inches below the surface of the earth, dogs being trained to discover them by their scent. The truffle has a very rich, tart, and high flavour when fresh and in season, but loses it when dried, or out of season. They are not very common in America, but they are found in great quantities in France and Italy. A writer in Rees's Cyclopædia informs us, that "truffles are generally in seed about August, when they are of a fine high flavour and agreeable smell; continue good till the beginning of winter, and sometimes as late as March; but those gathered between March and July are small, white, and of a poor flavour. The same authority, in the same article, intimates that truffles are tenderest and best in spring, though easiest found in autumn; the wet swelling them and the thunder and lightning disposing them to throw out their scents: hence by the ancients they were called thunder-roots. Hogs are fond of them; hence the common people call them swine-bread." It is now, the editor may observe, a well-established fact, that truffles are not good after March, or before August. They require a great deal of washing and brushing, in several waters, before they can be applied to culinary purposes. When fresh and fine they are very rich, and are a very delicious addition to some dishes. They may be, and frequently are, stewed like mushrooms, and prepared in other ways, and eaten by themselves.

435. *Cucumbers* may be stewed in the same way as celery, with the addition of some sliced onions; or the cucumbers and onions may

be first floured and fried in butter; then add the gravy, and stew till tender; skim off the fat.

436. *Parsnips.*—Clean and dress just the same as carrots, they require boiling from one hour to two, according to their size and freshness; they should be drained well, and set on the hob in a dry saucepan to steam; they are sometimes mashed with butter, pepper, salt, and cream, or milk, the same as turnips; they are eaten alone, or with salt beef or salt pork. Sauce, melted butter and vinegar.

POTATOES.

437. In our directions for dressing vegetables, we speak lastly of potatoes—not because the cooking of this every-day food is of the least importance, but because, on the contrary, it is of the greatest. There are few persons, simple as the process may appear to be, who can cook potatoes well with *certainty.* Potatoes from the same ground, and of the same kind, dressed by the same cook, may come to table one day palatable and nutritious, and the next the very reverse of these qualities. How does this happen? The cook acts upon no principle. By accident the potatoes may be boiled well, and by accident they may be boiled bad: in one word, the boiling of potatoes is, with the generality of cooks, all chance work. A friend of ours, Mr. John Barker, the attorney, no mean judge in such matters, always averred, that a woman who could boil potatoes and melt butter *well*, was a good cook; he never requires any other proof of the capabilities of a cook. The fact is, those who thoroughly understand the elements of any art or science, find little or no difficulty in what are called the higher branches. It is for this reason that we have, in our little work, dwelt so much upon elementary principles, in preference to filling it up with long receipts, which every body may obtain, but which do not teach any principle of the art of cookery. Dr. Kitchiner observes, that "the vegetable kingdom affords no food more wholesome, more easily procured, easily prepared, and less expensive, than the potatoe." This is perfectly true, and yet how few are there that can boil potatoes properly! In Ireland, as every body knows, potatoes constitute almost entirely the food of the great mass of the people; in Ireland, therefore, necessity must have taught the people the best mode of cooking them. Their process is this: the potatoes, unpeeled, that is with their jackets on, after being washed, are put into a cast-iron pot of cold water, which is placed on the fire. When the water boils, a small quantity of cold water is put into the pot to check the boiling; this is once or twice repeated. When the potatoes are done, or nearly done, the water is poured away from the potatoes, which are again subjected to the fire to let the steam evaporate, and make the potatoes mealy. They are then served up in the usual way, (we are speaking of the tables of the middling classes,) and each person takes as many potatoes as he chooses; he peels them, depositing the skins by the side of his plate. In the course of the

dinner the potatoes on the table will become cold, when a fresh supply is ordered, and when furnished, the host calls out to his guest, "a hot potatoe, Sir." Before the dinner is finished, you will have two or three supplies of hot potatoes, and the last, though all from the same pot, are to our taste better than the first. They are all the time kept on the fire; the action of the heat completely evaporates the moisture from the potatoes, and those at the bottom of the iron pot become partially roasted. Such is the Irish mode of dressing potatoes, and if we could reconcile ourselves to the "*bother*" of peeling them, and to the disagreeable appearance of a table-cloth nearly covered with potatoe skins, there is no doubt that we should consider the Irish way of dressing and serving potatoes the best. The generality of modern cookery books recommend the dressing of potatoes with their skins on, like the Irish, but direct that they should be peeled before sent to the table; this mode spoils the potatoes by cooling them; when so dressed, they should be eaten hot. We recommend that potatoes, excepting when young, for the table, should be always pared, *carefully* pared, before they are boiled: that they should be put into cold water with salt, and boiled quickly, till they are nearly done; that then the water should be poured off, and the potatoes again subjected to the fire, covered with close lid, till they are quite done, when the lid ought to be removed, and the moisture evaporated. They may be then mashed, or served whole. The cook should take care to have potatoes pretty much of an equal size, or, if this be not practicable, she should divide the large ones. We ought, however, to add, with regard to peeling potatoes, that most people very fond of this root insist upon it, that you do not get the true flavour if you do not dress it with the skin on. Let it be always remembered, that potatoes differ very much in quality, and that no cook can dress a bad potatoe into a good one.

This brings us to the choice of potatoes. We can lay down no rule, notwithstanding what former writers have said, for the choice of potatoes. As it is with pudding, so it is with potatoes—the proof is in the eating. The dealers in nuts say, "Crack and try before you buy," and we say as regards potatoes, Boil and try before you buy; the expenditure of one half-penny will enable you to do this. Dr. Kitchiner says, that "reddish coloured potatoes are better than the white, but the yellowish ones are the best." The colour of a potatoe is no criterion of its goodness or badness; there are good of all colours, and there are bad of all colours. You should never buy washed potatoes; they should never be washed till they are to be used, and as little as possible exposed to the open air. When frost-bitten, they are good for nothing as regards culinary purposes. There are various directions given by writers for dressing potatoes, some of which we subjoin. Kitchiner says, that "most boiled things are spoiled by having too little water; but potatoes are often spoiled by too much." It is sufficient to just cover them with water. Potatoes may be boiled well according to either of the subjoined methods; but after trying all, we prefer our own.

438. *Potatoes to boil.* —To boil, choose them all of a size, that they may be all done together; put them on with cold water, and a spoonful of salt, in a saucepan larger than they require, without the lid, and with not quite water enough to cover them. When they boil, put in a little cold water; do this twice or three times as they come to boil. When a fork will easily go into them, strain off, and put the saucepan on the hob for two minutes, for the steam to evaporate. If done too soon, fold a coarse cloth and cover them up immediately, to keep them hot and mealy; but they are best served immediately they are done.

Another Method. The best method in the opinion of some, is to wash the potatoes quite clean and put them in the saucepan with a large table-spoonful of salt, and cover them with water; but when they boil up, pour three parts of the water away, put the lid on the saucepan, and set them where they will boil, but not very fast. Observe if the skins are cracked; if not, carefully crack them with a fork to let the watery matter contained in the potatoe out; this you cannot do until they are nearly done. When they are boiled sufficiently, drain all the water away; take off the lid, and hold them over the fire for a minute, giving them a gentle shake. They are best served immediately, while they are dry and hot. This method is good in a small family, but where there are a great many to dine it would be best to pare them, and take out all the eyes with the point of your knife; wash them, put them in the saucepan with a large table-spoonful of salt, cover them with water, and when they boil, pour three parts of the water off, close the saucepan, and let them boil gently; when done, dry them over the fire. As potatoes should be always served hot, by this method you lose no time in taking off the skins.

439. *Potatoes to steam.* —Let the potatoes be washed, and put into the steamer, when the water boils in the saucepan beneath; they will take about three-quarters of an hour to steam, and should be taken up as soon as done, or they become watery.

440. *To roast.* —Wash and dry potatoes all of a size; put them in a dutch oven, or cheese toaster, or in the oven by the side of the fire; take care that the heat is not too great, or they will burn before they are baked through. They may be parboiled first; in that case they will take less time in baking.

441. *Potatoes mashed.* —When the potatoes are thoroughly boiled or steamed, drain them dry, pick out every speck, and while hot rub them through a colander into a clean saucepan, in which warm them, stirring in half an ounce or an ounce of butter, and a table-spoonful of milk, with a little pepper and salt; do not make them too wet; then put them into the scallop shells, or pudding shells buttered, the tops washed over with the yolk of an egg, and browned in an oven by the side of the fire; but best in a dutch oven. Some people consider a mixture of boiled onions an improvement.

442. *Potatoes roasted under meat.* — Parboil large potatoes; peel them, and put them in an earthen dish, or small tin pan, under meat that is roasting. They will partake of the basting, salting, and flouring, that are put on the meat; when one side is brown, turn and brown the other. They may be baked in the same manner in an oven.

443. *Potatoes fried or broiled.*—Cut cold potatoes into slices a quarter of an inch thick, and fry them brown in a clean dripping-pan. Some people like them shaved in little thin pieces, sprinkled with salt and pepper, and stirred about in the frying-pan till hot through. They are very good fried whole; first dip them in egg and roll them in bread crumbs; they are likewise very good broiled on a gridiron, after being partially boiled. Cold potatoes, which are generally thrown away, are very good when broiled.

444. *Potatoe Balls.*—Mix mashed potatoes with a beaten egg, roll them in balls and fry them, either with or without crumbs.

445. *Potatoe Snow.*—Wash very clean some potatoes of a white mealy sort; set them on in cold water, and boil them according to the first direction; when done, strain the water from them, crack the skins, put them by the fire until they are quite dry and fall to pieces; then rub them through a wire sieve on the dish they are to be served on, and do not disturb them.

SALADS.

446. Among the principal salad herbs we may reckon lettuce, of which the white cos in summer, and in winter the brown Dutch cos and brown cos, are the best; endive, of which the curled leaf is preferred; corn-salad and water-cress, both of which are preferred when the leaves have a brownish cast; mustard and cress, or small salading, of which a succession may be kept up through the spring months; celery, young, crisp, and well blanched. All or any of these may be united in the composition of a salad. Cucumbers, either sliced by themselves, or mixed with other articles. Radishes give a lively appearance, by way of garnish, to a salad, but are not themselves improved by dressing. Red-beet also is much in request for winter salads, especially mixed with endive. Young onions or escalions are liked by many people, but much disliked by others; therefore they should not be mixed in the bowl, but sent up on a small dish by themselves. Sorrel gives a pleasing acid taste; and pimpernel, or burnet, gives flavour resembling that of cucumber. Dandelion, if well grown and well blanched with a tile or slate (in the same manner as endive), is equally good and wholesome.

Let the ingredients of the salad be well picked, and washed and dried; but do not add the dressing till just before eating, as it is apt to make the salad flabby. The most simple way of dressing a salad is, perhaps, the best; certainly the most wholesome; merely salt, oil, and vinegar, to taste; one table-spoonful of the best olive oil to three of vinegar, is a good proportion. For those who do not like oil, or when it is not at hand, the following may be used as a substitute: The gravy that has dropped from roasted meat, good sweet thick cream, a bit of fresh butter rubbed up with fine moist sugar, or just melted, without either flour or water; great care must be taken in thus melting the butter, or it will be apt to oil or curdle; it must be shaken one way only, and kept near the fire no longer than is necessary to dissolve the lumps — on no account suffered to boil. Eggs boiled for salads require ten or twelve minutes boiling, and should immediately be plunged into cold water.

In the more complicated preparation of a salad, great care must be taken that every additional ingredient is thoroughly well blended before proceeding to add another.

Prepare the dressings in the bowl, and add the herbs; after stirring them in, take care that all the various colours are displayed. The coral of a lobster or a crab makes a beautiful variety with a lettuce, onion, radish, beet, and white of egg. The following are the ordinary proportions, but various tastes will suggest variety: The yolks of two eggs rubbed very smooth with a very rich cream; if perfectly rubbed and quite cold, they will form a smooth paste without straining; a tea-spoonful each of thick mustard, salt, and powdered loaf-sugar, or a little cayenne instead of mustard, less than half of the mustard; when these are well rubbed in, add two table-spoonfuls of oil (or whichever of its substitutes is adopted), and then four spoonfuls of the best white wine vinegar; then lay the herbs lightly on.

Cucumbers are only to be pared and sliced, with slices of onion, which correct their crudity, and render them less unwholesome; the pickle for them consists of pepper, salt, oil, and vinegar.

VINEGARS FLAVOURED.

Vinegar is employed in extracting flavours as well as spirits and wine. But such extracts are principally used with salads, or as relishes to cold meats, and in a few instances to flavour sauces and soups; but, in English cookery, flavours extracted by sherry wine are preferred for soup.

447. *Vinegar for Salads.* — Take three ounces each of tarragon, chives, eschalots, savoury, a handful of the tops of balm and mint, all dry and pounded; put these into a wide-mouthed bottle, with a gallon of the best vinegar, cork it close and set it in the sun, and in a fortnight strain it off, and press the herbs to get out all the juice; let it stand a day to settle, and then strain it through a filtering bag.

448. *Basil Vinegar or Wine.* — Sweet basil is in perfection about the middle of August; gather the fresh green leaves, quite free from stalk, and before it flowers; fill a wide-mouthed bottle with them, fill it with vinegar or wine, and steep them ten days; if you want a very strong essence, strain the liquor, put it on some fresh leaves, and let them steep fourteen days more; strain it and bottle, cork it close; it is a very agreeable addition to cold meat, soups, sauces, and to the mixture generally made for salads. A table-spoonful, when the soup is ready, impregnates a tureen-full with the basil and acid flavours at a very little expense, when fresh basil and lemons are very dear.

CATSUPS.

The flavour of other sweet or savoury herbs may be preserved in the same manner, by infusing them in wine or vinegar.

449. *Burnet Vinegar* is made exactly in the same way as the above, and imparts the flavour of cucumbers so exactly, when steeped in vinegar, that the nicest palate could not distinguish it from the fruit itself. This is a nice relish to cold meat, salads, &c. Burnet is best in season from Midsummer to Michaelmas.

450. *Cress or Celery Vinegar.* — Pour over a quart of the best vinegar to an ounce of celery or cress seeds, when dried and pounded; let them steep ten days, shake it every day, then strain and bottle in small bottles.

451. *Horse-radish Vinegar.* — Pour a quart of best vinegar on three ounces of scraped horse-radish, one drachm of cayenne, and an ounce of shred eschalot; let it stand a week. This is very cheap, and you have an excellent relish for cold beef, salads, &c. Horse-radish is in perfection in November.

452. *Garlic, Onion, or Eschalot Vinegar.* — Put and chop two ounces of the root, pour over them a quart of the best vinegar, in a bottle, shake it well every day for ten days; then pour off the clear liquor into half-pint bottles. A few drops of the garlic will flavour a pint of gravy, as it is very powerful.

453. *Tarragon Vinegar.* — Fill a wide-mouthed bottle with fresh gathered tarragon leaves. They should be gathered on a dry day, just before it flowers, between Midsummer and Michaelmas. Pick the leaves off the stalks, and dry them a little before the fire; cover them with the best vinegar, and let them steep fourteen days; then strain them through a flannel jelly-bag till it is fine, then pour it into half-pint bottles, cork them tight, and keep them in a dry place.

454. *Elder Flower Vinegar* is prepared in the same manner as above, and other herbs also.

455. *Green Mint Vinegar* is made exactly the same way, and the same proportions, as basil vinegar. In housed lamb season, green mint is sometimes not to be got, it is then a welcome substitute.

456. *Camp Vinegar.*—Take four table-spoonfuls of soy, a quarter of an ounce of cayenne pepper, six anchovies, bruised and chopped, walnut pickle a quarter of a pint, a clove of garlic shred fine; steep the whole for a month in a quart of the best vinegar, shake it four or five times a week, strain it through a tamis, and put it in half-pint bottles, close corked and sealed, or dipped in bottle cement.

457. *Capsicum, Cayenne, or Chili Vinegar.* — Pound fifty fresh red chilies, or capsicums, or a quarter of an ounce of cayenne pepper; steep in a pint of the best vinegar for a fortnight.

CATSUPS.

These rank high, and deservedly so, amongst the lists of flavourings, particularly mushroom catsup, with the directions for the making of which we have been at considerable pains. You cannot be certain of having it good, unless you make it yourself, for no article is more adulterated and diluted than this most delicious and useful flavourer.

458. *Walnut Catsup.*—Take three half sieves of walnut shells, put them into a tub, mix them up well with common salt, about a pound and a half. Let them stand six days, frequently beating and washing them; by this time the shells become soft and pulpy; then by banking them up on one side of the tub, raising the tub on the same side, the liquor will run clear off to the other; then take that liquor out. The mashing and banking may be repeated as long as any liquor runs. The quantity will be about three quarts. Simmer it in an iron pot as long as any scum rises; then add two ounces of allspice, two ounces of ginger, bruised, one ounce of long pepper, one ounce of cloves, with the above articles; let it boil slowly for half an hour; when bottled, take care that an equal quantity of spice goes into each bottle; let the bottles be quite filled up, cork them tight, and seal them over. Put them into a cool and dry place, for one year before they are used.

459. *Oyster Catsup.*—Take fine large fresh oysters, open them carefully, and wash them in their own liquor, to take any particle of shell that may remain, strain the liquor after. Pound the oysters in a mortar, add the liquor, and to every pint put a pint of sherry, boil it up and skim, then add two anchovies, pounded, an ounce of common salt, two drachms of pounded mace, and one of cayenne. Let it boil up, skim it, and rub it through a sieve. Bottle it when cold, and seal it. What remains in the sieve will do for oyster sauce.

460. *Cockle and Muscle Catsup.*—The same way as oyster catsup.

461. *Mushroom Catsup.*—The juice of mushrooms approaches the nature and flavour of gravy meat more than other vegetable juices. Dr. Kitchiner sets a high value, and not without reason, upon good mushroom catsup, "a couple of quarts of which," he says, "will save some score pounds of meat, besides a vast deal of time and trouble." The best method of extracting the essence of mushrooms, is that which leaves behind the least quantity of water. In all essences, it is quality, not quantity, to which we ought to look. An excess of aqueous fluid in essences renders them less capable of keeping; while in flavouring sauces, &c. a small quantity is sufficient, so that by this means you do not interfere with the thickness or consistency of the thing flavoured. Mushrooms, that is, field mushrooms, begin to come in about September. There are several varieties of these fungi, and they differ very much, both in their wholesomeness and flavour. The best and finest flavoured mushrooms are those which grow spontaneously upon rich, dry, old pasture land. The following is the mode of making good mushroom catsup, or, as Dr. Kitchiner calls it, "double catsup."

Take mushrooms of the right sort, fresh gathered and full grown, but not maggoty or putrescent; put a layer of these at the bottom of a deep earthen pan, and sprinkle them with salt; then put another layer of mushrooms, sprinkle more salt on them, and so on alternately, mushrooms and salt. Let them remain two or three hours, by which time the salt will have penetrated the mushrooms, and have made them easy to break; then pound them in a mortar, or break them well with your hands; then let them remain in this state for two days, not more, mashing them well once or twice a day; then pour them into a stone jar, and to each quart add an ounce and a half of whole black pepper, and half an ounce of allspice; stop the jar very close, and set it in a saucepan or stew-pan of boiling water, and keep it boiling for two hours at least. Take out the jar, and pour the juice clear from the settlings, through a hair sieve into a clean stew-pan. Let it boil very gently for half an hour; but to make good or double catsup, it should boil gently till the mushroom juice is reduced to half the quantity, or, in other words, till the more aqueous part is evaporated; then skim it well, and pour it into a clean dry jar or jug; cover it close, and let it stand in a cool place till next day, then pour it off as gently as possible (so as not to disturb the settlings at the bottom of the jug,) through a tamis, or thick flannel bag, till it is perfectly clear; add a table-spoonful of good unflavoured spirits (brandy is dear and not a whit better than common spirits of wine of equal strength) to each pint of catsup, and let it stand as before. A fresh sediment will be deposited, from which the catsup is to be poured off gently, and bottled in half pints; washed with spirit. Small bottles are best, as they are sooner used, and the catsup, if uncorked often, is apt to spoil. The cork of each bottle ought to be sealed or dipped in bottle cement. Keep it in a dry cool place; it will soon spoil if kept damp. If any pellicle or skin should appear upon it when in the bottle, boil it up again with a few peppercorns. It is a question with us, whether it would not be best to dispense with the spice altogether, and give an addition of spirits. When a number of articles are added to the catsup, such as different spices, garlic, eschalot, anchovy, &c. &c., the flavour of the mushroom is overpowered, and it ceases to be, properly speaking, mushroom catsup.

462. *Mushroom Catsup without Spice* is made thus:—Sprinkle a little salt over your mushrooms. Three hours after, mash them; next day, strain off the liquor, and boil it till it is reduced to half. It will not keep long, but an artificial mushroom bed will supply sufficient for this, the very best of mushroom catsup, all the year round.

463. *Mushroom Powder* may be made of the refuse of the mushrooms, after they have been squeezed, by drying them well in a dutch oven, or otherwise, and then reducing them to powder. If the mushrooms themselves are dried and pounded, the powder will be much stronger. Tincture or essence of mushrooms, we apprehend, might be made, by steeping dried mushrooms in spirits.

CLARIFYING.

464. *Clarified Butter.*—Put the butter in a clean saucepan over a very clear, slow fire, and when it is melted, carefully skim off the butter-milk, which will swim on the top; let it stand for a minute or two for the impurities to sink to the bottom, then pour the clear butter

through a sieve into a basin, leaving the sediment at the bottom of the pan.

465. *Burnt Butter.*—Put two ounces of fresh butter into a frying-pan; when it becomes a dark brown colour, add a table-spoonful and a half of good vinegar and a little salt and pepper. This is used for sauce to boiled fish or poached eggs.

466. *Oiled Butter.*—Put two ounces of fresh butter into a sauce-pan, melt it gradually till it comes to an oil, and pour it off quietly from the dregs. This will supply the place of olive oil.

467. *To clarify Dripping.*—Be careful that no cinders or ashes fall into the dripping-pan, and empty the well before the meat is salted or floured, as the dripping will be more valuable. The Nottingham ware are the best vessels for keeping dripping in; where much dripping is made, however, keep one general receiving pot; do not put in seasoned dripping, or dripping of game and poultry; this should be kept by itself; it answers very well to baste similar articles again, or it makes very good common crust for meat pies, or for frying; it is not fit for delicate pastry. The cook will find at the bottom of the receiving pot, after it has stood a few days, some gravy which may be useful to make gravy, and if not removed will spoil the colour of the dripping; then put the dripping into a saucepan over a clear slow fire, at a good distance; when it is nearly boiling skim it well, then let it boil, and immediately put it aside; when cool, and a little settled, pour it steadily through a sieve into the pan; this is very nice dripping for pastry. What remains may be put into the receptacle of seasoned dripping, or kept by itself, and will do for basting meat.

In this manner the fat that settles on the top of stews and boils and soups may be clarified and turned to use. Remove the fat before you add the vegetables or seasoning. Nothing makes a lighter piecrust than this sort of fat. It should be used soon, as the moisture hanging about it will turn it sour.

468. *To clarify Suet and Fat.*—Take away whatever fat or suet that is not likely to be used off a loin of mutton, loin of veal, or sirloin of beef. An inch thickness of fat may be taken from a loin or neck of mutton, and a good deal of fat from the kidney; then shave it into very thin slices, or chop it up as suet; pick out all veins and skin, then put it into a stone jar or saucepan, and set it in a slow oven, or over a stove till it is melted; then strain it through a hair sieve into jars or pots; when quite cold, tie over the jars. Be careful not to put this or dripping into a warm place.

469. *Hog's Lard.*—The inside fat or leaf of a pig should be beaten with a lard-beater, or rolling-pin; then put it into a jar or earthen pot, in a large kettle of boiling water, till it is melted; add a little salt and a little rosemary—the last may be left out if not preferred. When melted, pour it into jars or bladders, nicely cleaned. The bits of skins that are left are called crittens, and chopped up with apples or currants to make fritters, or a pie. Lard is frequently melted in a brass kettle over a slow fire. It is better to surround it with water.

470. *Clarified Sugar* is merely brought to a syrup in the following

manner:—Break up the sugar in large lumps, and allow a pint of water to every two pounds of sugar: but whatever quantity is employed, keep out a quarter of a pint cold. Put the sugar and water in the preserving pan, with the white of one egg well beaten, to every two pounds of sugar. When the sugar is dissolved, set it on the fire, and when it boils fast, throw in the quarter of a pint of cold water; this is intended to throw up the scum. When it boils again, take the vessel from the fire and let it stand to settle; then remove all scum, and place it in a hair sieve; what runs through may be returned to the rest: give it another boil, and again settle and skim. It should not be stirred after the sugar is dissolved and syrup begins to warm. In this manner sugar is clarified for jelly which is to be put in glasses.

PICKLES.

Like Dr. Kitchiner, we are not fond of pickles. They are, indeed, for the most part, mere vehicles for taking up vinegar and spice—and very unwholesome, indigestible vehicles they are. By pounding them, as they do in India, they are rendered less indigestible. Those who are fond of relishes, and who are wise enough not to gratify their tastes at the expense of their stomachs, will find the various flavoured vinegars, mixed to each individual's liking, an excellent substitute for pickles.

471. There are three methods of pickling; the most simple is, merely to put the articles into cold vinegar. The strongest pickling vinegar of white wine should always be used for pickles; and for such as are wanted for white pickles, use distilled vinegar, which is as white as water. This method we recommend for all such vegetables as, being hot themselves, do not require the addition of spice, and such as do not require to be softened by heat, such as capsicums, chili, nasturtiums, button onions, radish-pods, horse-radish, garlic, and eschalots. Half fill the jars with best vinegar, fill them up with the vegetables, and tie down immediately with bladder and leather. One advantage of this plan is, that those who grow nasturtiums, radish-pods, and so forth, in their own gardens, may gather them from day to day when they are exactly of the proper growth. They are very much better if pickled quite fresh, and all of a size, which can scarcely be obtained if they be pickled all at one time. The onions should be dropped in the vinegar as fast as peeled; this secures their colour. The horse-radish should be scraped a little outside, and cut up in rounds half an inch deep. Barbaries for garnish; gather fine full bunches before they are quite ripe; pick away all bits of stalk and leaf and injured berries, and drop them in cold vinegar; they may be kept in salt and water, changing the brine whenever it begins to ferment: but the vinegar is best.

472. The second method of pickling is that of heating vinegar and spice, and pouring them hot over the vegetables to be pickled, which are previously prepared by sprinkling with salt, or immersing in brine. It is better not to boil the vinegar, by which process its strength is

evaporated. Put the vinegar and spice into a jar, bung it down tightly, tie a bladder over, and let it stand on the hob, or on a trivet by the side of the fire, for three or four days, well shaken three or four times a day; this method may be applied to gherkins, French beans, cabbage, brocoli, cauliflowers, onions, and so forth.

473. The third method of pickling is when the vegetables are in a greater or less degree done over the fire. Walnuts, artichokes, artichoke bottoms, and beet-roots, are done thus, and sometimes onions and cauliflowers.

474. *Gherkins or young Cucumbers* should be the size of a finger; if smaller they have not attained their flavour, if much larger they are apt to be seedy; put them in unglazed stone jars; cover them with brine, composed of a quarter of a pound of salt dissolved in a quart of boiling water, and left to become cold; cover down the jars and put them on the hearth before the fire for two or three days, till they become yellow; then pour off the brine, drain the cucumbers, scald and dry the jars, return the cucumbers and cover them with vinegar: set them again before the fire and let them remain until they become green, which will be in eight or ten days; then pour off the vinegar, and put to them a pickle of fresh vinegar (prepared for gherkins, French beans, and so forth, as directed.) To each quart, black pepper two ounces, ginger one ounce, salt one ounce, cayenne half a drachm, mustard-seed one ounce.

The vinegar in which the cucumbers were greened should be bottled: it will make good sauce for cold meat or salads. Cucumbers are often steeped in vinegar on purpose to give it a flavour.

475. *French Beans.*—The best sort for this purpose are white-runners. They are very large long beans, but should be gathered quite young, before they are half grown; they may be done in the same way as gherkins, but will not require so long a time, and the first vinegar is not so nice as that from cucumbers.

476. *Onions.*—Onions should be chosen about the size of marbles, the silver-skinned sort are the best. Prepare a brine and put them into it hot; let them remain one or two days, then drain them, and, when quite dry, put them into clean dry jars, and cover them with hot pickle, in every quart of which has been steeped one ounce each of horse-radish sliced, black pepper, allspice, and salt, with or without mustard-seed. In all pickles the vinegar should always be two inches or more above the vegetables, as it is sure to shrink, and if the vegetables are not thoroughly immersed in pickle they will not keep.

477. *Red Cabbage.*—Choose fine firm cabbages: the largest are not the best; trim off the outside leaves; quarter the cabbage, take out the large stalk, slice the quarters into a colander, and sprinkle a little salt between the layers; put but a little salt, too much will spoil the colour; let it remain in the colander till next day, shake it well that all the brine may run off; put it in jars, cover it with a hot pickle composed of black pepper and allspice, of each an ounce; ginger pounded, horse-radish sliced, and salt, of each half an ounce

to every quart of vinegar (steeped as above directed); two capsicums may be added to a quart, or one drachm of cayenne.

478. *Garlic and Eschalots.*—Garlic and eschalots may be pickled in the same way as onions.

479. *Melons, Mangoes, and long Cucumbers,* may all be done in the same manner. Melons should not be much more than half grown; cucumbers full grown, but not overgrown. Cut off the top, but leave it hanging by a bit of rind, which is to serve as a hinge to a box-lid; with a marrow-spoon scoop out all the seeds, and fill the fruit with equal parts of mustard-seed, ground pepper, and ginger, or flour of mustard instead of the seeds, and two or three cloves of garlic. The lid which encloses the spice may be sewed down or tied, by running a white thread through the cucumber, and through the lid, and then, tying it together, cut off the ends. The pickle may be prepared with the spices directed for cucumbers, or with the following, which bears a nearer resemblance to India. To each quart of vinegar put salt, flour of mustard, curry powder, bruised ginger, turmeric, half an ounce of each, cayenne pepper one drachm, all rubbed together with a large glassful of salad oil; eschalots two ounces, and garlic half an ounce, sliced; steep the spice in the vinegar as before directed, and put the vegetables into it hot.

480. *Brocoli or Cauliflowers.*—Choose such as are firm, yet of their full size; cut away all the leaves, and pare the stalk; pull away the flowers by bunches, steep in brine two days, then drain them; wipe them dry and put them into hot pickle; or merely infuse for three days three ounces of curry powder in every quart of vinegar.

481. *Walnuts.*—Be particular in obtaining them exactly at the proper season; if they go beyond the middle of July, there is danger of their becoming hard and woody. Steep them a week in brine. If they are wanted to be soon ready for use, prick them with a pin, or run a larding pin several times through them; but if they are not wanted in haste, this method had better be let alone. Put them into a kettle of brine, and give them a gentle simmer, then drain them on a sieve and lay them on fish drainers in an airy place, until they become black, which may be two days; then add hot pickle of vinegar in which has been steeped, in the proportion of a quart, black pepper one ounce, ginger, eschalots, salt, and mustard-seed, one ounce each. Most pickle vinegar, when the vegetables are used, may be turned to use, walnut pickle in particular; boil it up, allowing to each quart four or six anchovies chopped small, and a large table-spoonful of eschalots, also chopped. Let it stand a few days, till it is quite clear, then pour off and bottle. It is an excellent store sauce for hashes, fish, and various other purposes.

482. *Beet-roots.*—Boil or bake gently until they are nearly done; according to the size of the roots they will require from an hour and a half to two hours; drain them, and when they begin to cool peel and cut in slices half an inch thick, then put them into a pickle composed of black pepper and allspice, of each one ounce, ginger pounded, horse-radish sliced, and salt, of each half an ounce to every

quart of vinegar, steeped. Two capsicums may be added to a quart, or one drachm of cayenne.

483. *Cauliflowers or Brocoli.*—Choose firm full-grown cauliflowers and brocoli, cut away all the leaves and pare the stalk, and instead of steeping in cold brine, set them over the fire in cold brine, and let it heat gradually. Just before it comes to boil, take them up in a wire ladle, and spread them on a cloth before the fire; when quite dry, put them into glass or jars, and add cold pickle, according to the second method of making pickle (472).

484. *Artichokes.*—Gather young artichokes as soon as formed; throw them into boiling brine, and let them boil two minutes; drain them; when cold and dry put them in jars, and cover with vinegar, prepared as method the third, but the only spices employed should be ginger, mace and nutmeg.

485. *Artichoke Bottoms.*—Get full-grown artichokes and boil them, but not so much as for eating, but just until the leaves can be pulled; remove them and the choke; in taking off the stalk, be careful not to break it off so as to bring away any of the bottom; it would be better to pare them with a silver knife, and leave half an inch of tender stalk coming to a point; when cold, add vinegar and spice, the same as for artichokes.

486. *Mushrooms.*—Choose small white mushrooms; they should be but one night's growth. Cut off the roots, and rub the mushrooms clean with a bit of flannel and salt; put them in a jar, allowing to every quart of mushrooms one ounce each of salt and ginger, half an ounce of whole pepper, eight blades of mace, a bay leaf, a strip of lemon rind, and a wine-glassful of sherry; cover the jar close, and let it stand on the hob or on a stove, so as to be thoroughly heated, and on the point of boiling; so let it remain a day or two, till the liquor is absorbed by the mushrooms and spices; then cover them with hot vinegar, close them again, and stand till it just comes to a boil; then take them away from the fire. When they are quite cold divide the mushrooms and spice into wide-mouthed bottles, fill them up with the vinegar, and tie them over. In a week's time, if the vinegar has shrunk so as not entirely to cover the mushrooms, add cold vinegar. At the top of each bottle put a tea-spoonful of salad or almond oil; cork close, and dip in bottle resin.

487. *Samphire.*—On the sea-coast this is merely preserved in water, or equal parts of sea-water and vinegar; but as it is sometimes sent fresh as a present to inland parts, the best way of managing it under such circumstances, is to steep it two days in brine, then drain and put it in a stone jar covered with vinegar, and having a lid, over which put thick paste of flour and water, and set it in a very cool oven all night, or in a warmer oven till it nearly, but not quite boils. Then let it stand on a warm hob for half an hour, and let it become quite cold before the paste is removed; then add cold vinegar, if any more is required, and secure as other pickles.

488. *Indian Pickle.*—The vegetables to be employed for this favourite pickle, are small hard knots of white cabbage sliced, cauli-

PICKLES.

flowers or brocoli in flakes, long carrots not larger than a finger, or large carrots sliced (the former are far preferable,) gherkins, French beans, small bottom onions, white turnip radishes half grown, radish-pods, eschalots, young hard apples, green peaches when the trees are thinned before the stones begin to form, vegetable marrow not larger than a hen's egg, small green melons, celery, shoots of green elder, horse-radish, nasturtiums, capsicums, and garlic. As all these vegetables do not come in season together, the best method of doing this is to prepare a large jar of pickle at such time of the year as most of the things may be obtained, and add the others as they come in season. Thus the pickle will be nearly a year in making, and ought to stand another year before using, when, if properly managed, it will be excellent, but will keep and continue to improve for years. For preparing the several vegetables, the same directions may be observed as for pickling them separately, only take this general rule—that, if possible, boiling is to be avoided, and soaking in brine to be preferred; be very particular that every ingredient is perfectly dry before putting into the jar, and that the jar is very closely tied down every time that it is opened for the addition of fresh vegetables. Neither mushrooms, walnuts, nor red cabbage, are to be admitted.

For the pickle. To a gallon of the best wine vinegar add salt three ounces, flour of mustard half a pound, turmeric two ounces, white ginger sliced three ounces, cloves one ounce, mace, black pepper, long pepper, white pepper, half an ounce each, cayenne two drachms, eschalots peeled four ounces, garlic peeled two ounces; steep the spice in vinegar on the hob or trivet for two or three days. The mustard and turmeric must be rubbed smooth with a little cold vinegar, and stirred into the rest when as near boiling as possible. Such vegetables as are ready may be put in; when cayenne, nasturtiums, or any other vegetables mentioned in the first method of pickling, come in season, put them in the pickle as they are; any in the second method, a small quantity of hot vinegar without spice; when cold pour it off, and put the vegetables into the general jar. If the vegetables are greened in vinegar, as French beans and gherkins, this will not be so necessary, but will be an improvement to all. Onions had better not be wet at all; but if it be desired not to have the full flavour, both onions, eschalots, and garlic, may be sprinkled with salt in a colander, to draw off all the strong juice; let them lie two or three hours.

The elder apples, peaches, and so forth, to be greened as gherkins. See method the second (472.)

The roots, radishes, carrots, celery, are only soaked in brine and dried. Half a pint of salad oil, or of mustard oil, is sometimes added. It should be rubbed with the flour of mustard and turmeric. It is not essential to Indian pickle to have every variety of vegetable here mentioned; but all these are admissible, and the greater variety the more approved.

11*

PASTRY.—GENERAL OBSERVATIONS.

We are no friends to pastry, particularly what is called the rich flaky pastry. It is decidedly indigestible, and consequently unwholesome. A crisp, short paste, however, we consider nutritious; the butter, lard, &c. being thoroughly incorporated with the flour in the process of making it. Oleaginous substances, such as lard, become not only perfectly innocuous, when well mixed with farina, and well baked or boiled, but very nourishing and wholesome; and this we take to be the best way of preparing such things for human food.

In making pastry, the cook, as indeed she ought to be on all occasions, should be particularly clean and neat. Her utensils should be kept in "apple-pie order," and when they are done with, they should be carefully cleaned and put in their places. Her paste-board and rolling-pin, let it be remembered, should, after using, be well scoured with hot water *alone*. She should not use soap, sand, or stone dust of any kind. A marble slab is preferable to a board for rolling paste. Both are generally made too small to be convenient. Three feet long by two feet wide is a good size. In making a paste, a good cook will have no waste of any kind, and particularly she will not make more at one time than she wants, under the idea that she can keep it in flour till the next time of making; for it is ten to one but that the old paste will spoil the new. No flour except the very best can be used for fine descriptions of pastry, and in damp weather it should be dried before the fire, but not scorched. Clarified dripping, good lard, marrow, salt butter well washed, may be used for ordinary pastry; indeed, if they are pure and sweet they will form good pastry, with good flour and good management. In wealthy families, however, where economy is not an object, and every thing for the table is required to be of the first quality, the safest plan is to use the best fresh butter. The fat that settles on stews, and on the broth in which meat has been boiled, may be used for pastry, that is, provided it is tasteless. Suet is sometimes used for meat pies, but though it makes a light crust, when hot, it does not eat well when cold.

A most wholesome crust is made without butter or any other oily matter. For this purpose take half a quartern of dough, work in an egg, and cover your pie. This will be sufficient for a large one. A great deal more butter, or fat of some kind or other, was formerly directed to be used in making pastry than at present. For ordinary purposes, half the weight of lard, or butter, is sufficient, but in the richest crusts the quantity should never exceed the weight of flour. Eggs may be added to enrich the crust; use no more water or other liquid in making paste than is absolutely necessary, or, in other words, take care not to "put out the miller's eye," that is, to make the paste too moist. The great thing is to incorporate the flour well with the fat, which you cannot do if you allow too much water or milk in the first instance.

The under or side crust, which should be thin, should not be made so rich as the top crust, as otherwise it will make the gravy or syrup greasy. All dishes in which pies are to be baked should be buttered or greased round the edges to prevent the crust from sticking, and if there be an under crust, all over the inside: — the same must be done with tins or saucers.

There is a number of other little things to be attended to in making pastry, which we will enumerate in as few words as we can. Fruit pies or large tarts should have a hole made in the middle of the crust, and it is a good plan in a family pie to place a small tea-cup in the middle of the pie; this will form a receptacle for the syrup, and prevent its boiling over. For the same reason meat pies should have holes round their edges, but they do not require a tea-cup. The thickness of the crust must be regulated by the judgment of the cook with reference to the nature of the pie, and the circumstances of the party by whom it is to be eaten. Top crusts vary in thickness from half an inch to an inch or more. Of course a meat pie will require a longer time to bake than a fruit one, and some descriptions of fruit again longer than others. The edges of pies are sometimes crimped or jagged, and some persons further *ornament* them with leaves, or stars cut out of paste, and laid on the top of the crust. Pigeon and game pies, &c. are generally washed over with finely beaten yolk of eggs, simply to give them a nice appearance, but they are just as nice without it. We ought to add, that where the paste is wanted to adhere, as in the upper and under crusts of a pie, it is a good plan to touch the parts with the white of an egg; a little water will do, but not so well.

489. *Flaky and Short Crusts.*—In making a *flaky crust* a part of the fat should be worked with the hand to a cream, and then the whole of the flour well rubbed into it before any water or milk is added. The remaining fat must be stuck on the paste and be rolled out. For *crisp crust*, by far the most wholesome, the whole of the fat should be rubbed in and thoroughly incorporated with the flour. Water or milk must be added when this is done, and the dough, or rather paste, made up. The pie-board and rolling-pin should be well dusted with flour, and the dough should be well beaten with the pin to thoroughly mix it, and render it light. Mind, in rolling out paste do not drive the pin backwards and forwards, but *always keep rolling from you.* In making flaky crusts the paste must be rolled out thin, and the fat or butter laid all over it; then roll it up and beat it till it puffs up in little bladders: it should be then finally rolled out, and put in the oven as quickly as possible.

490. *Raised Crust.* — Put two pounds and a half of flour on the paste-board, and put on the fire in a saucepan three-quarters of a pint of water, and half a pound of good lard; when the water boils, make a hole in the middle of the flour, pour in the water and lard by degrees, gently mix it with a spoon, and when it is well mixed, then knead it with your hands till it becomes stiff; dredge a little flour to prevent it sticking to the board, or you cannot make it smooth; then set it aside for an hour, and keep it cool: do not roll it with your rol'ing-pin, but roll it with your hands, about the thickness of a quart pot;

cut it into six pieces, leaving a little for the covers; put the left hand, clenched, in the middle of one of the pieces, and with the other on the outside work it up against the back of the left to a round or oval shape. It is now ready for the meat, which must be cut into small pieces with some fat, and pressed into the pie; then cover it with the paste previously rolled out to a proper thickness, and of the size of the pie; put this lid on the pie and press it together with your thumb and finger, cut it all round with a pair of scissors, and bake for an hour and a half. Our good old country housewives pride themselves very much upon being able to raise a large and high pork pie. This crust will answer for many meat and other pies baked in dishes or tins.

491. *Puff Paste.*—This paste is nearly the same as what we have called (489) flaky crust, and, of course, made upon the same principles. If eggs are desired, allow three yolks to a pound of butter or lard. Rub a fourth part of the fat to a cream, then mix the eggs with it, and afterwards the flour. A very little water will suffice to wet it. Beat it with the pin to make it flaky; roll it out thin three times, putting in a portion of the fat each time, and roll it from you: after each rolling, beat it well.

492. *Sweet Paste.*—This is suitable to fruit tarts generally, apples perhaps excepted, for which we recommend a puff paste. To three-quarters of a pound of butter put a pound and a half of flour, three or four ounces of sifted loaf-sugar, the yolks of two eggs, and half a pint of new milk. Bake it in a moderate oven; if required to be iced, see 500.

493. *Crust for Savoury Pies.*—To two pounds of flour, one and a half of butter, or lard, and the yolks of three eggs; rub part of the fat to a cream with the eggs, then rub in the flour; wet with cold water, and roll out with the remainder of the butter. This crust is suitable for pigeon, rabbit, hare, and other savoury pies.

494. *A rich Short Crust.*—Rub to a cream a quarter of a pound of butter; add one pound of well-dried and very fine flour, and two ounces or more of pounded loaf-sugar; rub together till they are thoroughly incorporated; then add the yolks of two good-sized eggs, and as much boiling hot cream as will bring it to a proper consistence. Bake in a moderate oven.

495. *Biscuit Paste.*—Take six yolks of eggs, a quarter of a pound of loaf-sugar, a pound of flour, and a tea-cup full of milk. Rub these ingredients into a stiff paste. This paste is only fit for light preserved fruits that require scarcely any baking. It is sometimes cut out in rounds, a bit of jam or jelly placed on each, and baked in tins.

496. *Crust for Venison Pasty.*—Raised crust (490) will do, but if a richer be required, increase the quantity of butter, and add eggs. Let the top crust be substantial, and line the sides of the dish, but not the bottom.

497. *Stringing Paste* must be made more tenacious than the other descriptions. A quarter of a pound of flour to one ounce of butter,

PIES, TARTS, AND PUFFS.

with a very little water, will make paste which may be drawn out in fine strings, and laid across the tartlets.

498. *Potatoe Paste.*—Boil your potatoes; rub through a colander, and while quite hot add butter and an egg. Use plenty of flour on the pie-board and rolling-pin; cover your pie, and put it into the oven while quite warm.

499. *Rice Paste.*—Simmer the rice in water or milk till quite soft and pulpy; drain it well off; stir in yolks of eggs, one to a quarter of a pound of rice, and a little butter, if you like. Roll out the paste with a dust of flour. Cover your pie and bake without suffering to cool. This paste will do for either savoury or sweet pies.

500. *Icing Pastry.*—When nearly baked enough, take the pastry out of the oven and sift fine powdered sugar over it. Replace it in the oven and hold over it, till the sugar is melted, a hot salamander or shovel. The above method is preferred for pastry to be eaten hot: for cold, beat up the white of two eggs well, wash over the tops of the pies with a brush, and sift over this a good coating of sugar; cause it to adhere to the egg and pie crust; trundle over it clean brush dipped in water till the sugar is all moistened. Bake again for about ten minutes.

PIES, TARTS, AND PUFFS.

501. *Perigord Pie.*—Make a force meat chiefly of truffles, a small quantity of basil, thyme, parsley, knotted marjoram, the liver of any kind of game (if of woodcocks, that and the entrails, except the little bag), a small quantity of fat bacon, a few crumbs, the flesh of wild or tame fowls, pepper, and salt. Lard the breasts of pheasants, partridges, woodcocks, moor-game, or whatever game you have, with bacon of different sizes; cut the legs and wings from the backs, and divide the backs; season them all with white pepper, a little Jamaica pepper, mace, and salt; make a thick raised crust to receive the above articles; it is thought better than a dish, but either will do. Line it closely with slices of fine fat bacon, then cover it with stuffing, and put the different parts of the game lightly on it, with whole green truffles, and pieces of stuffing among and over it, observing not to crowd the articles, so as to cause them to be underbaked. Over the whole lay slices of fat bacon, and then a cover of thick common crust. Bake it slowly, according to the size of the pie, which will require a long time.

Some are made with a pheasant in the middle whole, and the other game cut up and put round it.

502. *Sole Pie.*—Split the soles from the bone, and cut the fins close; season with a mixture of salt, pepper, a little nutmeg, and pounded mace, and put them in layers with oysters. They eat excellently. A pair of middling sized ones will do, and half a hundred of oysters; put in the dish the oyster liquor, two or three spoonfuls of broth, and some butter. When the pie is baked, pour in a cupful of thick cream boiled up with a tea-spoonful of flour.

503. *Eel Pie.*—Cut the eels in lengths of two or three inches, after skinning them; season with pepper and salt, and place in the dish with some bits of butter and a little water, and cover it with paste. Middle-sized eels do best.

504. *Oyster Pie.*—Open the oysters and strain the liquor from them; parboil them after taking off the beards. Parboil sweetbreads, cut them in slices, lay them and the oysters in layers, season them very lightly with salt, pepper, and mace, then put half a tea-cup full of liquor, and the same of gravy. Bake in a slow oven, and before you serve, put a tea-cup full of cream, a little more of oyster liquor, and a cup of white gravy, all warmed, but not boiled.

505. *Pilchard Pie.*—Clean and skin the white part of large leeks; scald in milk and water, and put them in layers into a dish, and, between the layers, two or three salted pilchards which have been soaked for two or three hours the day before. Cover the whole with a good plain crust. When the pie is taken out of the oven, lift up the side crust with a knife and empty out all the liquor; then pour in half a pint of scalded cream.

506. *A remarkably fine Fish Pie.*—Boil two pounds of small eels; having cut the fins quite close, pick the flesh off and throw the bones into the liquor with a little mace, pepper, salt, and a slice of onion, and boil till rich, and strain it; make force meat of the flesh, an anchovy, parsley, lemon peel, salt, pepper, and crumbs, and four ounces of butter warmed, and lay it at the bottom of the dish. Take the flesh of soles, small cod, or dressed turbot, and lay it on the force meat, having rubbed it with salt and pepper; pour the gravy over, and bake. Observe to take off the skins and fins, if cod or soles.

507. *Beef-steak Pie.*—Take beef-steaks that have been well hung, beat them gently with a circular steak-beater, season them with pepper, salt, and a little eschalot minced very fine. Roll each steak with a good piece of fat, and fill your dish. Put some crust on the edge an inch below it, and a cup of water or broth in the dish. Cover with rather a thick crust, and set in a moderate oven.

508. *Beef-steak and Oyster Pie.*—Prepare the steaks as above, without rolling, and put layers of them and of oysters. Stew the liquor and beards of the latter, with a bit of lemon peel, mace, and a sprig of parsley. When the pie is baked, boil with above three spoonfuls, and an ounce of butter rolled with flour. Strain it, and put it into the dish.

509. *Veal, Chicken and Parsley Pie.*—Cut some slices from the neck or leg of veal; if from the leg, about the knuckle; season them with salt, scald some parsley that is picked from the stems and press it dry; cut it a little and lay it at the bottom of the dish, then put the meat, and so on, in layers. Fill the dish with milk, but not so high as the crust: cover it with crust, and when baked, pour out a little of the milk, and put in half a pint of good scalded cream. Chickens may be cut up and cooked in the same way.

510. *Veal Olive Pie.*—Make the olives in the following manner: Cut long thin slices of veal, beat them, lay on them thin slices of fat

bacon, and over them a layer of force meat, seasoned high with shred eschalot and cayenne. Roll them tight, about the size of two fingers, but not more than two or three inches long; fasten them round with a small skewer, rub egg over them. Put them round and round the dish, making the middle highest; fill it up almost with water, and cover it. Add gravy, cream, flour, and mushroom powder, when baked.

511. *Veal Pie.*—Take some of the middle or scrag of a small neck; season it with pepper and salt, and either put to it, or not, a few slices of lean bacon or ham. If it is wanted of a high relish, add mace, cayenne, and nutmeg, to the salt and pepper, and also force meat and eggs, and if you choose add truffles, morels, mushrooms, sweetbreads cut into small bits, and cocks'-combs blanched, if liked. Have a rich gravy to pour in after baking; it will be very good without any of the latter additions.

512. *A rich Veal Pie.*—Cut steaks from the neck or breast of veal; season them with pepper, salt, and nutmeg, and a very little clove in powder. Slice two sweatbreads, and season them in the same manner. Lay a puff paste on the edge of the dish; then put the meat, yolks of hard eggs, the sweetbreads, and some oysters, up to the top of the dish. Lay over the whole some very thin slices of ham, and fill up the dish with water; cover, and when it is taken out of the oven pour in at the top, through a funnel, some veal gravy and rich cream, warmed together. Lay a paper over the crust, that it may not be too brown.

513. *Calf's Head Pie.*—Stew a knuckle of veal till fit for eating, with two onions, a few isinglass shavings, a bunch of sweet herbs, a blade of mace, and a few peppercorns, in three pints of water. Keep the broth for the pie. Take off a bit of the meat for the balls, and let the other be eaten; butter, simmer the bones in the broth till it is very good. Half boil the head, and cut it into square bits; put a layer of ham at the bottom of the dish, then some head, first fat, then lean, with balls and hard eggs cut in half, and so on till the dish is full; and take care not to place the pieces close, or the pie will be too solid, and there will be no space for the jelly. The meat must be first pretty well seasoned with salt, pepper, and a scrape or two of nutmeg. Put a little water and a little gravy into the dish, and cover it with a tolerably thick crust; bake it in a slow oven, and when done, pour in as much gravy as it will hold, and do not cut it till perfectly cold, in doing which observe to use a very sharp knife, and first cut out a large piece, going down to the bottom of the dish, and when cut thus, thinner slices can be cut. The different colours and the jelly have a beautiful marble appearance. A small pie may be made to eat hot, which, with high seasoning, oysters, mushrooms, truffles, and morels, has a very good appearance. The cold pie will keep many days; slices make a pretty side dish. Instead of isinglass, use a calf's foot or a cow-heel, if the jelly is not likely to be stiff enough. The pickled tongues of calves' heads may be cut instead of, or in addition to, ham.

514. *Excellent Pork Pies to eat cold.*—Cut the trimmings off a hog when cut up, and if you have not sufficient, take the meat off a sweet-bone. Beat it well with your rolling-pin; season with salt and keep the lean and fat separate. Raise common crust either in a round or oval form; put a layer of lean and then a layer of fat, or mix your fat and lean, and so on till you have filled the pie to the top; lay on the lid, cut the edge smoothly round, and pinch it close. Bake in a slow oven, as the meat is very solid. Do not put any water or bone into pork pies. The outside pieces will be hard unless they are cut small and pressed close. See raised crust, 490.

515. *Lamb Pie.*—Make it of the breast, neck, or loin; it should not be seasoned much with salt and pepper; the bone taken out, but not the gristles; a small quantity of jelly gravy should be put in hot; put two spoonfuls of water before baking. This pie should not be cut until cold. House lamb is one of the most delicate things that can be eaten. Grass lamb makes an excellent pie, and may either be boned or not, but not to bone it is perhaps the best. Season with only pepper and salt; put two spoonfuls of water before baking, and as much gravy when taken out of the oven. Meat pies being fat, it is best to pour out the liquor on one side, take the fat off, and put it in again and a little more to it (by means of a funnel), at the top.

516. *Mutton Pie.*—Take steaks from the loin or neck of mutton that has been kept some time hanging; beat them and cut off some of the fat; add pepper, salt, and a small onion; put a little water at the bottom of the dish, and paste on the edge, put in the steaks, and cover it over with rather a thick crust. If you make raised small pies, break the bones in two; season and cover them over, pinch the edges. When baked, pour into each a little gravy made of mutton, seasoned with pepper, salt, and a small bit of onion.

517. *Chicken Pie.*—Take two young fowls, cut them up and season them with salt, a little mace, nutmeg, and white pepper very finely powdered; add a small bit of cayenne. Put the chickens, force meat balls, slices of ham or gammon, and hard eggs, in turn by layers. If they are to be made into raised pies, add no water; if in a dish, put a little at the bottom. Make gravy of the scrag or a knuckle of veal, with some shank bones of mutton, seasoned with mace, white pepper, an onion, a small bunch of sweet herbs, and a little salt. Add morels, truffles, mushrooms, and so forth, if eaten hot; but not, if eaten cold. Should you make this pie in a dish, put as much gravy as it will hold; but if in a raised crust the gravy must be strained, and then put in cold, as jelly. Make the jelly clear by boiling with it the whites of two eggs well beaten; take away the meat previous to adding the whites; strain it through a muslin sieve.

Young Rabbits are prepared in the same way; their legs should be cut short, and the breast-bones must not be put in; they will help to make the gravy.

519. *Giblet Pie.*—Nicely clean goose or duck giblets; stew them in a little water with a bunch of sweet herbs, black pepper, onion, a little salt, till nearly done; let them stand till cold. If you have not

enough to fill the dish, put a veal or beef-steak, or two or three mutton chops, at the bottom. Put the liquor that you have stewed your giblets in into the dish; put in the giblets, and when baked, pour into it a tea-cup full of cream.

520. *Green Goose Pie.*—Pluck and singe two young green geese of a good size; bone them and wash; season them well with allspice, mace, pepper, and salt. Put one inside the other and press them as close as you can, drawing the legs inwards. Butter them well, and bake either with or without crust. If made a pie of, the cover must fit the dish close, to keep the steam in. It will keep many days. Gravy-jelly may be put in when served.

521. *Staffordshire Goose Pies.*—Bone, wash, and season the birds with allspice, mace, pepper, and salt. Put rather a small turkey inside a goose, duck, fowl, and then less birds, tongue or force meat. Force meat may fill up the spaces between the crust and fowls, and be omitted within. Ornament the crust, and put a knob or flower at the top by which to lift it, as it must not be cut, but kept to cover the pie. A less expensive and smaller pie may be made by omitting the goose and turkey. All pies made of white meats or fowls are improved by a layer of fine sausage meat.

522. *Hare Pie to cut cold.*—Cut up the hare; season it; and bake it with force meat and egg, in a raised crust or dish. When served, cut off the lid, and cover it with jelly gravy.

523. *Partridge Pie.*—Pick and singe four partridges; cut off the legs at the knees; season them with chopped parsley, thyme, mushrooms, pepper, and salt. Put a slice of ham and a veal cutlet at the bottom of the dish; put the partridges in, and half a pint of good broth. Put puff paste on the edge of the dish; cover it; brush it over with eggs; and bake an hour.

524. *A French Pie.*—Lay a puff paste on the edge of a dish; put into it either chickens jointed, veal in slices, or rabbits, with force meat balls, sweetbreads cut in pieces, a few truffles, and artichoke bottoms.

525. *Pigeon Pie.*—Rub the pigeons with salt and pepper, inside and out; put a bit of butter inside, and, if approved, some parsley chopped fine, with the livers, salt, and pepper. Lay a beef-steak at the bottom of the dish, and place the birds on it. Between every two a hard egg. Lay a bit of ham on each pigeon; put a cup of water at the bottom of the dish. When ham is cut for pies or gravy, take the under part rather than the prime. Season the gizzards and two joints of the wings, and place them in the middle of the pie; and over them, in a hole made in the crust, three feet, nicely cleaned, to show what pie it is.

526. *Squab Pie.*—Cut apples, and lay them in rows, with mutton chops, a little sugar, and an onion; cut fine, and put among them.

527. *Duck Pie.*—Bone a fowl and a full-grown duck; wash them, season with a small quantity of mace and allspice, in the finest powder, with salt and pepper. Put the fowl within the duck. Put a calf's tongue, pickled red, boiled very tender, and skinned, into the

fowl; press the whole close. The skins of the legs should be drawn inwards, that the body of the fowl may be quite smooth. The space between the sides of the crust and fowl may be filled with a fine force meat, if approved.

Bake it in a slow oven, either in a raised crust or dish, with a thick crust ornamented.

528. *Rabbit Pie.*—Cut up two young rabbits; take a pound of fat pork, that has been in pickle a week; cut it into small bits; season it with salt and pepper, and put into a dish. Parboil the livers and brains, and beat them in a mortar with a quarter of a pound of fat bacon or ham; add mace, salt, pepper and sweet herbs, chopped fine. Make this into small balls, and distribute in the dish, with artichoke bottoms, cut in dice. Grate half a small nutmeg over, and add half a pint of port, and the same quantity of water. Cover with a tolerably thick crust, and bake it an hour in a quick oven.

529. *Vegetable Pie.*—Cut young carrots, artichoke bottoms, lettuces, mushrooms, turnips, broad beans, scalded and blanched, onions, celery, parsley, and add peas. Or use any of them you may chance to have. Make them into a stew, with some good veal gravy; season with salt and pepper. Bake a crust over a dish, with some paste over the edge, and a cup turned bottom upwards, to prevent its sinking when baked. Pour the stew into the dish, and lay the crust over it. Winter vegetables may be used in the same way. A cup of cream is a great improvement.

530. *An Herb Pie.*—Take one handful of spinach, two handfuls of parsley, from the stems, some mustard and cress, two lettuces, a few leaves of borage, and white beat leaves. Wash and boil them a little, and then drain out all the water; cut them small; mix, and lay in a dish; sprinkle with some salt; mix a batter with two eggs well beaten, a pint of cream, and half a pint of milk, as much flour as will bring it to a paste not very thick, and pour it on the herbs; cover with a good crust, and bake.

531. *To prepare Venison for Pasty.*—Take the bones out; season and beat the meat; lay it in a stone jar in large pieces; pour upon it some plain drawn beef gravy, rather weak. Put the bones on the top; then set the jar in a saucepan over the fire; simmer between three and four hours. Put it in a cold place until next day. Then remove the cake of fat. Lay the meat in handsome pieces on a dish. Put some of the gravy in, and keep the remainder for the time of serving. Venison thus prepared will require less time in baking, and a thinner crust.

532. *Venison Pasty.*—A boned and skinned shoulder makes a good pasty. It must be beaten and seasoned. Add the fat of a loin of mutton, well hung, as the shoulder is lean. Steep twenty-four hours in equal parts of vinegar and port. Rub the shoulder well with sugar for two or three days, as it is sinewy. Wipe it clean from the sugar and wine when it is used. Either in the shoulder or side the meat must be cut in pieces, and laid with fat between, that it may be proportioned to each person, without breaking up the pasty to find it.

Dust some salt and pepper at the bottom of the dish, put a bit of butter; then the meat, nicely packed, so as not to be hollow. Bake between three and four hours in a slow oven. Take some fine old mutton, and boil with the bones of the venison to make gravy: season it with salt, pepper, and a little mace; put half a pint of this gravy, cold, into the dish; butter the venison; line the sides of the dish with a thick paste; lay a thick crust over the top. Put the remainder of the gravy, hot (when it is baked,) into it, with a funnel, through the hole at the top.

533. *To make a Pasty of Beef or Mutton, to eat as well as Venison.*—Bone a sirloin, or a small rump of beef, or a fat loin of mutton, after hanging several days; beat it well with a rolling-pin; then rub ten pounds of meat with four ounces of sugar; then pour over it a glass of vinegar, and a glass of port wine. Let it lie five days and then wash and wipe the meat very dry, and season it very high with salt, Jamaica pepper, nutmeg, &c. To ten pounds of meat, one pound, or nearly, of butter; spread it over the meat. Lay it in the dish. Put a crust round the edges, rather thick, and cover. It must be baked in a slow oven. Put the bones in a pan in the oven, with no more water than will cover them, and one glass of port wine, a little salt and pepper, in order that you may have a little rich gravy to add to the pasty when baked. Put it in the pie, through a funnel, at the top of the pasty. Sugar gives shortness and better flavour to meat than salt (too great a quantity of salt hardens it,) and is quite as good a preservative, except from flies.

534. *Apple Pie.*—Wipe the outside of some apples, pare, and core them; boil the parings and cores in a little water till it tastes well; strain, and put a bit of bruised lemon, a little sugar and cinnamon, and simmer again. Put a paste round the edge of the dish; place the apples in it; when one layer is made, sprinkle half the sugar, shred lemon peel, and squeeze some juice, or a glass of cider. Put in the liquor that you have boiled. Cover with paste. Add butter when cut, if hot. To flavour the pie you may add quince, marmalade, orange paste, or cloves, to flavour.

535. *Cherry Pie* should have a mixture of currants or raspberries, or both.

536. *Currant Pie.*—With or without raspberries.

537. *Mince Pies.*—Of scraped beef or tongue, free from skin and string, two pounds, four pounds of beef suet chopped fine, two pounds of jar raisins stoned and chopped, six pounds of currants nicely cleaned, perfectly dry, of chopped apples three pounds, the peel and juice of two lemons, a pint of sweet wine, a quarter of a pint of brandy, a nutmeg, a quarter of an ounce of cloves, the same of mace, the same of pimento, in fine powders. Press the whole into a deep pan when well mixed, and keep it covered in a cool place. Have orange, and lemon peel, and citron, ready, and put some of each in the pies when made. Half, or a quarter of the quantity may be made, unless for a very large family.

538. *Tarte de Moie.*—Put a light paste into a dish, then layers of

all kinds of sweetmeats, biscuits, marrow, and butter. Add a moderately rich custard, not very sweet, and seasoned with orange flower water; give it a scald, and pour over the whole. It will take half an hour to bake. Turn it out. It is good hot or cold.

539. *Rhubarb Tart.*—Take the skin off the rhubarb, and cut the stalks in lengths of four or five inches. Make a syrup for a quart basin. Take a pound of common lump sugar; boil it in nearly half a pint of water to a thin syrup; skim it, and put in the rhubarb, and as it simmers shake the pan over the fire. It will turn yellow at first, but keep it very gently simmering till it greens, and then take it off. When cold, put in a tart dish, with as much syrup as will make it very moist. Put a light crust over, and when that is done, the tart will be sufficiently baked. Quarter the crust, and fill the dish with custard or cream.

540. *To prepare Cranberries for Tarts.* — Simmer them in moist sugar, without breaking, twenty minutes; and let them become cold before used; a pint will require nearly three ounces of sugar. The Russian and American sorts are larger and better flavoured than those of England. The juice, when pressed from the baked fruit and sweetened, makes a fine drink in fevers. Stewed with sugar, they eat exceedingly nice with bread.

541. *Lemon Tart.* — Take the rind of four lemons, pared rather thick, boil it in water till tender, and beat fine. Add to it four ounces of lump sugar, four ounces of blanched almonds cut thin, the juice of the lemon, and a little grated peel. Simmer to a syrup; when cold turn it into a shallow tin, lined with a thin rich puff paste, and lay bars of the same over. As soon as the paste is baked, take it out.

542. *Orange Tartlets* or *Puffs.* — Line patty-pans; when baked, put in orange marmalade made with apple jelly.

543. *Fried Patties.*—Mince a bit of cold veal and six oysters with a few crumbs of bread, nutmeg, pepper, salt, and a small bit of lemon peel; add the liquor of the oysters; warm all in the tosser, but do not boil it; let it get cold. Make a good puff paste, roll thin, and cut it in round or square bits; put the meat between two of them, pinch the edge to keep in the gravy, and fry them of a fine brown. This is a very good thing — and baked, is a fashionable dish. Wash all patties over with egg before baking.

544. *Oyster Patties.*—Put a fine puff paste into small patty-pans; put a bit of bread in each, and cover with paste; bake them; and in the mean time make ready the oysters. Take off the beards of the oysters; cut the other parts in small bits, put them in a small tosser, with a grate of nutmeg, a little white pepper and salt, a bit of lemon chopped very fine, a little cream, and a little of the oyster liquor; take the bread out of the patties, and fill them, after simmering them a few minutes. Observe to put a bit of bread into all the patties, to keep them hollow while baking.

545. *Beef Patties.* — Cut very fine some underdone beef with a little fat, season with pepper, salt, and a little onion or eschalot. Make plain paste, thin, in an oval shape; fill it with mince, pinch

the edges, and fry them of a fine brown. The paste should be made with a small quantity of butter, egg, and milk.

546. *A good Mince for Patties.*—Two ounces of ham, four of chicken or veal, one egg boiled hard, a blade of mace, salt, and pepper, three cloves in powder. Just before you serve, warm it with four spoonfuls of rich gravy, four spoonfuls of cream, and an ounce of butter: fill as usual.

547. *Apple Puffs.*—Pare and core the fruit, and either stew them in a stone jar, or bake them. When cold, mix the pulp of the apple with sugar and lemon peel shred fine, taking as little of the apple juice as you can. Bake them in a thin paste, in a quick oven; a quarter of an hour will do them, if small. Orange or quince marmalade is a great improvement; cinnamon pounded, or orange flower water, in change.

548. *Lemon Puffs.*—Beat and sift a pound and a quarter of double refined sugar, grate the rind of two large lemons and mix it with the sugar; then beat the whites of three new-laid eggs a long time, add them to the sugar and peel, and beat them for an hour. Make it up in any shape you please, and bake them on paper; put on tin plates, in a moderate oven. Do not remove the paper till cold. Oiling the paper will make it come off with ease.

549. *Excellent light Puffs.*—Mix two spoonfuls of flour, half a spoonful of brandy, one egg, a little grated lemon peel, a little loaf-sugar, some nutmeg; then fry, but not brown; beat it in a mortar with five eggs; put a quantity of lard in a frying-pan, and when quite hot, drop a dessert spoonful of batter at a time; turn as they brown. Serve them immediately with sweet sauce.

550. *Cheese Puffs.*—Strain cheese curd from the whey, and beat half a pint of it fine in a mortar, with three eggs, a spoonful and a half of flour, only one white of the eggs, a quarter of a nutmeg, orange flower water, and sugar to make it sweet. Put a little of this paste in very small round cakes on a tin plate. A quarter of an hour will bake them, if the oven is hot. Serve with pudding sauce.

PUDDINGS, CHEESECAKES, &c.

The first thing to be learnt, with regard to making puddings, is the composition of the batter. Without good batter, you cannot have good pudding; and without good eggs, flour, and milk, you cannot have either. For all kinds of puddings and pastry, it is of great importance that your flour should be of the very best quality. Your milk too should be good. The goodness or badness of milk depends much on the kind of food upon which the cow is fed; but cows fed upon the same food do not yield milk of the same quality. A cow that gives a large quantity of milk does not always produce a proportionate quantity of cream, and of course poor milk will not make so good a pudding as rich. Flour is not the better for being fresh ground, as Dr. Kitchiner intimates, but on the contrary. It should, however, be perfectly sweet. The goodness of well-manufactured flour depends upon the quality of the wheat from which it is made. Without good wheat you can have no good flour. In one word, to ensure a good pudding, your eggs must be new laid, your butter rich and fresh, your flour of the first quality, and all your ingredients of the same character. In the making of a pudding—a *good* pudding—the cook must observe the utmost cleanliness, both as respects herself and the utensils which she uses. The eggs directed to be used in the following receipts are full-sized hen eggs; if pullet eggs are used, two will be required for one hen egg. There is no substitute, that we know of, for eggs in pudding making. We have heard *male* and *female* old women talk about using, as substitutes for eggs, *snow* and *small beer*. Dr. Kitchiner says, truly, " that they will no more answer this purpose than as substitutes for sugar or brandy." Batter puddings in all their varieties are composed of milk, eggs, and flour. As has been properly observed, " the proportions may vary, and other articles may be added, by which the name is changed, but the great matter is to know how to mix eggs, flour, and milk, and then you may easily adopt any variety that is directed." In using eggs, you should always break them, one by one, into separate cups, or at any rate take care not to spoil all your eggs by the admission of one that is bad into the mass. Let the eggs be well beaten, and then add the flour, with a pinch of salt, and a little nutmeg, and mix the eggs and flour thoroughly before any milk is added; then by degrees put in as much milk as will bring the batter to the consistency you wish. It ought, indeed, it *must* be, well stirred immediately before being put into the basin or dish.

The vessel in which a batter pudding is to be dressed must be well buttered. Dripping, or lard, will answer as well for a baked pudding. The cloth tied over the basin must be buttered, or dipped in boiling water, wrung out, and dredged with flour, but buttering is best.

The pudding will break in boiling, if the batter do not exactly fill the vessel. In baking, the pudding is sure to swell considerably, and therefore the batter should not fill the vessel by about an inch. Before putting the pudding into the pot, take care that the water boils rapidly, and afterwards make the water boil as soon as possible, which must be kept up till the pudding is done. Just after putting the pudding into the pot, it should be shook two or three times to prevent it settling.

The length of time that a pudding requires to be boiled depends upon its size, and, in some degree, upon the material of which it is made. The less flour, the shorter time is required for boiling. A one-egg pudding, not exceeding three parts of half a pint in quantity, in a tea-cup, will require about twenty or twenty-five minutes boiling; or with three eggs about half an hour; and so on in proportion. But the best way of ascertaining when a pudding is done, is to run your fork into the middle of it, and if the fork comes out *clear*, the pudding is done.

551. *To make Pudding Paste.*—Beat one egg, mix it with half a

pound of suet, well chopped, add one pound of flour; well mix; then add as much cold water as is requisite to bring it to a stiff paste; flour the pie-board and rolling-pin, and beat the paste till it puffs up; roll it out to the size desired, and put in the fruit. If boiled in a basin, it should be well buttered, and the cloth well floured before tying it over. This paste is used for all kind of fresh fruit. A very small quantity of sugar should be put in with the fruit to draw the juice, but not much, or it will become so juicy as to burst the crust. A fruit pudding is lighter boiled in a cloth, but it should be well secured to prevent the juice from escaping. An hour and a half will boil a pudding of this size, if boiled in a cloth; if in a basin, allow another quarter of an hour or twenty minutes. The same paste will do for a roll pudding and meat puddings.

552. *Plum Pudding.*—To make a rich plum pudding take a pound of marrow, or suet, well chopped, a pound of fine flour dried, eight or ten eggs beaten well; half a nutmeg grated; as much mace, cinnamon, and ginger, all powdered very fine; a pinch of salt; mix these well together, and beat up into a batter; then add one pound of currants, one pound of raisins, stoned and chopped a little; the currants should be rubbed in a cloth, and well picked, or well wash and dry them; two ounces of candied citron peel, or part lemon, and orange, cut small; and two ounces of sweet almonds, blanched and cut up in bits; two ounces of loaf-sugar grated; then add these to the batter, and put in a wine-glass of brandy; well mix them together. It may be boiled in a buttered basin or mould; if the batter should be too stiff, put a glass of white wine in it. It will take four or five hours boiling. Strew over it powdered loaf-sugar; garnish with sliced lemon. Sauce, containing half a glass of best brandy, a glass of white wine, a little rind of lemon grated, and a little powdered cinnamon, half an ounce of grated loaf-sugar, mixed with an equal quantity of very thick melted butter. It is a good plan to make and keep by you a little of this sauce, and then it is ready at any time. In a bottle containing a pint of sherry, and half a pint of best brandy, add two ounces of loaf-sugar, a quarter of an ounce of mace, half an ounce of shaved lemon rind, with kernels of apricots, peaches, and nectarines, and steep in a little white wine; when steeped, pour it off clear, and put to the wine and brandy; and add half a quarter of a pint of capillaire. Two table-spoonfuls of this sauce will flavour a boat-full of thick melted butter.

553. *A plain family Plum Pudding.*—Beat up three eggs, six ounces of suet chopped, a pound of flour, a third part of a pound of raisins, and the same weight of currants; one ounce of candied orange or lemon peel, cut small; half a tea-spoonful of ground allspice, a little salt, two ounces of brown sugar: make a stiff batter with water, and mix the fruit and spice well in. If boiled in a basin, allow three hours and a half; if in a cloth, three hours.

554. *A common Plum or Currant Pudding* is nothing more than a suet pudding, with the addition of plums, or currants, and allspice.

555. *Very light Plum Pudding.*—Mix grated bread, suet, and stoned raisins, four ounces each, with two well-beaten eggs three or

four spoonfuls of milk, and a little salt: boil four hours. Sauce, a spoonful of brandy, sugar, and nutmeg, in melted butter.

556. *National Plum Pudding.*—Mix suet, jar raisins, and currants, one pound each, four ounces of crumbs of bread, two table-spoonfuls of sugar, one table-spoonful of grated lemon peel, half a nutmeg, a small blade of mace, a tea-spoonful of ginger, and six well-beaten eggs. Boil it five hours.—*N. B.* If you want to keep plum puddings good for a long time, say some months, hang them in a cold place in the cloth in which they were boiled. When wanted to be used, take them out of the cloth, cover them with a clean one, and warm them through with hot water; they will then be fit for the table.

557. *Potatoe Pudding.*—Boil mealy potatoes in their skins, according to the rule laid down, skin and mash them with a little milk, pepper, and salt: this will make a good pudding to bake under roast meat. With the addition of a bit of butter, an egg, milk, pepper, and salt, it makes an excellent batter for a meat pudding baked. Grease a baking dish; put a layer of potatoes, then a layer of meat cut in bits, and seasoned with pepper, salt, a little allspice, either with or without chopped onions; a little gravy of roast meat is a great improvement: then put another layer of potatoes, then meat, and cover with potatoes. Put a buttered paper over the top to prevent it from being burnt, and bake it an hour or an hour and a half.

558. *Cottage Potatoe Pudding.*—Two pounds of mashed potatoes rubbed through a colander, two or three eggs well beaten, two ounces of moist sugar, three-quarters of a pint of milk, a little nutmeg and salt, three ounces of raisins, or currants. It is very good without the fruit, and will take three-quarters of an hour to bake. Omitting the milk and adding three ounces of butter, it makes a very nice cake.

559. *For a rich sweet Potatoe Pudding.*—Rub a pound of potatoe meal through a colander; add half a pint of cream, nutmeg, cinnamon, and from two to four ounces of loaf-sugar, from two to four ounces of fresh butter or marrow, from three to six eggs, two ounces of sweet almonds, blanched and cut, one ounce of candied citron, cut small, a few dried currants, a spoonful of ratafia or brandy: put a crust round the edge of the dish and entirely line the dish: if baked, put in the batter, bake, and when it is brown, it is done. Only substituting potatoe for flour, a very good family plum pudding may be made, but it should be baked.

560. *Carrot Pudding.*—Grate a raw red carrot; mix with double the weight of bread crumbs, or Naples biscuit, or part of each; to a pound and a half put half a pint of new milk or cream.

561. *A Black-cap Pudding.*—Rub three table-spoonfuls of flour smooth by degrees into a pint of milk, strain it, and simmer it over the fire until it thickens; stir in two ounces of butter; when cold, add the yolks of four eggs well beaten and strained, and half a pound of currants rubbed and picked; put the latter into a cloth well buttered, tie it tight, and plunge it into boiling water; keep it in motion for five minutes, that it may be well mixed.

562. *Sago Pudding.*—Boil a pint and a half of new milk with four spoonfuls of sago nicely washed and picked, lemon peel, cinnamon, nutmeg; sweeten to taste, then mix four eggs; put a paste round the dish, and bake slowly.

563. *A very good Pudding.*—Mix one pound and a half of suet, cut small, and free from skin, with two pounds of flour, a pound of currants picked and rubbed in a coarse cloth, six eggs well beaten, a table-spoonful of infusion of saffron, a glass of brandy, a little grated ginger, a pinch of salt, and a pint of milk; put it into a basin that will just hold it, tie a floured cloth tight over it, and put it into a pot of boiling water. Boil it four hours.

564. *Bread and Butter Pudding.*—Slice bread, and butter it, and lay it in a dish with currants between each layer, and sliced citron, orange, or lemon peel; pour over an unboiled custard of milk, two or three eggs beaten, a little grated nutmeg, a little ratafia; two hours at least before it is baked, to soak the bread.

565. *Almond Pudding.*—Beat half a pound of sweet and a few bitter almonds with a spoonful of water, then mix four eggs, four ounces of butter, two spoonfuls of cream put warm to the butter, one spoonful of brandy, a little nutmeg and sugar to taste. Butter some cups, half fill, and bake the puddings. Serve with pudding sauce.— Or, beat fine, four ounces of almonds, four or five bitter almonds, with a little wine, yolks of six eggs beaten, peel of two lemons grated, six ounces of melted butter, nearly a quart of cream, and juice of one lemon. When well mixed, bake it half an hour, with paste round the dish.

566. *Kitchiner's Pudding.* — Beat up three eggs, strain them through a sieve, and gradually add to them a quarter of a pint of new milk; stir them well together; rub together in a mortar two ounces of moist sugar, and as much nutmeg as will lie on a sixpence; stir these to the eggs and milk, then add four ounces of flour, and beat it to a smooth batter (the only way of doing this is, by adding a little of the milk, &c., and mixing that to a smooth paste, then gradually thinning it). Stir to it by degrees seven ounces of suet chopped fine, and three ounces of bread crumbs; mix the whole half an hour or more before boiling; well butter a mould or basin, tie over a pudding cloth very tight, and boil it three hours. Half a pound of muscatel raisins, cut in half, and a little grated lemon peel, will make the above a good plum pudding: or without the plums, by adding half a pint more milk, it bakes well under meat as a Yorkshire pudding; or it may be baked in saucers or tin patty-pans, and served with wine sauce. An hour will bake it the size of a saucer.—Or, simmer for ten minutes half a pint of milk with a roll of lemon peel, and two blades of mace,; strain it into a basin, and put it away to cool; beat three eggs with three ounces of loaf-sugar, the third part of a nutmeg, and three ounces of flour; mix well with the eggs, add the milk by degrees; then three ounces of butter broken in bits, three ounces of bread crumbs, three ounces of currants rubbed and picked, three ounces of raisins stoned and chopped; mix all well together

butter a mould, tie a cloth tightly over and boil it two hours and a half. Serve with melted butter, two table-spoonfuls of brandy, and a little loaf-sugar.

567. *A Dutch Rice Pudding.*—Soak four ounces of rice in warm water half an hour, then drain the water from it, and throw the rice into a stew-pan, with half a pint of milk, half a stick of cinnamon, and simmer till tender; when cold, put four whole eggs, well beaten, two ounces of butter melted in a tea-cup full of cream (or milk where cream is scarce or dear), and put three ounces of sugar, a quarter of a nutmeg, and a good piece of lemon peel. Put a light puff paste in a mould or dish, or grated tops and bottoms, and bake in a quick oven.

568. *Rice Puddings.*—It will be well to make a few observations on rice before we enter upon rice puddings. Large long corn which is quite white and clear is the best; though this may cost a little more money, it will be found the cheapest. Bad rice has a dingy red and yellow appearance, and is dusty; in this state it is almost sure to turn the milk with which it is used. The best rice takes less sugar to sweeten it, and the flavour of it is much superior to the inferior sort. Good rice will soon become tender and swell, and when this is the case it is done. Inferior rice may be used for broths, or stews, as thickeners, but it is not so wholesome as the best. Rice should be kept in a vessel closely shut, and in a dry place. It does not keep well after grinding; it is almost sure to become sour. It should be ground as it is wanted.

569. *A Rice Pudding.*—Take two parts of a pound of rice, put it in a cloth or bag that would hold three times the quantity; put it into boiling water, and let it boil an hour. Take it up, and beat two eggs and add to it; mix and beat with the rice a little sugar, nutmeg, and one ounce of suet, or butter, with or without currants; flour a cloth and tie it tight in it, and let it boil half an hour. Sauce, boiled milk with a little sugar and nutmeg, or wine sauce.

570. *A baked Rice Pudding.*—The above may be used, enriched by slices of bread and butter laid at the top, with a little sugar and nutmeg strewed over. — Or, scald the rice in a small quantity of water; when all the water is absorbed by the rice, add a quart of new milk, and let it boil up, with a stick of cinnamon for flavour;* beat three or four eggs with fine moist sugar, stir to them gradually the boiling milk and rice; add one ounce of beef suet or butter; when it is in the pan, or dish, which should be buttered before putting in, grate nutmeg over the top; put it in the oven as soon as made, and bake an hour.

571. *Ground Rice Pudding.*—Put on the fire a quart of new milk; put into it five or six young laurel leaves, a stick of cinnamon, a pinch of salt; when it boils, stir into it a quarter of a pound of ground rice, which has been previously wetted with a little cold water; stir

---

* Laurel leaves are usually directed; but they are decidedly poisonous, and we strongly disapprove of the use of them.

till it boils and thickens. As it is apt to burn, a double saucepan is the best for this purpose. Take the flavourings out, and stir into it three or four eggs, well beaten, with an ounce of sugar, and a little grated nutmeg: three-quarters of an hour will bake it. This pudding (if desired) can be very much enriched by adding one or two more eggs, two ounces of fresh butter or marrow, a tea-cup full of cream, and a large spoonful of brandy, ratafia, or noyeau.

572. *Rice Snow Balls.*—Pick and wash half a pound of the best rice, boil it in water for ten minutes or a quarter of an hour, drain it quite dry; there should be more water than the rice will take up: after it is well drained through a sieve, divide it into six parcels; take apples as for dumplings, surround each with rice; tie them in a cloth separately, and rather loosely; boil one hour. Sauce, sugar and butter, or wine sauce.

573. *Plain Rice Pudding.*—If you wish to boil it, take half a pound of ground rice, put it into a bag that would hold three times as much, put it into the saucepan containing boiling water; let it boil an hour and a quarter. For baking, take a third part of a pound of rice, put it into a deep dish with two quarts of skim milk; it will take an hour and a half baking. Sauce, cold butter, and sugar and nutmeg, or preserved fruit.

574. *Rice Bignets.*—In a pint of new milk simmer three ounces of rice till it becomes a stiff paste; add half a tea-cup full of thick cream, the grated rind of half a lemon, two ounces of loaf-sugar, and a little powdered cinnamon, mace, and nutmeg, and two eggs well beaten; grate a small tea-cup full of bread crumbs; when the rice is cold, cut it into bits and roll it into small balls, dip each in the egg, roll in the bread crumbs, and fry them quickly. Sauce, wine sauce.

575. *Vermicelli, Sago, Tapioca, and Russian Seed Puddings.*—These are all made in the same way as rice puddings. Arrow-root pudding is made as ground rice pudding. It is generally baked in a dish lined with paste, and turned out.

576. *Yeast Dumplings.*—Procure half a quarter of dough from the baker's. Keep it covered over by the fire till it is wanted. Should it be wished to make the dough at home, set half a quarter, or rather less, of the best flour, with a wine glass full of fresh yeast, stirred into half a tea-cup full of milk, just warm. Let it rise, in a warm place, for about an hour. Then make your dumplings, and boil. Each dumpling should be about the size of an egg. Put them in a large saucepan of boiling water, or in a steamer, which is much better; they should boil or steam twenty minutes. Stick in a fork; if done, the fork will come out clean. Take them up, and they should be eaten directly, as they become hard in their own steam. Tear them apart with your fork; if cut with your knife it will make them close. French baker's dough is always very light, and is much better for dumplings. Sauce, cold butter and sugar, or wine sauce.

577. *Suet Pudding.*—Shred a pound of suet; mix with a pound and a quarter of flour, two eggs beaten separately, a little salt, and as little milk as will make it. Boil it four hours. It eats well the

next day, cut in slices and broiled. The outward fat of loins and necks of mutton, finely shred or chopped, makes a more delicate pudding than suet; and both are far better for the purpose than butter, which causes the pudding to be heavy or close.

578. *Hunter's Pudding.*—Mix a pound of suet, a pound of flour, a pound of currants, a pound of raisins, stoned and a little cut, the rind of half a lemon, shred as fine as possible, six Jamaica peppers, in fine powder, four eggs, a glass of brandy, a little salt, and as little milk as will make it of a proper consistence; boil it in a flannel cloth, or a melon mould, eight or nine hours. Sweet sauce. Add sometimes a spoonful of peach water, for change of flavour. This pudding will keep, after it is boiled, six months, if tied up in the same cloth, and hung up, folded in a sheet of cap paper, to preserve it from dust, being first cold. When used, it must first be boiled a full hour.

579. *Marlborough Pudding.*—Cover the dish with a thin puff paste; then take candied citron, orange, and lemon peel, each one ounce; slice these sweetmeats very thin, and lay them all over the bottom of the dish; dissolve six ounces of butter, without water, and six ounces of powdered sugar, and the yolks of four eggs, well beaten; stir them over the fire until the mixture boils, then pour it on the sweetmeats, and bake the pudding three-quarters of an hour in a moderate oven.

580. *Custard Pudding.*—Boil a quart of milk until it is reduced to a pint; take from it a few spoonfuls, and let it cool, mixing with it, very perfectly, one spoonful of flour, which add to the boiling milk, and stir until it is quite cool. Beat four yolks and two whites of eggs, strain them, and stir them into the milk, two ounces of sifted sugar, two or three spoonfuls of wine, and a little grated nutmeg. Put it into a basin, tie a cloth over it, and boil it half an hour; untie the cloth, cool the basin a little, lay a dish upon the top of it, and turn it out.

581. *Custard.*—Boil half a pint of new milk, with a piece of lemon peel, and two peach leaves, and eight lumps of white sugar. Should cream be used instead of milk, there will be no occasion to skim it; beat the yolks and whites of three eggs, strain the milk through coarse muslin, or a hair sieve; then mix the eggs and milk very gradually together, simmer it gently on the fire, and stir it till it thickens.

582. *Almond Custard.*—Boil in a pint of milk or cream two or three bitter almonds, and cinnamon, and a piece of lemon peel, pared thin, with eight or ten lumps of sugar; let it simmer to extract the flavour, then strain it, and stir it till cool. Beat the yolks of six eggs, mix them with the milk, and stir the whole over a slow fire, until of a proper thickness, adding one ounce of sweet almonds, beaten fine in rose water.

583. *Rice Custard.*—Take a cup of whole Carolina rice, and seven cups of milk; boil it, by placing the pan in water, which must never be allowed to go off the boil until it thickens; then sweeten it, and add an ounce of sweet almonds pounded.

584. *Baked Vermicelli Pudding.*—Simmer four ounces of vermicelli in a pint of new milk ten minutes; then put into it half a pint of cream, a tea-spoonful of pounded cinnamon, four ounces of butter warm, the same of white sugar, and yolks of four eggs, well beaten. Bake it in a dish without a lining.

585. *Marrow Pudding.*—Four ounces of marrow, four of biscuits, or French biscuits, three of jar raisins, stoned, candied orange peel, sugar and nutmeg to the taste. Place these articles in layers in a dish surrounded by paste; then beat up four eggs, leave out the whites of two, in half a pint of cream, or good milk, and pour it over the other ingredients. It will take an hour and a half to bake.

586. *The Conservative Pudding.*—Take four sponge biscuits, a quarter of a pound of ratafia and macaroone cakes, mixed, the yolks of eight eggs, a glass of brandy, half a pint of cream, well beaten together, the cakes being soaked in the brandy and cream. Butter a quart mould, place dried cherries or stoned raisins in a pattern over it, pour in the mixture, and place the mould in a stew-pan, surrounded by water, and let it simmer an hour and a half over charcoal.

587. *Economical Pudding.*—In families where there are loose pieces of bread, they can be made into a pudding instead of throwing them on one side. Boil as much milk as the size of your dish will require, put in a bit of lemon peel, and two or three of young laurel leaves; cut up the bread crust too in thin slices. When the milk boils, take out the flavourings, put in the bread, cover it up, and set it by the fire to swell; then beat it up fine, and stir to it two or three eggs well beaten, with a little moist sugar and ground allspice, a bit of butter or suet, chopped fine, or a bit of good beef dripping. A few currants or not; currants are apt to turn the milk wheyey. Three-quarters of an hour will bake it. It is a very wholesome pudding for children.

588. *A delicate Bread Pudding.*—Take fine bread, grated fine, and rich new milk. When the milk boils, put in the bread crumbs; for every table-spoonful of bread, allow one egg, well beaten; sweeten it with loaf-sugar to your taste, and grate in a little nutmeg. Put it into a buttered basin, and boil it from twenty minutes to fifty, according to the size of the pudding. If baked, rather less time will do it. It only requires to be a light brown.

589. *Barley Pudding.*—Take a quarter of a pound of Scotch or pearl barley. Wash, and simmer it in a small quantity of water; pour off the water, and add milk and flavourings as for rice puddings. Beat up with sugar and nutmeg, and mix to the milk and barley in the same way. It may be more or less rich of eggs; and with or without the addition of butter, cream, or marrow. Put it into a buttered deep dish, leaving room for six or eight ounces of currants, and an ounce of candied peel, cut up fine, with a few apples cut in small pieces. An hour will bake it.

590. *Hard Dumplings.*—Mix flour and water, with a bit of salt, to the consistency of dough. Make it into dumplings, and boil them half an hour. Serve them with butter and salt. Skimmer cakes are made

in the same way, and flatted to the thickness of half an inch, and boiled on the skimmer, which should be previously buttered; when done, it will slip off the skimmer. They are eaten with sugar and butter.

591. *Newmarket Pudding.*—A pint of new milk, half a lemon rind, a little cinnamon, and a bay leaf; simmer a few minutes, sweeten with loaf-sugar, and strain by degrees to five well-beaten eggs (leaving out two whites;) pour this over thin slices of bread and butter strewed with currants. Bake half an hour.

592. *A light Pudding*—Take a pint of new milk, eight eggs, and half a pint of cream, to two spoonfuls of flour. Beat the yolks and whites of the eggs separately; beat up the batter without the whites, but, just before putting it in the pot, or oven, stir in the whites, with one ounce of fine loaf-sugar, a little powdered cinnamon, or nutmeg, and half a glass of brandy or ratafia. Butter the basin or mould which it will exactly fill. Put it into the water fast boiling, and keep it shaking about several minutes, lest the eggs should settle on one side. Half an hour will boil it. When turned out, grate over the top fine sugar and nutmeg, with melted butter, or wine sauce, round it; or stick bits of raspberry jam, or red currant jelly, at top. If baked, it will not require more than twenty minutes. A rich puff paste, put round the edge of any baked pudding, greatly improves the appearance.

593. *A Yorkshire Pudding.*—Beat up four eggs, and mix with them, by degrees, four spoonfuls of flour; beat it to a smooth paste, and add a pint of new milk and a pinch of salt. Put it into a shallow square tin, under roast meat. It should not be put down until the meat is warmed through, and begins to drip; or till the fire is become clear and fierce, so that the batter shall soon boil. The tin should be very hot when the pudding is put in, to keep the floury part from settling.

594. *A nice Suet Pudding.*—Take two or three eggs, well beaten, with half a pound of suet, chopped fine, a pound of flour, a pinch of salt, and some grated ginger and nutmeg. Beat these up very smooth with cold water to rather a thick batter. A few currants may be added. Two hours will boil it. White wine sauce.

595. *Mother Eve's Pudding.*—Take equal weights of suet, plums, currants, sugar, apples chopped up, bread crumbs, and flour, with an egg to an ounce of the ingredient, candied peel, spice, and salt. Boil six hours.

596. *Newcastle Pudding.*—Butter half a melon mould, or quart basin, and stick all round with dried cherries, or fine raisins, fill up with bread and butter—and steam it half an hour.

597. *Hasty Pudding.*—Boil a quart of new milk, cinnamon or bay leaves. While boiling, shake in from a flour dredger two tablespoonfuls of flour, and stir it until it thickens. Then pour it into a deep dish, stir in an ounce of butter, the same of moist sugar, and grate nutmeg over the top.

598. *Arrow-root Pudding.*—Arrow-root pudding is made in the

same way as hasty pudding, with the exception of shaking the arrow-root in, which should be stirred into a little cold milk, and then stirred into the boiling milk.

599. *A Friar's Omelet.*—Boil a dozen apples, as for sauce; stir in a quarter of a pound of butter, and the same of white sugar; when cold, add four eggs, well beaten; put it into a baking dish thickly strewed over with crumbs of bread, so as to stick to the bottom and sides; then put in the apple-mixture; strew crumbs of bread over the top; when baked, turn it out, and grate loaf-sugar over it.

600. *A Swiss Pudding.*—Put layers of crumbs of bread and sliced apples, with sugar between, until the dish be as full as it will hold; let the crumbs be the uppermost layer; then pour milk over it, and bake.

601. *Oxford Puddings.*—Take a quarter of a pound of grated biscuit, the same quantity of currants, the same of suet, finely chopped, a spoonful of sugar, and a little nutmeg; mix them well together. Take the yolks of three eggs, and make up the puddings into balls. Fry them a light colour in fresh butter, and serve with white wine sauce.

602. *Muffin or Cabinet Pudding.*—Cut three or four muffins in two, pour over them boiling milk sufficient to cover them, cover them up until they are tender. Make a rich custard with eight eggs (only four whites,) a pint of cream, a quarter of a pound of loaf-sugar, an ounce of almonds, blanched and cut, lemon peel and nutmeg grated, and a glass of ratafia or brandy. Butter a tin mould for boiling—for baking, a dish. Put a layer of dried cherries, greengages, apricots, or French plums; cover with custard, add more fruit, then custard, until the mould or dish is quite full. Boil an hour and a half, and serve with wine sauce. It should not float in the water, but stand in a stew-pan, and only water enough to reach half way up the mould. If for baking, it will not take so long. Lay a puff paste round the edges of the dish.

Stale muffins are very good boiled in milk and eaten with wine sauce.

603. *French and Italian Puddings.*—These puddings are composed of sliced French rolls, eggs, and cream. Five or six eggs to a pint of cream, and as much roll as will thicken it; sweeten it with loaf-sugar; a pound of suet, chopped fine, may be added or omitted. Line the dish with puff paste; lay at the bottom six or eight apples, cut up, a pound of raisins stoned, a few dates sliced, or a few French plums, some candied orange peel, sugar, and spice. Pour the pudding over this, grate nutmeg at top, and bake of a fine pale brown.

604. *A Cheese Pudding.*—Half a pound of cheese grated, butter two ounces, four eggs, a little cayenne and nutmeg. Butter a dish, and bake twenty minutes.

605. *A very rich Pudding of prime ripe Fruit.*—This is made sometimes by pressing the fruit through a sieve, if apricots, greengages or peaches; sweet juicy apples, or rich mellow pears, may be grated; or the fruit may be scalded a few minutes in white wine;

then the skins and stones removed, and beaten in a mortar. When cold mix with rich custard, cream, eggs, and bread crumbs, or Naples biscuit, with loaf-sugar to taste; the kernels blanched, and a glass of brandy or Madeira wine. Then bake in a dish edged with puff paste, and call it according to the fruit employed—apricot pudding, peach pudding, and so forth. If the cook is ordered to make such a pudding, it is fit she should know how to do it; but it is a great pity to spoil good things by such incongruous mixtures; the batter alone would make a much better pudding; and the fruit and wine might be saved for dessert. For these rich delicate puddings, the tinctures are preferable to the spice in substance.

606. *Chesnut Pudding.*—Roast chesnuts, or boil them a quarter of an hour; blanch, peel, and grate, or pound in a mortar, with a little white wine. To a dozen chesnuts, add six eggs, well beaten, a pint and a half of cream, and a quarter of a pound of butter; mix it well together; sweeten to taste; add a little salt and nutmeg; simmer over the fire till it thickens, stirring it well. Then bake it in a dish, edged and lined with puff paste.

607. *Rusk Pudding* is exactly the same thing as bread and butter pudding, except that the butter is spread on rusks instead of bread. The richness may be varied at pleasure. Let it steep two hours or more before putting in the oven.

608. *Portugal Pudding.*—Rub up four table-spoonfuls of ground rice, or semilina, with three ounces of butter, and stir in it a pint of cream; stir it till it boils and is quite thick. Then stir in two whole eggs, and the yolks of three more, well beaten, with a quarter of a pound of loaf-sugar, a little salt and nutmeg. Butter a dish, and bake it an hour. When it is done, have ready another dish of the same size, or a very little deeper; on the bottom of this spread a layer of raspberry jam, then the pudding, and then a layer of apricot jam. This pudding is very delicate without the mixture of fruit, with wine or lemon sauce instead.

609. *Tansey Pudding.*—Make a rich batter with Naple-biscuits, eggs, cream, and a little sugar; chop up a very few tansey leaves, and a few of spinach; enough to give the whole a green colour. Set it in a double saucepan, over boiling water, till it becomes quite thick; then pour it into a buttered basin or mould; tie it up securely; and let it boil three-quarters of an hour. Let it stand a few minutes after taken up; then turn out, and serve with wine sauce.

610. *To make Curd for Cheesecakes, and other purposes.*—Milk is turned to curds and whey by means of rennet, which is the stomach of a calf, taken out as soon as it is killed, well cleansed from its contents, then scoured inside and out with salt, and when thoroughly salted stretched on a stick to dry. A bit of this is to be soaked in boiling water for several hours, and the liquor put in milk warm from the cow, or made that warmth. Use alone can prescribe the exact quantity. Never use more than enough to turn it, as it hardens the curd. The gizzard skin of fowls and turkeys may be prepared in

the same way, and answer the same purpose; or the curd for cheesecakes may be bought of the regular dairy people.

611. *Cheesecakes.*—The basis of cheesecakes is professedly the curd of milk as turned for cheese; but many are made entirely without it. The following recipe is much approved: Take the curd of eight quarts of new milk; rub the curd in a coarse cloth till quite free from whey; then work into it three-quarters of a pound of butter, three biscuits, and an equal quantity of bread crumbs, a little salt, and such spices as you choose, finely powdered. Beat ten eggs (half the whites) with three-quarters of a pound of fine loaf-sugar, a wine-glass full of brandy or ratafia, and a pint of rich cream. Having well mixed all these ingredients, rub them with the hand through a coarse hair sieve; then add a pound of currants, rubbed in a coarse cloth, and picked, and an ounce of candied citron, cut as small as possible. Line tin patty-pans with rich puff paste, put in the mixture, and either entirely cover with paste, or put on only bars or leaves. They will take about twenty minutes to bake in rather a quick oven. By substituting half a pound of sweet almonds for currants, and half an ounce of bitter, blanched, and beaten to a paste, almond cheesecakes may be made; or lemon orange cheesecakes, by substituting for the currants two or three candied lemons or oranges, pounded in a mortar.

612. *Potatoe Cheesecakes.*—Take half a pound of mashed potatoes, rubbed through a colander, or a quarter of a pound of mucilage, or potatoe starch; mix with a quarter of a pound of butter, a tea-cup full of cream, a quarter of a pound of loaf-sugar, and two eggs, finely beaten, a quarter of a pound of candied peel, either chopped fine or beaten in a mortar, and a little nutmeg or cinnamon; well mix these ingredients. Put in patty-pans, or saucers, lined with paste. Do not more than half fill, as the substance will swell. Sift over fine sugar, and bake in a quick oven a quarter of an hour. Four or six ounces of currants may be substituted for part or all of the candied peel, or the grated rind and juice of a lemon or Seville orange may be added; also a little brandy or ratafia: but do not make the mixture too moist.

613. *A plain Cheesecake.*—Turn three quarts of milk to curds; break it, and drain the whey; when dry, break it in a pan, with two ounces of butter, till perfectly smooth; put to it a pint and a half of thin cream, or good milk, and add sugar, cinnamon, nutmeg, and three ounces of currants.

614. *Bread Cheesecakes.*—Pour a pint of boiling cream on a penny loaf; let it stand two hours; mix half a pound of butter, warm, with eight eggs, and a grated nutmeg; beat the whole in a mortar; then add half a pound of currants rubbed and picked, two ounces of sugar, a spoonful of wine, and the same of brandy.

615. *Common Pancakes.*—Make a light batter of eggs, flour, and milk; fry in small pan, in hot dripping or lard; a little salt, nutmeg, and ginger, may be added. Sugar and lemon should be served to eat with them.—Or, when eggs are scarce, make the batter with

small beer, ginger, and so forth; or water, with flour, and a very little milk, will serve, but not nearly so well as eggs and all milk.

616. *Pancakes of Rice.*—Boil half a pound of rice to a jelly, in a small quantity of water; when cold, mix it with a pint of cream, eight eggs, a bit of salt and nutmeg; stir in eight ounces of butter, just warmed, and add as much flour as will make the batter thick enough. Fry in as little lard or dripping as possible.

617. *Cream Pancakes.*—Mix the yolks of two eggs, well beaten, with a pint of cream, two ounces of sifted sugar, a little nutmeg, cinnamon, and mace. Rub the pan with a bit of butter, and fry the pancakes thin.

618. *Fritters.*—Make them of any of the batters directed for pancakes, by dropping a small quantity into the pan; or make the plainer sort, and put pared apples, sliced and cored, into the batter, and fry some of it in each slice. Currants, or sliced lemon as thin as paper, make an agreeable change. Fritters for company should be served on a folded napkin in the dish. Any sort of sweetmeat, or ripe fruit, may be made into fritters.

619. *Oyster Fritters.*—Make a batter of flour, milk, and eggs; season a very little with nutmeg. Beard the oysters, and put as many as you think proper in each fritter.

620. *Potatoe Fritters.*—Boil two large potatoes, scrape them fine, beat four yolks and three whites of eggs, and add to the above one large spoonful of cream, another of sweet wine, a squeeze of lemon, and a little nutmeg. Beat this batter well half an hour. It will be extremely light. Put a good quantity of fine lard into a stew-pan, and drop a spoonful at a time of the batter into it. Fry them; and serve as a sauce, a glass of white wine, the juice of a lemon, one dessert-spoonful of peach-leaf or almond water, and some white sugar, warmed together; not to be served in the dish.

BAKING.

621. *Bread.*—Put a quartern of flour into a large basin, or small pan, with two tea-spoonfuls of salt; make a hole in the middle, then put in a basin four table-spoonfuls of good yeast, stir in a pint of milk lukewarm; put it in the hole of the flour, stir just to make it of a thin batter, and then strew a little flour over the top; then set it on one side of the fire, cover it over with a cloth, let it stand till the next morning; add half a pint more of warm milk, and make it into dough, knead it for ten minutes, then set it in a warm place by the fire for one hour and a half, then knead it again, and it is ready for either loaves or bricks.

622. *Sally Lunn Tea Cake.*—Take a quarter of a pint of thick small-beer yeast, and one pint of warm milk, and put into a pan with flour sufficient to make it of a thick batter; let it stand by the fire till it has risen as high as it will, about two hours. Two ounces of lump sugar, dissolved in a pint of new milk, a quarter of a pound of butter rubbed in the flour very fine; then make your dough; let it

stand half an hour, then make your cakes and put them on tins; when they have stood to rise, put them in a quick oven. When eggs are plentiful you may put four eggs instead of milk—they will make it much lighter.

French rolls are made much in the same way; instead of using all milk put half water, and use only butter and a little salt.

623. *A Plum Cake.*—A quartern of dough, half a pound of moist sugar, half a pound of butter, a tea-cup full of cream and two eggs, a pound of currants (add raisins if you please) a tea-spoonful of allspice, two ounces of candied orange peel cut small, and an ounce of carraway seeds. Roll the dough out several times, and spread over the several ingredients; flour the pan well, and set it on one side the fire to rise; bake an hour and a half. A richer cake may be made by adding more sweetmeats, butter, eggs, and almonds, and so forth. The dough made as bread; when risen, melt the butter in warm milk and put to it with the other ingredients, and put to rise.

624. *A plain Pound Cake.*—One pound each of butter, loaf-sugar, and flour, and nine eggs; work the butter to a cream, pound the sugar, and add then the eggs; beat all together twenty minutes, then lightly add the flour; mix, put in a tin or hoop lined with buttered paper. Bake an hour in a moderate oven.*

AMERICAN MODE OF COOKING INDIAN CORN, PUMPKINS, &c.

Maize or Indian corn has never been extensively used in Great Britain, and the editor has every reason to believe that this has arisen from the almost total ignorance of the English people as to the mode of preparing it for human food. It is, perhaps, the most productive crop that can be grown, and its nutritious qualities, when properly prepared, are equal to its productiveness. We are satisfied that it may be grown in that country, or, at any rate, in the south and eastern parts of it, with great advantage; indeed, the experiment has been tried, and with decided success. The late Mr. Cobbett grew an average crop of the dwarf kind on Barn Elms farm, Surrey, for three or four years, as the editor can testify from his own personal inspection, and he himself has succeeded in rearing the large sort to perfection, the cobs or ears, when quite ripe, averaging eight or nine inches; this, however, was effected upon a small scale, and in a garden.

625. *Indian Cake, or Bannock.*—This, as prepared in our own country, is cheap and very nice food. Take one quart of Indian meal, dressed or sifted, two table-spoonfuls of treacle or molasses, two tea-spoonfuls of salt, a bit of "shortening" (butter or lard) half as big as a hen's egg, stirred together; make it pretty moist with scalding water, put it into a well-greased pan, smooth over the surface with a

---

* Full directions for these and all other similar preparations are given in "The Baker," by the same Editor.

spoon, and bake it brown on both sides before a quick fire. A little stewed pumpkin, scalded with the meal, improves the cake. Bannock split and dipped in butter, makes very nice toast.

626. *Green Indian Corn.*—This is a most delicious vegetable. When used as a vegetable the *cobs*, or ears, are plucked about the time that the corn has arrived at a milky state, or just before it assumes a solid substance. A part of the leaves or filaments by which the cob, or ear, is surrounded, is taken away, and the cobs boiled from twenty to forty minutes, "according to its age." When it is done, it is served with cold or melted butter, and eaten (after being stripped of its remaining leaves) by taking the two ends of the cob in the hands, and biting off the corn. The editor can bear testimony to its delicious quality from having grown it in his own garden and partaken of it.

627. *Indian Corn, or Maize Pudding, baked.*—Scald a quart of milk (skimmed milk will do,) and stir in seven table-spoonfuls of sifted Indian meal, a tea-spoonful of salt, a tea-cup full of molasses or treacle, or coarse moist sugar, and a table-spoonful of powdered ginger or sifted cinnamon; bake three or four hours. If whey is wanted, pour in a little cold milk after it is all mixed.

628. *Boiled Maize Pudding.*—Stir Indian meal and warm milk together " pretty stiff;" a little salt and two or three " great spoonfuls" of molasses added; also a spoonful of ginger, or any other spice that may be preferred. Boil it in a tight-covered pan, or in a very thick cloth; if the water gets in, it will ruin it. Leave plenty of room, for Indian meal swells very much. The milk with which it is mixed should be merely warmed; if it be scalding hot, the pudding will break to pieces. Some chop suet very fine, and warm in the milk; others warm thin slices of apple to be stirred into the pudding. Water will answer instead of milk.

629. *Pumpkin and Squash Pie.* — The usual way of dressing pumpkins in England in a pie is to cut them into slices, mixed with apples, and bake them with a top crust like ordinary pies. A quite different process is pursued in America, and the editor can testify to the immense superiority of the Yankee method. In England, the pumpkin is grown for show rather than for use; nevertheless, when properly dressed, it is a very delicious vegetable, and a universal favourite with our New England neighbours.

The following is the American method of making a pumpkin pie: Take out the seeds, and pare the pumpkin or squash; but in taking out the seeds do not scrape the inside of the pumpkin; the part nearest the seed is the sweetest; then stew the pumpkin, and strain it through a sieve or colander. To a quart of milk for a family pie, three eggs are sufficient. Stir in the stewed pumpkin with your milk and beaten-up eggs till it is as thick as you can stir round rapidly and easily. If the pie is wanted richer make it thinner, and add another egg or two; but even one egg to a quart of milk makes " very decent pies." Sweeten with molasses or sugar; add two tea-spoonfuls of salt, two table-spoonfuls of sifted cinnamon, and one of powdered ginger; but allspice may be used, or any other spice that may be preferred. The peel of a lemon grated in gives it a pleasant flavour. The more eggs, says our American authority, the better the pie. Some put one egg to a gill of milk. Bake about an hour in deep plates, or shallow dishes, without an upper crust, in a warm oven.

There is another method of making this pie, which, we know from experience, produces an excellent dish: Take out the seeds, and grate the pumpkin till you come to the outside skin. Sweeten the pulp; add a little ground allspice, lemon peel, and lemon juice; in short, flavour it to your taste. Bake without an upper crust.

630. *Carrot Pies.*—These pies are made like pumpkin pies. The carrots should be boiled very tender, skinned, and sifted.

631. *American Custard Puddings*, sufficiently good for common use, may be made by taking five eggs beaten up and mixed with a quart of milk, sweetened with sugar and spiced with cinnamon, allspice, or nutmeg. It is well to boil your milk first, and let it get cold before using it. "Boiling milk enriches it so much, that boiled skim milk is about as good as new." (We doubt this assertion; at any rate, it can only be improved by the evaporation of the water.) Bake fifteen or twenty minutes.

632. *American Plum Pudding.*—Pound six hard fine biscuits (crackers), soak them for some hours in milk sufficient to cover the mass; add three pints of milk, beat up six eggs, and mix; flavour with lemon brandy, and a whole nutmeg grated; add three-quarters of a pound of stoned raisins, rubbed in flour. Bake not quite two hours.

633. *Rennet Pudding or Custard.*—A pudding may be made of this description in five minutes. Take a wine-glass full of wine, in which a small portion of calf's rennet has been kept soaking; put it into a quart of cold new milk, and a sort of custard will be the result. This sweetened with loaf-sugar and spiced with nutmeg is very good. It should be eaten immediately, for in a few hours it begins to curdle.

634. *American Apple Puddings.*—Take your apples, and bore out the core without cutting them in two. Fill up the holes with washed rice. Tie up each apple very tight, and separately in the corners of a pudding bag. Boil an hour, or an hour and a half.

635. *Bird's Nest Pudding.*—If you wish to make what is called a bird's nest pudding, prepare your custard; take eight or ten pleasant apples, prepare them and take out the core, but leave them whole; set them in a pudding-dish, pour your custard over them, and bake about thirty minutes.

636. *American Souse.*—Take pigs' feet, ears, &c. well cleaned, and boil or rather simmer them for four or five hours, until they are too tender to be taken out with a fork. When taken from the boiling water it should be put into cold water. After it is packed down tight, boil the jelly-like liquor in which it was cooked with an equal quantity of vinegar; salt as you think fit, and cloves, allspice, and cinnamon,

at the rate of a quarter of a pound to a hundred weight, must be mixed with it when scalding hot.

637. *American dry Bread.*—As far as possible, have bits of bread eaten up before they become hard. Spread those that are not eaten, and let them dry, to be pounded for puddings, or soaked for brewis. *Brewis* is made of crusts and dry pieces of bread, soaked a good while in hot milk, mashed up, and salted, and buttered like toast.

638. *Another sort of Brewis.*—The author of Domestic Cookery observes, that a very good meal may be bestowed on poor people in a thing called *brewis*, which is thus made: Cut a very thick upper crust of bread, and put it into the pot where salt beef is boiling, and nearly ready; it will attach some of the fat, and when swelled out, will be no unpalatable dish to those who rarely taste meat.

639. *Salt Fish.*—The New England mode of dressing salt fish is an excellent one, and ought to be generally adopted. Keep the fish many hours (at least seven or eight) in scalding hot water, which must never be suffered to boil.

640. *To preserve Cheese.*—Cover the cheese carefully with paper, fastened on with paste, so as totally to exclude the air. In this way cheese may be kept for years.

641. *American Mince Meat.*—Take the good bits of vegetables, and the cold meat left after dinner. Mash your vegetables fine, and chop your meat very fine. Warm it with what remains of gravy, or roast meat dripping. Two or three apples, sliced and fried to mix with it, are considered an improvement. Some like a little sifted sage sprinkled in it. After it is warmed, lay it upon a large slice of toasted bread. Potatoes should not be used in the preparation of American mince meat.

GRUELS, CREAMS, SYLLABUBS, JELLIES, &c., &c.

642. *Common Flummery* is merely water gruel flavoured, and eaten cold. Soak in cold water a pint of very fine white oatmeal; when it has steeped a day and a night, pour off the water quite clear. Then put upon the oatmeal three pints of fresh water, and let that stand also a day and a night; then strain it through a hair sieve, and boil it till it is as thick as hasty pudding, stirring it all the time; sweeten it with loaf-sugar, and put a spoonful of ratafia or noyeau, or a few drops of essence of lemon. Pour it into saucers or shallow dishes. It is eaten with sugar and cream, or wine, or cider.

643. *Rice Flummery* is ground rice thickened with milk, the same as for good rice pudding. In a pint of new milk, simmer three ounces of ground rice till it is become a very thick paste, sweeten it with loaf-sugar, flavour with ratafia or peach water, put it in a bason or a mould; when it is cold, turn it out. Sauce; half a pint of new milk, a glass of white wine, a large tea-cup full of cream, the juice of a small lemon, sweetened with loaf-sugar. Or you may pour round it cream or custard.

644. *French Flummery.*—Take two ounces of isinglass to a quart

GRUELS, CREAMS, &C. 163

of cream; simmer them a quarter of an hour; sweeten with loaf sugar; flavour with rose water; strain it into a mould; when cold, turn it out, and put round it baked or dried pears.

645. *Dutch Flummery* is composed of isinglass boiled in water, enriched with lemon, eggs, and wine. Take two ounces of isinglass, boil it half an hour in a pint and a half of water, and grate off with loaf-sugar the yellow rind of two lemons; sweeten with loaf-sugar, a pint of white wine, and the juice of three lemons. Beat up seven eggs, and strain the above to them, stirring all the time. Put it into the saucepan a minute or two to scald—by no means let it boil. Then pour it into a basin, and stir it till nearly cold, and then let it stand a few minutes to settle, and put it into a tin mould previously dipped in cold water.

646. *Blancmange.*—If for a sick person, boil an ounce of the best isinglass, with a stick of cinnamon, in half a pint of water. The isinglass will become a very thick jelly in half an hour's boiling. Then mix to it a pint of new milk, and sugar to taste. Let it boil up once, and strain through a tamis, or swan-skin jelly-bag, into a bason. Pour it into a mould, or custard cups, when nearly cold; pour it very steadily, and keep back any sediment. When turned out, raise it all round the edges with a silver knife; turn the mould on a dish, shake it once or twice. If properly prepared, it will turn out a beautiful white jelly, like marble; garnish with flowers or with sweetmeats, or sliced lemon.

647. *A richer Blancmange.*—Simmer an ounce or little more of fine isinglass in a pint and a half of new milk; add the rind of half a lemon, shred very fine a blade or two of mace, a stick of cinnamon, and sweeten with two ounces and a half of loaf-sugar. Blanch and pound, with a spoonful of rose water, half an ounce of sweet almonds, and eight or ten bitter; put to the milk, and mix. When the isinglass is quite dissolved, strain through a linen flannel, to half a pint of rich cream, and stir together well. When it has stood an hour, pour it off into another bason, leaving the sediments at the bottom, and when nearly cold, pour it into moulds, jelly glasses, or custard cups. Two table-spoonfuls of noyeau will answer the purpose of the almonds. And the isinglass may be dissolved in a pint of water and half a pint of milk.

648. *Arrow-root Blancmange.*—Put two tea-cups full of arrow-root to a quart of milk. Flavour it with an ounce of sweet almonds, and fifteen or sixteen bitter, blanched and pounded; or with noyeau. Moisten the arrow-root with a little cold milk, and pour to it the boiling milk, stirring all the time. Then put it in the saucepan, and boil it a minute or two, still stirring. Dip the moulds in cold water. Turn it out when cold.

649. *Italian Cream.*—Rub on a lump of sugar the rind of a lemon, and scrape it off with a knife into a deep dish or china bowl; add two ounces and a half of sifted sugar, a gill of brandy, the juice of a lemon, and a pint of double cream; then beat it up well with a whisk; boil an ounce of isinglass in a gill of water till quite dissolved; strain

it to the other ingredients; beat some time, and fill the mould; and when cold and set well, turn it out on a dish. The above may be flavoured with any kind of liquor; strawberry, raspberry, or any kind of fruit; coloured with prepared cochineal, and named to correspond with the flavour given.

650. *Clouted or Clotted Cream.*—The milk which is put into the pan one morning stands till the next; then set the pan on a hot hearth, half full of water; put this over a stove from ten to twenty minutes, according to the quantity of the milk; it will be done enough when bladders rise on its surface; this denotes that it is nearly boiling, which it must by no means do, but must be instantly removed from the fire, and placed in a cool place till the next morning, when the cream is thrown up, and is ready for the table, or for butter, into which it may be converted by stirring it with the hand, but not very readily. This is sometimes called Devonshire cream, and it is imagined by those who do not know better, to be much richer than the common cream. The artificial process employed in raising this cream causes the milk to yield a greater quantity, but the quality and flavour are inferior to cream raised naturally, and so is the butter made from it.

651. *Cream for Fruit Pies.*—There are many ways of preparing cream. For fruit pies, simmer a pint of new milk, rind of Seville orange or lemon, cinnamon, either, or all, as you may choose. Whisk up the yolks of three eggs, with half a spoonful of flour, and one or two of cream; gradually add the boiling milk, set it over the fire, and whisk till it is of the consistence of a thick cream. When it is removed from the fire, and rather cool, add a table spoonful of rose or orange water, or a tea-spoonful of syrup of clove gilly flowers. When quite cold, take off the top of the pie and pour in the cream; return the cover, either whole or cut in quarters. If eggs are dear, one whole egg will whisk up with a spoonful of rice flour or arrow-root, and will answer for thickening. Richer cream may be prepared with an equal quantity of cream and milk, flavoured with almond, lemon, sack, ratafia, or brandy, and called by the name of the article by which it is flavoured principally. Be careful not to let your creams boil, or they will curdle. Creams may be prepared with fresh or preserved fruits. Luscious fruits are improved by the addition of lemon juice.

652. *Birch's Receipt for Mock Cream.*—Mix half a spoonful of flour with a pint of new milk; let it simmer five minutes to take off the rawness of the flour; then beat up the yolk of one egg, stir it into the milk while boiling, and run it through a fine sieve. A tea-spoonful of arrow-root would do better than flour.

653. *Trifle.*—Mix in a large bowl a quarter of a pound of sifted sugar, a bit of lemon peel grated fine, and the juice of a whole lemon, half a gill of Lisbon or sweet wine, the same of brandy, and a pint and a half of good cream. Whisk the whole well, and take off the froth as it rises with a skimmer, and put it on a sieve; continue to whisk it till you have enough of the whip; set it in a cold

GRUELS, CREAMS, &c.

place to drain three or four hours. Then put in a dish six or eight sponge biscuits, two ounces of almonds, blanched and split, a quarter of a pound of ratafia, some grated nutmeg and lemon peel, currant jelly and raspberry jam, half a pint of sweet wine, and a little brandy; when the cakes have absorbed the liquor, pour over about a pint of custard, made rather thicker than for apple pie; and, when wanted, lay on plenty of the whip, and throw over a few nonpariel comfits.

654. *Whip Syllabub.*—Make a whip as in the last receipt; mix with a pint of cream half a pint of sweet wine, the juice of a lemon a glass of brandy, six ounces of sifted loaf-sugar, grated nutmeg; nearly fill the custard cups with the mixture, and put on with a spoon some of the whip.

655. *Gooseberry or Apple Fool.*—Stew green gooseberries or apples, peeled or cored; add to them a little moist sugar, enough to draw the juice, to two quarts of fruit a quarter of a pound of sugar. When quite tender, pulp through a coarse sieve; add what more sugar is necessary to your taste, and a quart of new milk warm from the cow; if not from the cow, warm it by the fire; a tea-cup full of cream; mix with it an egg, or two yolks, well beaten. Let it thicken in the milk; be careful it does not boil. When cold, mix the fruit, and stir all together till well united. A little grated ginger is an improvement, nutmeg and lemon rind also, and half a glass of brandy.

655. *Calves' Feet Jelly.*—Take our calves' feet, not from the tripe shop, which have been boiled till almost all the gelatine is extracted, but buy them at the butcher's. Slit them in two, take away the fat from between the claws, wash them well in lukewarm water, put them in a large saucepan or stew-pan, cover them with water; when the liquor boils, skim it well, and let them boil gently six or seven hours, that it may be reduced to about two quarts. Then strain it through a sieve, and put it by till next day. Then take off all the oily part which is at the top, with pieces of kitchen paper applied to it; by so doing you may remove every particle of the oily substance, without wasting any of the jelly. Put the jelly in the stew-pan to melt; add a pound of lump sugar to it, the juice of lemons, the peel of two, six whites and shells beat well together, and a bottle of Sherry or Madeira; whisk the whole together until it is on the boil; then put it by the side of the stove, and let it simmer a quarter of an hour. Then strain it through a jelly-bag; what is strained first must be put into the bag, and repeated until it is quite bright and clear. Then put the jelly in moulds till it is cold and firm. Put it in a cold place. If you wish to have it very stiff, add half an ounce of isinglass, when the wine is put in. It may be flavoured by the juice of various fruits and spices, &c., and coloured with cochineal, saffron, spinach juice, red beet-root juice or claret. It is sometimes made with cherry brandy, noyeau rouge, or essence of punch, instead of wine. Ten shank mutton bones, which may be bought for a trifle, will give as much jelly as a calf's foot.

656. *Whey.*—Boil a pint of milk, put to it a glass or two of white

wine; put it on the fire till it boils again; then pour it on one side till it has settled. Pour off the clear whey, and sweeten as you like. Cider is often used instead of wine, or half the quantity. When there is no fire in the sick room, it may be put hot into bottle, and laid between the bed and mattrass. It will keep warm several hours.

657. *Arrow-root.*—A dessert spoonful will thicken half a pint. It may be made with milk, and flavoured at pleasure, and according to circumstances, if for the sick. The method of mixing is, to moisten the arrow-root with a very little liquid, and stir it into a smooth paste; then pour the rest of the milk to it in a boiling state, stirring it one way all the time, and a minute or two afterwards. If it is not thick, return it to the saucepan, but that wastes it. If you pour it carefully, it will be thick by mixing the milk, and quite smooth.

658. *Gruel* is made of Scotch oatmeal, or cracked groats, or common oatmeal. The Embden, or cracked groats, or Scotch oatmeal, is preferable to the common, both for flavour and nutriment, but cannot be made so quickly. A block-tin saucepan, or a brass skillet, is the best for preserving the colour of the gruel; and a hair sieve to strain. Set on the groats in cold water, half a pint to three quarts of water. Let it boil three quarters of an hour. In that time it will be reduced to two quarts. Then strain it. The groats may be boiled up again, and will make another quart of gruel, but they must be boiled longer than at first. Scotch oatmeal may be made a mess at a time. To a pint of water two ounces of oatmeal; mix it with a little cold water, and stir it into the rest while boiling. This may be strained or not. Let it boil ten minutes.

659. *Robinson's prepared Groats* are prepared in the same way, but do not require so much boiling; a large spoonful of this will make a pint of gruel. A bit of butter and salt are generally stirred in gruel; or sugar and nutmeg, according to taste.

660. *Rice Gruel.*—This is principally used for bowel complaints, but is not so good as arrow-root. A table-spoonful of ground rice will thicken a pint of milk or water. Mix it in the same manner as oatmeal gruel; boil in a bit of dried orange or lemon peel, and a bit of cinnamon. Let it boil about ten minutes, sweeten with loaf-sugar, and add two glasses of port, or one of brandy, as may be required.

661. *Barley Gruel.*—This also is used to give to a person in a state of great debility. Either Scotch or pearl barley may be used; it requires a great deal of washing. If time allows, it should be boiled in a small quantity of cold water; when it boils up, pour off; add fresh boiling water for the gruel. To a quart of water put two ounces of barley; boil till reduced one half, then strain it off. Put to it half as much port wine, and sugar to taste; simmer it together two or three minutes. Rewarm it from time to time as wanted. The barley will do to put in broth.

662. *Thick Milk*, or *Flour Caudle*, is used for the same purpose. A large table-spoonful of flour will thicken a pint. It may be flavoured with cinnamon, or dried orange or lemon peel. Great care

GRUELS, CREAMS, &C.

must be taken that it does not burn. A double saucepan is best for the purpose, or a brass kettle. Half water may be used.

663. *Barley Water.*—Scotch or pearl barley may be used. Wash, or boil up, as for barley gruel; to a quart of water, barley two ounces. Simmer till of an agreeable thickness, and strain. Boil the barley up again, and it will make a pint more. This is a very cooling drink. It also is a pleasant thing to take medicine in. Lemon juice and peel, raisins, figs, liquorice root, sugar, honey, and gum arabic, with these additions it is often used either for complaints of the chest, confined bowels, or stranguary; or powdered nitre a drachm to a quart, is often found good for fever. (Merely for a drink, put sugar and lemon peel.) Rub up the nitre with honey or sugar, mix it with a little barley water, and then pour it on the whole quantity in a boiling state. Stir it well together.

665. *Beef Tea.*—Take a pound of fleshy beef, cut in slices (without the least bit of fat;) boil it up in a quart of water, and skim it well; then put it on one side to simmer twenty minutes. Season if approved, but generally only salt.

666. *Shank Jelly.*—Soak twelve shanks of mutton some hours. Brush and scour them well. Put them in a saucepan, put three quarts of water to them, add bunch of sweet herbs, thirty or forty black peppers, twenty Jamaica, three blades of mace, an onion, and a crust of bread toasted brown, and put them on a hot hearth, closely covered. Let them simmer five hours very gently; then strain it off, and put it in a cool place. It may have the addition of a pound of beef, if approved, for flavour. This is a very good thing for people who are weakly.

667. *Tapioca Jelly.*—Choose the largest sort. Pour cold water on, and wash it two or three times; then soak it in fresh water five or six hours, and simmer it until it becomes quite clear. Add wine, lemon juice, and sugar. Boil the peel of the lemon in it. It thickens very much.

667. *Posset.*—This is more potent than whey, and in which the curd is not separated. Either ale or wine will turn it. Put on the fire, in a kettle, a quart of new milk, with a stick of cinnamon; cut a slice of bread; as the milk boils, lay it at the top, and let it boil a minute or two; then put it aside to soften. Put a pint of very strong ale, with sugar and nutmeg, or white wine. Boil up the milk again, take the bread out with a slice, and lay on the ale or wine; then very gently pour over the boiling milk, and let it stand until the head rises like that of a syllabub. Then serve. A richer posset may be made by substituting Naples biscuits for bread. A brandy posset is a quart of rich custard poured over a glass and a half of brandy.

668. *Orgeat.*—Boil a quart of new milk with a stick of cinnamon. Put to it two ounces of loaf-sugar, and let it cool. Blanch and beat to a paste, with a little rose water, three ounces of sweet almonds, and two dozen bitter. Stir them to the milk; boil it up again, and continue stirring till cold. Then add half a glass of brandy.

669. *Orange Marmalade.*—Seville oranges are in perfection about

the end of March and beginning of April, at which time marmalade should be made. Allow two pounds of sugar to each pound of Seville oranges; grate the oranges lightly, and slice them down with a very sharp knife, as thin as possible, and straight through. Nothing must be kept out but the seeds. Clarify the sugar, put the fruit in, and boil it slowly for at least an hour, until the chips are perfectly tender and clear, and it will jelly; a little of the grate may be put in, if approved; the rest is good seasoning for puddings.

670. *Fruit Jelly.*—Put the fruit, carefully picked, into a stone jar; cover close; set it in a kettle of cold water, which reaches not more than three parts the height of the jar. Let it boil half an hour (more or less, according to the nature of the fruit; black currants are much longer running to juice than either red currants or raspberries). Strain through a jelly-bag or lawn strainer; or the juice may be strained more quickly, by setting on the fruit in a preserving pan, and carefully stirring round the sides as it begins to heat, that it may not burn; strain through a jelly-bag or lawn strainer. To every pint of juice allow a pound of loaf-sugar. Set on the juice over a clear fire; when it boils, put in the sugar. When it has boiled some time, and the scum thickens and gathers together, skim it on to a sieve, and continue to do so while the scum rises; what runs from it may be returned to the rest. When it has boiled forty minutes, try a few drops, by putting on a plate in a cool place. If this become stiff almost immediately, the jelly is done enough. If not, it must be boiled till it will. The jelly may then be strained through a hair sieve, but if it have been properly skimmed this is not necessary, and it is a great waste. The best way is to pour it into a spouted jug that will contain the whole, and then into small jelly pots or glasses. Be very careful not to pour aside, or smear the edges, as an accident of this sort, however carefully wiped away, renders the jelly apt to turn mouldy. White currant jelly should be strained through a muslin or lawn sieve.

PRESERVES.

671. *Jams.*—In making jam of very ripe juicy fruit, a portion of jelly may be taken from it which will improve the jam, taking care to have sufficient syrup to jelly round the fruit. Each quart of fruit and two pounds of sugar will admit the removal of half a pint of jelly without injury.

Strawberries, raspberries, gooseberries, and currants: put an equal weight of loaf-sugar and fruit; put the fruit in a preserving pan; bruise it a little and put it on the stove; stir it carefully to keep it from sticking to the bottom and sides of the pan. Let it boil before adding the sugar, and if there is plenty of juice from the fruit, so that there is no danger of it burning, let it boil a quarter of an hour before adding the sugar; it must boil half an hour afterwards. Skim on to a sieve, and add that which runs through to it. Try the stiffness of the jelly by putting a little on a plate and setting it in a cool place;

if it becomes stiff when quite cold, it has boiled sufficiently; if not stiff, boil it until it is.

The scarlet or mulberry strawberries are the best for preserving: they must be quite ripe and dry: to three pints of strawberries allow half a pint of red currant jelly. For gooseberry jam, take the small, dark hairy sort named Crystal, or a large bright hairy sort called the Warrington. Smooth gooseberries do not do well in preserving.

Lisbon sugar answers very well when the jam is wanted for immediate use, and in large families where it is much used. Put six pounds of Lisbon sugar to seven of fruit. Gooseberries and black currants should be boiled an hour; if not stiff in that time, boil it longer.

672. *Cherries.*—To preserve cherries without boiling, take fine ripe Morello cherries; cut the stalks an inch from the fruit, and put them into wide-mouthed bottles; when full, put powdered loaf-sugar over the top, and pour in a little brandy. Cork and cement, or tie over with leather and bladder. They will keep all the winter through, and do very well for desserts.

673. *To bottle Damsons or Gooseberries.*—Damsons should have attained their dark colour, but not be ripe. Be careful not to bruise them. Fill wide-mouthed bottles: shake them down so that you may get as many in as possible. To each bottle put a wine glass of good home-made wine, either ginger or raisin; no other sort is good. Tie them over with bladders, and put them to stand in a large pot with cold water to reach the necks of the bottles; put a fire under the pot, and let the water boil; when the bladders begin to rise and puff, prick them with a pin. As soon as the water boils remove the fire, and let the bottles remain there until they are quite cold. Next day remove the bladders, and put over the top a thick layer of powdered loaf-sugar and a spoonful of brandy; then cork them tight, and seal or cement them.

674. *Gooseberries.*—The same rules do for gooseberries, but they should be full grown, and gathered when green.

675. *Currants.*—Currants full grown, but not turned, may be preserved in the same way; cut the stalks off with scissors.

676. *To keep Codlins several months.*—Gather codlins at Midsummer of a middling size; put them into an earthen pan, pour boiling water over, and cover the pan with cabbage leaves; keep them by the fire till they would peel, but do not peel them; then pour the water off till both are quite cold. Place the codlins in a stone jar with a smallish mouth, and pour on them the water that scalded them. Cover the pot with bladder, and tie very close, and then cover it with coarse paper again. It is best to keep them in small pots, such as will be used at once when opened.

677. *To preserve Apricots in jelly.*—Pare the fruit very thin and stone it; weigh an equal quantity of sugar in fine powder and strew over it. Next day boil very gently till they are clear; move them into a bowl, and pour the liquor over. The following day pour the liquor to a quart of codlin liquor made by boiling and straining, and a

pound of fine sugar; let it boil quickly till it will jelly; put the fruit into it, and give one boil; skim well and put into small pots.

678. *A very nice preserve of Apricots.*—Choose the finest apricots when quite ripe; pare them as thin as possible, and weigh them; lay them in halves on dishes, with the hollow parts upwards; have an equal weight of good loaf-sugar finely pounded, and strew it over them; break the stones, and blanch the kernels; when the fruit has lain twelve hours, put it with the sugar and juice, also the kernels, into a preserving pan; let it simmer very gently till clear, then take out the pieces of apricots singly; put them into small pots, and pour the syrup and kernels over them. The scum must be taken off as it rises. Cover with brandy paper.

Greengages and egg-plums may be preserved in the same way.

679. *Dried Apricots.* — Proceed as above, but instead of pouring the syrup over them after the last boil, drain them close, strew over sifted sugar to cover them, and dry them on a wire sieve on a stove, or in a slow oven; they must be turned several times, but ought not to be cold till quite dry.

680. *Apricots or Peaches in brandy.*—Wipe and weigh the fruit, and take a quarter of the weight of fine powdered sugar; put the fruit into an ice-pot that shuts very close, throw the sugar over it, and then cover the fruit with brandy. Between the top and cover of the pot, put a piece of double cap-paper. Set the pot into a saucepan of water till the brandy be as hot as you can possibly bear to put your finger in, but it must not boil. Put the fruit into a jar, and pour the brandy on it. When cold, put a bladder over, and tie it down tight.

681. *Apricot Jam.*—Divide fine apricots that have become yellow, but are not over ripe; lay the hollow part uppermost on china dishes, and strew over twelve ounces of sifted sugar to every pound of fruit; let it lie until it becomes moist, then boil it twenty minutes, stirring it well. Blanch the kernels, and boil with the jam.

682. *To preserve Ginger.*—If your ginger can be had green, it is best. Pare it nicely with a sharp knife, and throw it into cold water as you pare it, to preserve the whiteness. If fresh ginger cannot be procured, have the finest large white races of Jamaica ginger. Boil it several times in water till tender, then pare and proceed as above; set on the ginger in cold water and boil it. Pour off the liquor, and put cold water; then boil it up again. Do this a third time, till the ginger is tender, then throw it into cold water; when quite cold, drain the ginger and put into a china bowl. Clarify sugar for preserving it, in the proportion of eight pounds of sugar to seven of ginger. Let the sugar become cold, then pour over the ginger enough to cover it. Let it stand two days, then strain the syrup from the ginger and boil it with the remainder of the sugar; let them boil together twenty minutes or half an hour. When cold, again pour it over the ginger, and let it stand three or four days; by this time the ginger will have finely swollen. Then strain the syrup, boil it up, and pour it hot over the ginger. If the ginger is well swollen, and the syrup quite rich, nothing more is necessary; but if not, boil it

again at the interval of three or four days. Wide-mouthed bottles are best for keeping it. Divide the syrup to each; cork and seal, or dip in bottle cement.

683. *Cherries in brandy.*—Weigh the finest Morellos, having cut off half the stalk; prick them with a new needle, and drop them into a jar or wide-mouthed bottle. Pound three-quarters of the weight of sugar or white candy; strew, fill up with brandy, and tie a bladder over them.

684. *Damson Cheese.*—It is sometimes made with the whole skins and pulp of the fruit, sometimes with the pulp only. In either case the fruit is first to be baked or boiled in a stone jar till it is tender, and the stones will separate. If the skins are to be used, merely take out the stones with a spoon, then measure it into the preserving pan. If the skins are objected to, rub it through a very coarse sieve, that so they may be retained with the stones. Having measured the fruit, set it over a clear brisk fire, and let it boil quick till the liquid has evaporated and the fruit becomes quite dry; then add loaf-sugar powdered, in the proportion of half a pound to a quart of fruit, and let it go on boiling till the jam candies to the sides of the pan. The stones should be cracked, and the kernels skinned and boiled in the jam; this gives it a very pretty appearance, but some people object to it. It should be put out in shallow vessels, such as potting jars, saucers, and so forth, and turned out when brought to table.

DIRECTIONS FOR CARVING.

In preparing meat for the table, and in laying out the table, reference ought to be had to the carving department—a very onerous one to all, and to many a very disagreeable one. The carving knife of course ought to be sharp, and if to be used by a lady, in particular, light and handy; dexterity and address in the manner of using it being more required than strength, either in the knife or the carver. When a lady presides, a seat sufficiently high for her to have a complete command over the joints should be provided, and the dish should be sufficiently deep and capacious, so as not to endanger the splashing of the gravy. It should also be placed as near to the carver as possible, leaving room for his or her plate. A knife with a long blade is required for a large fleshy joint; for ham or bacon a middling sized, sharp-pointed one is preferable, and for poultry or game a short knife and sharp-pointed is best. Some like this knife a little curved. We do not presume to give any directions as respects the serving of the guests; no one it is presumed would take the head of the table not acquainted with the common rules of politeness, which principally consist in endeavouring to please everybody.

685. *Fish.*—As fish is the first thing to be carved, or served, we shall first speak of it. In helping fish, take care not to break the flakes, which in cod and fine fresh salmon, and some other sorts, are large. A fish trowel is necessary, not to say indispensable, in serving many kinds of fish, particularly the larger sort.

686. *Turbot, &c.*—The trowel is to be carried flatways from the middle of the fish, and the carver should bring out as much meat as will lie upon it. The thick part is the best, and of course most esteemed. When one side is cleared, the bones ought to be taken away—which done, serve the under part. The meat on the fins is considered by some a great delicacy. Halibuts, plaice, and other large fish, are served in a similar way.

687. *A Cod's Head and Shoulders*, perhaps, require more attention in serving than any other. It is, too, considered a handsome dish. In carving, introduce the trowel along the back, and take off a piece quite down to the bone, taking care not to break the flakes. Put in a spoon and take out the sound, a jelly-like substance, which lies inside the back-bone. A part of this should be served with every slice of fish. The bones and glutinous parts of a cod's head are much liked by most people, and are very nourishing.

688. *Salmon*—Cut slices along the back-bone, and also along the flank. The flank or thin part is the best and richest, and is preferred by all accomplished gourmands. The back is the most solid and thick. The tail of salmon is not so fine as the other parts. The head is seldom used. The liver, melt, and roe, are generally served, but seldom eaten.

689. *Soles* are easily carved. You have only to cut through the middle part of the fish, bone and all, and subdivide and serve according to the size of fish. The thick parts are best; the roes when well done are very nice.

690. *Mackerel.*—The trowel should be carried under the meat, horizontally over the back-bone, so as to raise one side of the meat from the bone. Remove the bone, and serve the other side of the fish. When fresh, well cleaned, and well done, the upper end is considered the best. The roes are much liked.

691. *Eels, Whiting Jack, &c.*, when intended to be fried, are previously cut in pieces of a suitable size for serving. When they are boiled, cut through them in the same way as soles. Large jacks will admit of slices being taken off with a trowel without the bones. Small fish are served whole.

692. *Aitch Bone of Beef.*—Cut a slice an inch thick all through. Put this by, and serve in slices from the remainder. Some persons, however, like outside, and others take off a thinner slice before serving, for the sake of economy. The rich, delicious, soft fat, which resembles marrow, lies at the back of the bone: the firm fat is cut in horizontal slices at the edge of the meat. Some prefer one and some the other. The skewer used to keep the meat together when boiling, should be taken out before coming to the table, and, if necessary, be replaced by a silver one.

693. *A Round, or Buttock, and thick Flank of Beef*, are carved in horizontal slices, that is, in slices from the top. Pare and neatly cut all round. Some prefer the silver side.

694. *A Brisket of Beef* is cut lengthways, right down to the bone.

The soft mellow fat is found underneath. The upper part is firm, but gristly; if well done, they are equally good to our taste.

695. *Sirloin of Beef*, the glory of the dinner-table, may be commenced carving, either by beginning at the end, and cutting slices along the bones, or across the middle; but this latter mode wi drain the gravy from the remainder. The inside is very juicy and tender, but the outside is frequently preferred. The inside fat is rich and marrowy, and is considered too much so by many. The inside of a sirloin is frequently dressed (in various ways) separately.

696. *Fillet of Veal* is the corresponding part to the round in an ox, and is cut in the same way. If the outside brown be not desired, serve the next slice. Cut deep into the stuffing, and help a thin slice, as likewise of fat. A fillet of veal should be cut very smooth and thin.

697. *Breast of Veal* answers to the brisket of an ox. It should be cracked lengthways, across the middle of the bones, to divide the thick gristly part from the ribs. There is a great difference in these parts; and as some prefer the one, and some the other, the best way is to ask to which the preference is to be given. The burr, or sweetmeat, is much liked, and a part should be served with each slice.

698. *Necks and Loins* of all sorts of meat, if properly jointed by the butcher, require only to be cut through; but when the joints are too thick for one, cut a slice between each, that is, cut one slice without bone, and another with. Some prefer one, and some the other.

699. *Calf's Head* affords a great variety of excellent meat, differing in texture and flavour, and therefore requires a judicious and skilful carver properly to divide it. Cut slices longways under the eye, taking care that the knife goes close to the bone. The throat sweetbread, or kernel, lies in the fleshy part, at the neck end, which you should help a slice of with the other part. The eyes are considered great delicacies by some. They should be taken out with the point of your knife, and each cut into two. A piece of the palate (which lies under the head), a slice of the tongue, with a portion of the brains, should be given to each guest. On drawing out the jawbone, some delicious lean will be found. The heads of oxen, sheep, lambs, &c., are cut in the same way as those of calves.

700. *A Leg of Mutton, &c.*—Begin to cut in the midway, between the knuckle and farther end. The slices should be thin and deep. If the outside is not fat enough, cut some from the fat on the broad end, in slices. Many prefer the knuckle, or venison bit, to the middle part; the latter is the most juicy—the former, in good, well-done mutton, is gelatinous and delicately tender. There is some good meat on the back of the leg, or aitch bone; this should be cut lengthways. It is, however, seldom carved when hot. To cut out the cramp bone, take hold of the shank in your left hand, and steadily cut down to the thigh bone; then pass the knife under the cramp bone. Legs of lamb and pork are cut in the same way.

701. *A Saddle, or Collar of Mutton*, sometimes called the chine, should be cut lengthways, in long slices, beginning close to the back-

bone, and thus leaving the ribs bare. The fat is taken from the outer ends. The inside of the loin is very tender, and in the opinion of some gourmands is preferred to the upper part. It is best, perhaps, to cut the inside lengthways.

702. *Shoulder of Mutton.*—To carve this joint (which when properly dressed is very fine eating) economically for a very small family, the best way is to cut away the underneath part when hot, and if any more is required, to take it from the knuckle. This plan leaves all the gravy in the upper part, which is very nice when cold. The usual way, however, of carving a shoulder of mutton, is to cut slices deep to the bone, in the hollow part. The prime part of the fat lies on the outer edge, and is to be cut in thin slices. Some good delicate slices of lean may be taken from each side of the ridge of the blade-bone. No slices can be cut across the edge of the blade-bone.

703. *Haunch of Venison or Mutton.*—Cut down to the bone in circular slices at the narrow end, to let out the gravy. You may then turn the broad end of the haunch towards you; insert the knife in the middle of the cut, and cut thin deep slices lengthways to the broad end of the haunch. The fat of venison is much esteemed; those who help should take care properly to apportion both the fat and gravy.

704. *Fore-quarter of Lamb.*—Separate the shoulder from the scovel, or breast and ribs, by passing the knife under it (the shoulder). The shoulder of grass lamb, which is generally pretty large, should have a little lemon or Seville orange juice, squeezed over it, and be sprinkled with a little pepper and salt, and then placed upon another dish. If the lamb be small, it is usual to replace the shoulder. The breast and ribs should be cracked across by the butcher, and be divided. Help either from that, the ribs, or shoulder, according to choice.

705. *Ham.*—The most economical way of cutting a ham, which is seldom or never eaten at one meal, is to begin to cut at the knuckle end, and proceed onwards. The usual way, however, is to begin at the middle, and cut in long slices through the thick fat. By this means you come at once to the prime, but you let out the gravy. Another plan is to cut a small hole on the top of the ham, and with a very sharp knife enlarge the hole, by cutting thin circular slices. In this latter way you preserve the gravy, and of course keep the meat moist to be eaten when cold.

706. *Tongue.*—This much-esteemed relish, which often supplies the place of ham, should be cut in thin slices across, beginning at the thick middle part. Serve slices of fat and kernel from the root.

707. *A Sucking Pig* is generally slit down the middle in the kitchen, and the cook garnishes the dish with the jaws and ears. Separate a shoulder from the carcase on one side, and then do the same thing with the leg. Divide the ribs, which are frequently considered the most choice part, into two or three helpings, presenting an ear or jaw with them as far as they will go, and plenty of sauce. Some persons prefer the leg, because not so rich and luscious as the

ribs. The neck end between the shoulders is also sometimes preferred. The joints may be divided into two each, or pieces may be cut from them.

708. *A Fowl.*—The legs of a boiled fowl are always bent inwards, and tucked into the belly, but before it is put upon the table, the skewers by which they are secured ought to be removed. The fowl should be laid on the carver's plate, and the joints as they are cut off placed on the dish. In taking off the wing, the joint only must be divided with the knife, for, by lifting up the pinion of the wing with the fork, and then drawing it towards the legs, the muscles will separate in a much better form than you can effect by cutting with a knife. Next place the knife between the leg and body, and cut to the bone; turn the leg back with the fork, and the joint will give way, if the fowl be young and well done. The merrythought is taken out when the legs and wings are all removed; the neck-bones are taken off by putting in the knife, and pressing it under the long broad part of the bone, then lift the neck-bone up and break it off from the part that sticks to the breast. The breast itself has now to be divided from the carcase, by cutting through the tender ribs close to the breast, quite down to the tail; then lay the back upwards, put your knife into the bone half-way from the neck to the rump, and on raising the lower end it will readily separate. The last thing to be done is to turn the rump from you, and neatly to take off the two sidesmen. Each part should be neatly arranged on the dish, but it is almost impossible to give effectual written descriptions for carving fowls; the best plan is to observe carefully a good carver, and then, by a little practice, you will become perfect. The breast and the wings are considered the best parts.

709. *A Pheasant.*—Take out the skewers; fix your fork in the centre of the breast, slice it down; remove the leg by cutting in the sideway direction, then take off the wing, taking care to miss the neck-bone. When the legs and wings are all taken off, cut off slices of the breast. The merrythought is separated by passing the knife under it towards the neck; the other parts are cut as before directed in a fowl. The breast, wings, and merrythought, are the favourites, particularly the former, but the leg has a higher flavour.

710. *Partridges and Pigeons.*—Partridges are carved like fowls, but the breast and wings are not often divided, the bird being small. The wing is the prime bit, particularly the tip; the other choice parts are the breast and merrythought. *Pigeons* may be cut in two, either from one end to the other of the bird, or across.

711. *Goose or Duck.*—Cut off the apron of the goose and pour into the body a large spoonful of gravy, which should be mixed with the stuffing. Some persons put, instead of the gravy, a glass of port wine, in which a large tea-spoonful of mustard has been previously stirred. Cut as many slices from the breast as possible, and serve with a portion of the apron to each plate. When the breast is all served, and not till then, cut off the joints; but observe, the joints of water-fowl are wider spread and go farther back than those of land-fowl.

712. *A Turkey* should not be divided till the breast is disposed of; but if it be thought proper to divide, the same process must be followed as directed in a fowl. The following is the best mode of serving this delicious bird: Begin cutting close to the breast-bone, scooping round so as to leave the mere pinions. Each slice should carry with it a portion of the pudding, or force meat, with which the craw is stuffed.

713. *Hare.*—Put the point of the knife under the shoulder, and cut all the way down to the rump, on the side of the back-bone. By doing the same on the other side, the hare will be divided into three parts. The back should be cut into four parts: the shoulder must be taken off in a circular line. The pieces as they are cut should be neatly placed on the dish; in helping, some pudding and gravy should be given to each person. The above mode of carving is only applicable to a young hare; when the hare is old, it is not practicable to divide it down, but put the knife between the leg and back, and give it a little turn inwards at the joints, which you must endeavour to hit, and then cut, and with the fork turn it completely back. When both legs are taken off, you will find a fine collop on each side of the back, which back you may divide into as many pieces as are necessary. Take off the shoulders, which some persons are very fond of, and which are called the sportsman's pieces; but the legs and back are considered the prime. When all the guests are served, it is usual to take off the head, and by putting the knife between the upper and lower jaw, you may divide them; then lay the upper flat upon your plate, put the point of the knife into the centre, and cut the head into two; you will thus get at the brains, which may be served with the ears and tail to those who like them. Some persons direct the carver to serve with slices, as much as possible, off the sides of the back-bone, from the shoulder to the rump.

714. *Rabbits* are generally cut up in the same way as hares. The back and legs are considered the best parts. The back should be cut into two pieces.

GARNISHES.

Parsley is the most universal garnish to all kinds of cold meat, poultry, fish, butter, cheese, and so forth. Horse-radish is the garnish for roast beef, and for fish in general; for the latter, slices of lemon are sometimes laid alternately with heaps of horse-radish.

Slices of lemon for boiled fowl, turkey, and fish, and for roast veal and calf's head.

Carrot in slices for boiled beef, hot or cold.

Barberries fresh or preserved for game.

Red beet-root sliced for cold meat, boiled beef, and salt fish.

Fried smelts as garnish for turbot.

Fried sausages or force meat balls round roast turkey, capon, or fowl.

Lobster coral and parsley round boiled fish.

Fennel for mackerel and salmon, either fresh or pickled.
Currant jelly for game, also for custard or bread pudding.
Seville orange in slices for wild ducks, widgeons, teal and so forth.
Mint, either with or without parsley, for roast lamb, either hot or cold.
Pickled gherkins, capers, or onions, for some kinds of boiled meat and stews.

SETTING OUT A TABLE.

A prudent housekeeper, in providing for a family, or for company, will endeavour to secure variety, and avoid extravagance, taking care not to have two dishes alike, or nearly alike, such as ducks and pork, veal and fowls; and avoiding, when several sorts are required, to have such things as cannot be eaten cold, or cannot be warmed or re-cooked. There is a great waste occasioned if these principles are overlooked in providing for a party. When a table is to be set out, it is usual to place nearly the whole provisions at once; but if comfort is the object, it is better to have each dish and its accompanying sauces and vegetables sent in separately, hot from the kitchen.

For plain family dinners, soup or pudding is placed at the head of the table, and meat at the lower end; vegetables on each side of the middle, and sauce boats in the middle. Boiled meat at the top; roast meat at bottom; soup in the middle; then the vegetables and sauce boats at cross corners of the middle dish. Poultry or mutton at bottom; boiled poultry at top; roast poultry, or game, at bottom; vegetables and sauces so disposed as to give the appearance of the whole table being covered without being crowded.

When there are several courses, the first consists of soups, stews, boiled fish, fricassees; poultry with ham, bacon, tongue, or chine; and roast or boiled meat.

For second courses, birds and game of all sorts, fish fried, pickled, or potted; pigeon pies, patties, brawn, omelets, oysters stewed or scolloped, and lobsters or crabs. Tarts, cheesecakes, and sweet dishes of all kinds, are sometimes placed with the second course, but more frequently form separate courses by themselves.

The dessert is usually served in another room, which is a great accommodation both to the servants, who can prepare it at leisure, and to the guests in quitting the smell of a hot dinner. A d'oyley, a finger glass, two wine glasses, a china dessert plate, and silver knife and fork, and spoon, to each person. Every variety of fruit, fresh and preserved, is admissible; and biscuits, and pound-cake, with an epergne or stand of jellies in the middle. Varieties of wine are generally placed at each end.

The modern practice of dining late has added importance to the luncheon, and almost annihilated the supper meal. The following are suitable for either: soups, sandwiches of ham, tongue, dried sausage, or beef; anchovy, toast or husks; potted beef, lobster, or cheese; dried salmon, lobsters, crayfish or oysters, poached eggs;

patties; pigeon pies; sausages; toast with marrow (served on a water plate), cheesecakes; puffs, mashed or scolloped potatoes, brocoli; asparagus, sea-kale with toast, creams, jellies, preserved or dried fruits, salad, radishes, &c. If a more substantial supper is required, it may consist of fish, poultry, game; slices of cold meat, pies of chickens, pigeons, or game; lamb or mutton chops, cold poultry, broiled with high seasoning, or fricasseed; rations or toasted cheese.

MADE WINES, &c.—GENERAL DIRECTIONS FOR MAKING.

715. The best method of making these wines is to boil the ingredients, and ferment with yeast. Boiling makes the wine more soft and mellow. Some, however, mix the juice, or juice and fruit, with sugar and water unboiled, and leave the ingredients to ferment spontaneously. Your fruit should always be prime, and gathered dry, and picked clean from stalks, &c. The lees of wine are valuable for distillation, or making vinegar. When wine is put in the cask the fermentation will be renewed. Clear away the yeast as it rises, and fill up with wine, for which purpose a small quantity should be reserved. If brandy is to be added, it must be when the fermentation has nearly subsided, that is, when no more yeast is thrown up at the bung-hole, and when the hissing noise within is not very perceptible: then mix a quart of brandy with a pound of honey; pour into the cask, and paste stiff brown paper over the bung-hole. Allow no hole for a vent peg, lest it should once be forgotten, and the whole cask of wine be spoiled. If the wine wants vent, it will be sure to burst the paper; if not, the paper will sufficiently exclude all air. Once a week or so, it must be looked to; if the paper is burst renew it, and continue to do so till it remains clear and dry. A great difference of opinion prevails as to racking the wine, or suffering it to remain on the lees. Those who adopt the former plan do it at the end of six months; draw off the wine perfectly clear, and put it into a fresh cask, in which it is to remain six months, and then be bottled. If this plan is adopted, it may be better, instead of putting the brandy and honey in the first cask, to put it in that in which the wine is to be racked; but on the whole it is, perhaps, preferable to leave the wine a year in the first cask, and then bottle it at once. All domestic wines improve more in the cask than in the bottle. Have very nice clear and dry bottles; do not fill them too high. Good soft corks, made supple by soaking in a little of the wine; press them in, but do not knock. Keep the bottles lying in saw-dust. This plan will apply equally well to raspberries, cherries, mulberries, and all kinds of ripe summer fruits.

716. *Ginger Wine.*—To make eighteen gallons of wine—twenty gallons of water, fifty pounds of loaf-sugar, two and a half pounds of bruised ginger, hops a quarter of a pound, the shaved rinds of eighteen lemons or Seville oranges; let these boil together for two hours, carefully skimming. Pour it, without straining, on to seven pounds of raisins: when cool put in the juice of the lemons or oranges; rinse the pulp in a pint or two of the wine, and strain it to the rest. Fer

ment it with yeast; mix a quarter of a pint of solid yeast with a pint or two of the wine, and with that work the rest; next day tun it, raisins, hops, ginger and all together, and fill it up for a fortnight either with wine or with good new beer; then dissolve three ounces of isinglass in a little of the wine, and return it to the rest to fine it: a few days afterwards bung it close. This wine will be in full perfection in six months. It may be bottled, but is apt to fly; and if made exactly by the above directions, and drawn from the cask, it will sparkle like champaign.

717. *Mead, Metheglin, or Honey Wine.*—Boil honey in water for an hour: the proportion is from three to four pounds to each gallon: half an ounce of hops will both refine and preserve it, but is not commonly added: skim carefully, draining the skimmings through a hair sieve, and return what runs through. When a proper coolness, stir in yeast; a tea-cup full of solid yeast will serve for nine gallons. Tun it, and let it work over, filling it up till the fermentation subsides. Paste over brown paper, and watch it (see No. 725). Rich mead will keep seven years, and afford a brisk, nourishing, and pleasant drink. Some people like to add the thinly shaved rind of a lemon to each gallon while boiling, and put the fruit, free from pith, into the tub. Others flavour it with spices and sweet herbs, and mix it with new beer or sweet wort: it is then called Welsh Braggart.

718. *Parsnip Wine.*—To make a kilderkin: Set on double the quantity of water, and for every gallon of water allow four pounds of parsnips cleaned and sliced. When the water boils, put in the parsnips, and boil till they are perfectly tender; drain through a sieve or colander without pressing; immediately return it to the copper with fifty-six pounds of loaf-sugar; it will soon boil, being already hot, and what drips from the sieve may be added afterwards; six ounces of hops, and boil it two hours. Ferment with yeast; let it stand four days to work in a warm place; then tun and paste paper over. It is most likely it will work up and burst the paper, which must be renewed. It may be cleared with isinglass, but will not require any brandy.

719. *Malt Wine, or English Sherry.*—For an eighteen-gallon cask allow fifty-six pounds of good moist sugar, and sixteen gallons of water; boil them together two hours, carefully skimming. When the scum is all removed, and the liquor looks clear, add a quarter of a pound of hops, which should boil a quarter of an hour or twenty minutes. When the liquor is quite cool add to it five gallons of strong beer in the height of working: cover up, and let it work forty-eight hours; then skim and tun. If none remains for filling up, use new beer for that purpose. This method may be adopted with all boiled wines, and will be found to improve their strength, and promote their keeping. In a fortnight or three weeks, when the head begins to sink, add raisins (free from stalks) ten pounds, sugar-candy and bitter almonds of each half a pound, and a pint of the best brandy: brown paper as in former articles. It may be bottled in one year

but if left three years in the wood, and then bottled, it will be found equal in strength and flavour to foreign wine.

720. *Orange or Lemon Wine, boiled.*—(For quantity of fruit, see No. 726.) To make eighteen gallons, twenty gallons of water, fifty-six pounds of loaf-sugar, the whites and shells of a dozen eggs, a quarter of a pound of hops; boil together the sugar, water, and eggs; when it has boiled an hour, and become quite clear, add the hops and the thinly shaved rinds of two or three dozen of the fruit—more or less, according as the bitter flavour is desired. Let it boil, in all, two hours: meanwhile, remove all the peel and white pith of the fruit, and squeeze the juice. Pour a gallon or two of the hot liquor on the pulp; stir it well about, and, when cool, strain to the rest, and add the juice. (N. B. Some people strain off the hops, rind, and eggs; others prefer their remaining: it is by no means important which mode is adopted.) Work it with yeast, as the foregoing article, and refine with isinglass dissolved in a quart of brandy. This wine should be one year in wood, and one in bottles, when it will be found excellent.

721. *Grape Wine.*—The larger the proportion of juice, and the less of water, the nearer it will approach to the strength and richness of foreign wine. There ought not to be less than one-third of pure juice. Squeeze the grapes in a hair sieve, bruising them with the hand rather than any heavier press, as it is better not to crush the stones. Soak the pulp in water until a sufficient quantity is obtained to fill up the cask. As loaf-sugar is to be used for this wine, and it is not easily dissolved in cold liquid, the best plan is to pour over the sugar (three pounds in every gallon required) as much boiling water as will dissolve it, and stir till it is dissolved. When cold put it in the cask with the juice, fill up from water in which the pulp has been steeped. To each gallon of wine put half an ounce of bitter almonds, not blanched, but cut small. The fermentation will not be very great. When it subsides, proceed with the brandy and papering as 726.

722. *Raisin Wine.*—There are various modes of preparing this wine, which is, perhaps, when well made, the best of our domestic wines. The following receipts are considered good:—For raisin wine, without sugar, put to every gallon of soft water eight pounds of fresh Smyrna or Malaga raisins: let them steep a month, stirring every day; then drain the liquor and put it into the cask, filling up as it works over: this it will do for two months. When the hissing has in a great measure subsided, add brandy and honey, and paper as the former articles. This wine should remain three years untouched; it may then be drunk from the cask, or bottled, and will be found excellent. Raisin wine is sometimes made in large quantities, by merely putting the raisins in the cask, and filling it up with water: the proportion as above: carefully pick out all stalks. In six months rack the wine into fresh casks, and put to each the proportion of brandy and honey. In cider countries, and plentiful apple years, a most excellent raisin wine is made by employing cider instead of water, and

steeping in it the raisins. Proceed in every respect as in the last article.

723. *Raisin Wine with Sugar.*—To every gallon of soft water four pounds of fresh raisins; put them in a large tub; stir frequently, and keep it covered with a sack or blanket. In about a fortnight the fermentation will begin to subside: this may be known by the raisins remaining still. Then press the fruit and strain the liquor. Have ready a wine cask, perfectly dry and warm, allowing for each gallon one pound or one pound and a half Lisbon sugar; put this into the cask with the strained liquor: when half full, stir well the sugar and liquor, and put in half a pint of thick yeast; then fill up with the liquor, and continue to do so while the fermentation lasts, which will be a month or more. Proceed with brandy, &c., as in the foregoing articles.

724. *Raisin Wine, in imitation of Frontignac.*—For every gallon of wine required, allow two pounds of raisins; boil them one hour in water; strain the boiling liquor on loaf-sugar, two pounds for every gallon; stir it well together: when cool put it in the cask with a moderate quantity of yeast (as last article). When the fermentation subsides, suspend in the cask a muslin bag containing elder flowers, in the proportion of a quart to three gallons of wine. When perfectly clear, draw off the wine into bottles.

725. *Currant or Gooseberry Wine without boiling.*—Suppose the cask to be filled is a kilderkin, to make it rich you should have fifty quarts of fruit, bruise it, and add to it half that quantity of water. Stir it well together, and let it stand twelve hours; then strain it through a coarse canvass bag or hair sieve to fifty-six pounds of good Lisbon sugar, and stir it well. Put the pulp of the fruit into a gallon more water; stir it about, and let it stand twelve hours. Then strain to the above, again stirring it; cover the tub with a sack. In a day or two the wine will begin to ferment. When the whole surface is covered with a thick yeasty froth, begin to skim it on to a sieve. What runs through may be returned to the wine. Do this from time to time for several days, till no more yeast forms. Then put it into the cask.

726. *Orange or Lemon Wine without boiling.*—For an eighteen-gallon cask, half a chest of Seville oranges; they are most juicy in March. Shave the rinds of a dozen or two (more or less according as the bitter flavour is desired, or otherwise.) Pour over this a quart or two of boiling water: cover up, and let it stand twelve hours, then strain to the rest. Put into the cask fifty-six pounds of good Lisbon sugar. Clear off all the peel and white pith from the oranges, and squeeze through a hair sieve. Put the juice into the cask to the sugar. Wash the sieve and pulp with cold water, and let the pulp soak in the water twenty-four hours. Strain, and add to the last, continually stirring it; add more water to the pulp, let it soak, then strain and add. Continue to do so till the cask is full, often stirring it with a stick until all the sugar is dissolved. Then leave it to ferment. The fermentation will not be nearly so great as that of currant wine, but the hissing noise will be heard for some weeks; when this sub-

sides, add honey and brandy, and paste over with brown paper. This wine should remain in the cask a year before bottling.

727. *Cowslip, or Clary Wine.*—The best method of making these wines is to put in the pips dry, when the fermentation of the wine has subsided. This method is preferred for two reasons; first, it may be performed at any time of the year when lemons are cheapest, and when other wine is making; secondly, all waste of the pips is avoided; being light they are sure to work over if put in the cask while the wine is in a state of fermentation. For a kilderkin boil fifty-six pounds of good moist sugar, with twenty gallons of water, and a quarter of a pound of hops; shave thin the rinds of three dozen lemons or Seville oranges, or part of each; they may be put in the boil the last quarter of an hour, or the boiling liquor poured over them; squeeze the juice to be added when cool, and rinse the pulp in the hot liquor. Work with yeast as in the foregoing articles. In two days tun the liquor, and keep it filled up either with wine or new beer, as long as it works over; then paste brown paper, and leave it for four, six, or eight months. The quantity of flowers is one quart to each gallon of wine. Let them be gathered on a fine dry day, and carefully picked from every bit of stalk and green. Spread them thinly on trays, sheets, or papers, and turn them often. When thoroughly dry, put them in paper bags until the wine is ready to receive them. Put them in at the bung-hole; stir them down two or three times a day, till all the cowslips have sunk; at the same time add isinglass. Then paste over again with paper. In six months the wine will be fit to bottle, but will be improved by keeping longer in the cask; the pips shrink into a very small compass in drying; the quantity allowed is of fresh-gathered flowers. Observe also, that wine well boiled, and refined with hops and isinglass, is just as good used from the cask, as if bottled, which is a great saving of time and hazard. Wine made on the above principles has been often praised by connoisseurs, and supposed to have been bottled at least a year, which, in fact, had not been bottled half a day.

728. *Birch Wine.*—The liquor of the birch tree is to be obtained in the month of March, when the sap begins to ascend. One foot from the ground bore a hole in each tree, large enough to admit a faucet, and set a vessel under; the liquor will run for two or three days without injuring the tree. Having obtained a sufficient quantity, stop the holes with pegs. To each gallon of liquor add a quart of honey, or two and a half pounds of sugar; boil together an hour, stirring it well; a few cloves may be added for flavour, or the rind of a lemon or two; and, by all means, two ounces of hops to nine gallons of wine. Work it with yeast; tun, and proceed as in former recipes: refine with isinglass. Two months after making, it may be drawn off and bottled; and in two months more will be fit for use, but will improve by keeping.

729. *Elder Wine.*—The quantity of fruit required is one gallon of ripe elder-berries, and one quart of damsons or sloes, for every two gallons of wine to be produced; boil them in water till the damsons

burst, frequently breaking them with a flat stick; then strain and return the liquor to the copper. The quantity of liquor required for eighteen gallons of wine, will be twenty gallons: whatever, therefore, the first liquor proves short of this, add water to the pulp; run it about and strain to the rest: boil two hours with fifty-six pounds of coarse moist sugar; a pound and a half of ginger bruised, a pound of allspice, and two ounces of cinnamon, loosely tied in a muslin bag, and four or six ounces of hops. When quite cool work on the foregoing plan, tun in two days, drop in the spice and suspend the bag by a string not long enough to let it touch the bottom of the cask: fill it up for a fortnight, then paste over stiff brown paper: it will be fit to tap in two months; will keep for years, but does not improve by age like many other wines; it is never better than in the first year of its age.

730. *Damson or Black Cherry Wine*—may be made in the same manner, excepting the addition of spice, and that the sugar should be finer. If kept in an open vessel four days, these wines will ferment of themselves; but it is better to forward the process by the use of a little yeast, as in former recipes: they will be fit for use in about eight months. As there is a flatness belonging to both these wines if bottled, a tea-spoonful of rice, a lump or two of sugar, or four or five raisins, will tend to enliven it.

731. *Cherry Brandy.*—For this purpose use either morello cherries or small black cherries; pick them from the stalks; fill the bottles nearly up to the necks, then fill up with brandy (some people use whiskey, gin, or spirit distilled from the lees of wine.) In three weeks or a month strain off the spirit; to each quart add one pound of loaf-sugar clarified, and flavour with tincture of cinnamon or cloves.

732. *Raspberry Brandy.*—Scald the fruit in a stone jar set in a kettle of water, or on a hot hearth. When the juice will run freely, strain it without pressing: to every quart of juice allow one pound of loaf-sugar; boil it up and skim; when quite clear pour out; and when cold, add an equal quantity of brandy. Shake them well together and bottle.

733. *Sherbet.*—In a quart of water boil six or eight sticks of rhubarb ten minutes: strain the boiling liquor on the thin shaved rind of a lemon. Two ounces of clarified sugar, with a wine-glassful of brandy, stir to the above, and let it stand five or six hours before using.

734. *Raspberry Vinegar* may be made either by boiling down the juice with an equal weight of sugar, the same as for jelly, and then mixing it with an equal quantity of distilled vinegar, to be bottled with a glass of brandy in each bottle; or in a china bowl or stone jar (free from metallic glaze) steep a quart of fresh-gathered raspberries in two quarts of the best white wine vinegar. Next day strain the liquor on an equal quantity of fresh fruit, and the next day do the same. After the third steeping of fruit, dip a jelly bag in plain vinegar to prevent waste, and strain the flavoured vinegar through it into

a stone jar. Allow to each pint of vinegar a pound of loaf-sugar powdered. Stir in the sugar with a silver spoon, and, when dissolved, cover up the jar and set it in a kettle of water. Keep it at boiling heat one hour; remove the scum. When cold, add to each pint a glass of brandy, and bottle it. This is a pleasant and useful drink in hot weather, or in sickness: one pint of the vinegar to eight of cold water.

735. *Lemonade.*—For a quart of water six lemons, and two ounces of loaf-sugar. Shave half the lemons, or rub the sugar over them. Squeeze the juice of the lemons to the sugar, and pour the water boiling hot. Well mix the whole, and run it through a jelly-bag previously wrung out of scalding water. Lemonade may be obtained, when the fruit is not in season, by using the syrup of lemons; (simmer each pint of juice with three-quarters of a pound of loaf-sugar; strain and bottle:) or the citric acid—two drachms of citric acid, twenty drops of essence of lemon, a pint of clarified syrup or capillaire. This may be reduced at pleasure with boiling water.

736. *Pop, or Ginger Beer.*—The principal difference between ginger pop and ginger beer, is, that the former is bottled immediately, the other is first put in a barrel for a few days. It is also usual to boil the ingredients for ginger beer, which is not done for pop. Both are to be bottled in stone bottles, and the corks tied or wired down. If properly done, the corks and strings will serve many times in succession; the moment the string is untied the cork will fly out uninjured. The bottles as soon as empty should be soaked a few hours in cold water, shaken about and turned down, and scalded immediately before using. The corks also must be scalded. On one pound of coarse loaf or fine moist sugar, two ounces of cream of tartar, and one ounce of bruised ginger, pour a gallon of boiling water: stir it well and cover up to cool, as the flavour of the ginger is apt to evaporate. It is a good way to do thus for the last thing at night; then it is just fit to set working the first thing in the morning. Two large table-spoonfuls of yeast, stir to it a tea-cup full of the liquor; let it stand a few minutes in a warmish place, then pour it to the rest; stir it well, and cover up for eight hours. Be particular as to time. If done earlier, the bottles are apt to fly—if later, the beer soon becomes vapid. Skim, strain, bottle, cork, and tie down. The cork should not touch the beer. It will be fit for use next day. Lemon rind and juice may be added, but are not necessary.

737. *Ginger Beer.*—The proportions of this may vary. Loaf-sugar is preferable to moist; some say a pound to a gallon, others a pound and a half; some allow but half an ounce of ginger (sliced or bruised) to a gallon, others an ounce; a lemon to a gallon is the usual proportion, to which some add a quarter of an ounce or half an ounce of cream of tartar; the white of an egg to each gallon is useful for clarifying, but not absolutely necessary. Some people put a quarter of a pint of brandy to four gallons of beer by way of keeping it: half an ounce of hops boiled in it would answer the same purpose. Boil the sugar,

water, and whites of eggs well beaten; skim carefully. Then add the ginger, and shaved rind of lemons; let it boil half an hour; clear the lemons of the white pith and put them in the wine. When cool, stir in the yeast (two table-spoonfuls to a gallon,) put it in the barrel without straining, and bung close. In a fortnight draw off and bottle. It will be ready for use in another fortnight, and will keep longer than ginger pop. If cream of tartar is used, pour the boiling liquor over it, but do not boil it.

INDEX.

The figures at the beginning of the lines refer to the numbers of the paragraphs; those at the end, to the pages.

    Advice to Cooks (Dr. Kitchiner's) 15.
    American mode of cooking Indian corn, pumpkins, &c., 159.
625 .. Indian cake, or bannock, 159.
334 Anchovy, essence of, 99.
335 .. powder of, 99.
123 .. sauce, 55.
677 Apricots, to preserve in jelly, 169.
678 .. a very nice preserve for, 170.
679 .. dried, 170.
680 .. or peaches in brandy, 170.
681 .. jam, 170.
657 Arrow-root, 166.
426 Artichokes, 117.
424 .. Jerusalem, 117.
    Artificial preparation of meat, fish, &c., for dressing, salting, drying, &c., 106.
425 Asparagus, 117.

784 Bacon, to boil, 65.
621 Baking, bread, 158.
622 .. Sally Lunn tea cake, 458.
623 .. plum cake, 159.
624 .. a plain pound cake, 159.
    Baking meat, &c., 87.
283 .. general remarks on, 87.
284 Baking a pig, 87
285 .. a goose, 87.
286 .. buttock of beef, 87.
287 .. fish, 87.
288 .. time for, 88.
289 .. objection to, 88.
290 .. Kitchiner (Dr.) on, 88.
663 Barley Water, 167.
448 Basil vinegar, or wine, 124.
421 Beans, Windsor, 117.
422 .. French, 117.
423 .. harricot, 117.

397 Beef alamode, 113.
167 .. boiled, 61.
168 .. boiled salt, 62.
342 .. hashed, 101.
349 .. harricot of, 102.
350 .. salt, baked, 102.
351 .. baked like red deer, to be eaten cold, 102.
233 .. sirloin of, roasted, 76.
234 .. rump and round, roasted, 76.
236 .. ribs of, roasted, 76.
665 .. tea, 167.
736 Beer, ginger, 184.
427 Beer-root, red, 118.
428 .. white, 118.
259 Blackcock, roasted, 83.
319 Blanching, 94.
646 Blancmange, 163.
647 .. a richer, 163.
648 .. arrow-root, 163.
628 Boiled maize pudding, 160.
    Boiling, 20.
    .. general directions for, 58.
146 .. vessels for, 58.
147 .. water for, 58.
148 .. fire for, 58.
149 .. directions for putting in the pot, 59.
150 .. to scum, 59.
151 .. how long to do, 59.
152 .. meats just killed, 59.
153 .. frozen meat, 59.
154 .. salt meat, 59.
155 .. bacon, 59.
156 .. ham, beef, tongues, pork, 59.
157 .. by steam, 60.
158 .. without coming in contact with water, 60.
159 .. warming up, 60.
160 .. soaking before, 60.
161 .. meat just killed, 60.

(187)

INDEX.

162 Boiling: what meats may remain in the hot liquor, 60.
163 .. potatoes not to be boiled with meat, 61.
164 .. what vegetables may be, 61.
165 .. vegetables, 61.
166 .. old potatoes, 61.
.. butcher's meat, poultry, and general remarks on, 61.
321 Boning, 94.
281 Brain balls, 87.
316 Braising, glazing, blanching, larding, and boning, general remarks on, 93.
317 Braising, 93.
732 Brandy, cherry, 183.
731 .. raspberry, 183.
638 Brewis, American, 162.
191 Brill, to boil, 267.
411 Brocoli, 115.
356 Broiled rump steaks with onion gravy, 104.
Broiling, 92.
308 .. gridiron for, 92.
309 .. thickness of chops for, 92.
310 .. fire for, 92.
311 .. when done, 92.
.. general remarks on, 75, 92.
312 .. steaks, 92.
312 .. chops, 92.
313 .. kidneys, 93.
314 .. fowl, 93.
314 .. rabbit, 93.
315 .. pigeons, 93.
Broth or stock, and gravies, 49.
99 Broth, beef or stock, 50.
69 .. fish, 39.
76 .. chicken, 41.
77 .. mutton, 41.
78 .. mutton chop, 42.
322 Browning, 95.
357 Bubble and squeak, 104.
108 Butter, melted, 53.
464 .. clarified, 127.
465 .. burnt, 128.
466 .. oiled, 128.

Cabbage, 115.
412 .. cold, 115.
414 .. red, 115.
178 Calf's head, boiled, 63.

340 Calf's head, to hash, 100.
249 Capons, to roast, 80.
186 .. to boil, 65.
213 Carp, fried, 71.
214 .. stewed, 71.
420 Carrots, 117.
Carving, directions for, 171.
686 .. fish, 171.
686 .. turbot, &c., 172.
687 .. cod's head and shoulders, 172.
688 .. salmon, 172.
689 .. soles, 172.
690 Carving mackerel, 172.
691 .. eels, whiting, jack, &c., 172.
692 .. aitch-bone of beef, 172.
693 .. round, and flank of beef, 172.
694 .. brisket of beef, 172.
695 .. sirloin of beef, 173.
696 .. fillet of veal, 173.
697 .. breast of veal, 173.
698 .. necks and loins, 173.
699 .. calf's head, 173.
700 .. leg of mutton, 173.
701 .. saddle of mutton, 173.
702 .. shoulder of mutton, 174.
703 .. haunch of venison, 174.
704 .. fore-quarter of lamb, 174.
705 .. ham, 174.
706 .. tongue, 174.
707 .. sucking pig, 174.
708 .. fowl, 175.
709 .. a pheasant, 175.
710 .. partridges and pigeons, 175.
711 .. goose or duck, 175.
712 .. turkey, 176.
713 .. hare, 176.
714 .. rabbits, 176.
Catsups, 125.
458 .. walnut, 126.
459 .. oyster, 126.
460 .. cockle and muscle, 126.
461 .. mushroom, 126.
462 .. mushroom, without spice, 127.
463 .. mushroom powder, 127.
410 Cauliflowers, 115.
431 Celery, 118.
640 Cheese, to preserve, 162.
684 .. damson, 171.
611 Cheesecakes, 157.

INDEX. 189

610 Cheesecakes, to make curd for, 156.
612 .. potatoe, 157.
613 .. a plain, 157.
614 .. bread, 157.
672 .. Cherries, 169.
683 .. in brandy, 171.
186 Chickens to boil, 65.
    Choice and purchasing of butcher's meat, 26.
    .. general remarks on, 26—27.
21 .. beef, 27.
22 .. mutton, 27.
23 .. venison, 27.
24 .. veal, 28.
25 .. lamb, 28.
26 .. pork, 28.
27 .. bacon. 28.
28 .. hams, 29.
    .. summary of directions, 29.
    Choice of poultry, eggs, and fish, and seasons of fish, 29
    .. poultry of all kinds, 29.
29 .. rabbits, 29.
30 .. fowls, 29.
31 .. rabbits and pigeons, 30.
32 .. game, 30.
33 .. eggs, 30.
34 .. fish, 30.
35 . seasons of fish, 30.
    Clarifying, 127.
195 Cod to broil, 68.
676 Codlins, to keep for several months, 169.
413 Coleworts, young, 115.
347 Collops, minced, 101.
232 Colouring, 95.
    Colourings, thickenings, flavourings, seasonings, stocks, gravies, sauces, stuffings, force meats, and clarifying, remarks on, 94.
    Cookery, general remarks on, 16.
    .. importance of good, as regards health, &c., 16.
    .. Johnson (Dr.), his observations on, 17.
    .. Sylvester (Mr.) on, 17.
    .. Waterhouse (Dr.) on, 17.
    .. Milton's writings on, 17.

Cookery, Parr (Dr.) on, 18.
.. Prout (Dr) on, 19.
.. Philosophical, — Count Romford, 20.
Cooking, preparations for, 29.
180 Cow-heel, 64.
649 Cream, Italian, 163.
650 .. clouted or clotted, 164.
651 .. for fruit pies, 164.
652 .. Birch's receipt for mock, 164.
489 Crusts, flaky, short. 135.
490 .. raised, 135.
493 for savoury pies, 136.
494 .. a rich short, 136.
    Cucumbers, 124.
435 .. stewed, 119.
    Curing, &c., with pyroligneous acid, 110.
385 .. general remarks on, 110.
386 hams for, 110.
    .. salmon for, 110.
387 .. time it will keep, 110.
388 .. hams and beef require no previous soaking, 110.
389 .. herrings, cod, haddock, 111.
375 .. bacon, 108.
675 Currants, 169.
581 Custard, 152.
582 .. almond, 152.
583 .. rice, 152.

673 Damsons or gooseberries, to bottle, 169.
364 Devil, 106.
382 Dried or kippered salmon, 110.
383 .. herrings, 110.
384 .. haddock, cod, ling, &c., 110.
467 Dripping, to clarify, 128.
    Drying, smoking, &c., 109.
    .. general remarks on, 109.
252 Duck, to roast, 81.
    .. canvas back or red-neck 81.
576 Dumplings, yeast, 151.
590 .. hard, 153.
192 Dutch plaice, to boil, 67.
    Duties, relative, of mistress and maid, 13.

194 Eels, stewed, 68.

16

INDEX.

210 Eels, fried, 70.
211 .. boiled, 71.
280 Egg balls, 86.
  .. plums, to preserve, 170.
185 .. Eggs, to poach, 75.

253 Fawns to roast, 82.
216 Fish, salt, to boil, 71.
 56 .. cleaning, 35.
 57 .. eels, 36.
 58 .. without scales, 37.
 59 .. turbot, plaice, flounders, 37.
 60 .. cod, 37.
 61 .. oysters, 37.
639 Fish, salt, American mode of dressing, 162.
372 Flavoured salt meat, to make, 107.
325 Flavourings, 97.
  .. essences, powders, &c., 98.
642 Flummery, common, 162.
643 .. rice, 162.
644 .. French, 162.
645 .. Dutch, 163.
278 Force meat, for veal or fowls, 86.
279 .. light, 86.
320 Forcing, 94.
278 Fowls, to roast, 86.
363 Fried slices of ham or bacon, 105.
618 Fritters, 158.
619 .. oyster, 158.
620 .. potatoe, 158.
    Frying, 89.
294 .. Kitchiner (Dr.) on, 89.
295 .. what to use for, 89.
296 .. dripping for, 89.
297 .. the great secret in, 90.
298 .. to know when done, 90.
299 .. bread crumbs for, 90.
    Frying, general remarks on, 75, 89.
300 .. steaks, 90.
301 .. beef steaks and onions, 90.
302 .. sausages, 90.
303 .. veal cutlets, 90.
304 .. sweetbreads, 91.
305 .. lamb chops, 91.
305 .. mutton chops, 91.
306 .. pork chops, 91.
307 .. eggs, 91.

 61 .. oysters, 36.
216 .. salt fish, to boil, 71.
    Fuel, waste of, 21.

    Garnishes, 176.
682 Ginger, to preserve, 170.
102 Glaze, 51.
318 Glazing, 94.
250 Goose, to roast, 81.
244 .. mock, 78.
674 Gooseberries, 169.
655 Gooseberry, or apple fool, 165.
103 Gravy beef, 51.
104 .. for roast meat, 51.
105 .. for boiled meat, 52.
106 .. for roast veal, 52.
107 .. rich brown for poultry, ragout, or game, 52.
 97 Green turtle soup, 48.
    Greengages, to preserve, 170.
659 Groats, Robinson's prepared, 166.
259 Grouse, to roast, 83.
    Gruels, creams, syllabubs, jellies, &c., &c., 62.
658 Gruel, 166.
660 .. rice, 166.
661 .. barley, 166.
206 Gudgeons, 70.

259 Guinea fowl, to roast, 83.
197 Haddock, to boil, 69.
344 Haggis, a good Scotch, 101
191 Halibut, to boil, 67.
376 Hams, curing, 108.
377 .. Yorkshire, 109.
379 .. mutton, 109.
184 .. to boil, 65.
235 Hare, mock, 76.
256 .. to roast, 82.
353 .. stewed, 102.
354 .. jugged, 103.
341 Hashed meat, remarks on, 100
326 Herbs, sweet, to prepare for keeping, 98.
337 .. spirit of, mixed, 100.
333 .. essence, or tinctures of, 99.
429 .. to fry, 118.
 68 Hotch-potch, 39.
380 Hung or Dutch beef, 109.

625 Indian cake, or bannock, 159

INDEX.

626 Indian corn, green, 160.
627 .. corn pudding, 160.

671 Jams, 168.
635 Jelly, calves' feet, 165.
666 .. shank, 167.
667 .. tapioca, 167.
670 .. fruit, 168.
374 Jerked beef, 108.

430 Kale, sea and Scotch, 118.
Keeping fresh meat, 111.
390 .. general remarks on, 111.
391 .. slightly roasted for, 111.
392 .. best method for, 111.
393 .. Franklin (Dr.) on, 111.
393 .. to kill fowl for, 111.
394, 395 recipes for, 112.
255 Kid, to roast, 82.
Kitchen, rules and maxims of, 24.
.. what must always be done, and what must never be done, 25.
290 .. grates, 88.

174 Lamb, a leg, boiled, 63.
175 .. neck of, boiled, 63.
242 .. roasting, 77.
176 Lamb's head and pluck, 63.
.. browned, 63.
469 Lard, hog's, to clarify, 128.
320 Larding, 94.
735 Lemonade, 184.
196 Ling, to boil, 69.

202 Mackerel, boiled, 69.
203 .. broiled, 69.
204 .. baked, or pickled, 70.
Made dishes, remarks on, 100.
365 Marrow bones, 106.
641 Mince meat, American, 162.
259 Moor game, to roast, 83.
433 Morels, 119.
209 Mullets, red, 70.
432 Mushrooms, 118.
169 Mutton, a leg, boiled, 62.
170 .. neck of boiled, 62.
171 .. shoulder, boiled, 62.
172 .. breast, boiled, 62.
237 .. roasted, 76.
238 .. venison fashion, 77.

342 Mutton, hashed, 101.
346 .. chops delicately stewed, 101
346 .. broth, good, 101.

599 Omelet, friar's, 155.
338 Orange or lemon peel tincture of, 100.
332 .. preserved, 99.
669 .. marmalade, 167.
668 Orgeat, 167.
219 Oysters, stewed, 72.
221 .. fried, 73.
218 .. au gratin, 72.
222 .. broiled, 73.

615 Pancakes, common, 157.
616 .. rice, 158.
617 .. cream, 158.
120 Parsley and butter, 55.
436 Parsnips, 120.
259 Partridges, to roast, 83.
491 Paste, puff, 136.
492 .. sweet, 136.
495 .. biscuit, 136.
497 .. stringing, 136.
498 .. potatoe, 137.
499 .. rice, 137.
Pastry, general observations on, 134.
500 .. icing, 137.
496 Pastry, crust for venison, 136.
531 .. to prepare venison for, 142.
533 .. of beef or mutton, to eat as well as venison, 143.
543 Patties, fried, 144.
544 .. oyster, 144.
545 .. beef, 144.
546 .. a good mince for, 145.
259 Pea fowl, to roast, 83.
418 Peas, green, 116.
419 .. to stew, 116.
215 Perch, to boil, 71.
258 Pheasant, to roast, 82.
Pickles, general remarks on, 19.
471 Pickling, first method of, 129.
472 .. second method of, 129.
473 .. third method of, 130.
474 .. gherkins, 130.
475 .. French beans, 130.
476 .. onions, 130.
477 .. red cabbage, 130.
478 .. garlic and eschalots, **131**.

INDEX.

479 Pickling, melons, mangoes, and long cucumbers, 131.
480 .. brocoli or cauliflowers, 131.
481 .. walnuts, 131.
482 .. beet-roots, 131.
483 .. cauliflowers and brocoli, 132.
484 .. artichokes, 132.
485 .. artichoke bottoms, 132.
486 .. mushrooms, 132.
487 .. samphire, 132.
488 .. Indian, 132.
373 Pickling meat, 107.
378 .. tongues, 109.
378 .. chines, 109.
378 .. chops, 109.
501 Pie, perigord, 137.
502 .. sole, 137.
503 .. eel, 138.
504 .. oyster, 138.
505 .. pilchard, 138.
506 .. a remarkable fine fish, 138.
507 .. beef-steak, 138.
508 .. beef-steak and oyster, 138.
509 .. veal, chicken, and parsley, 138.
510 .. veal olive, 138.
511 .. veal, 139.
512 .. a rich veal, 139.
513 .. calf's head, 139.
514 .. excellent pork to eat cold, 140.
515 .. lamb, 140.
516 Pie, mutton, 140.
517 .. chicken, 140.
   .. young rabbits, 140.
519 .. giblet, 140.
520 .. green goose, 140.
521 .. Staffordshire goose, 141.
522 .. hare to eat cold, 141.
523 .. partridge, 141.
524 .. a French, 141.
525 .. pigeon, 141.
526 .. squab, 141.
527 .. duck, 141.
528 .. rabbit, 142.
529 .. vegetable, 142.
530 .. an herb, 142.
534 .. apple, 143.
535 .. cherry, 143.
536 .. currant, 143.
537 .. mince, 143.

629 Pie, pumpkin, 160.
630 .. carrot, 161.
   Pies, tarts, and puffs, 137.
247 Pig, sucking, roasted, 79.
181 Pig's Pettitoes, boiled, 64.
262 Pigeons, to roast, 83.
212 Pike, 71.
736 Pop, 184.
243 Pork, roasting, 78.
244 .. leg of, roasted without the skin, 78.
245 .. spare rib of, 78.
246 .. loin of, roasted, 79.
182 .. salt, boiled, 64.
183 .. pickled, boiled, 64.
667 Posset, 167.
437 Potatoes, 120.
438 .. to boil, 122.
439 .. to steam, 122.
440 .. to roast, 122.
441 .. mashed, 122.
442 .. roasted under meat, 122.
443 .. fried or broiled, 123.
444 .. balls, 123.
445 .. snow, 123.
248 Poultry to roast, 79.
38 .. time of killing, 31.
39 .. drawing, 31.
41-42 Poultry, trussing, 31.
45 .. ducks, 32.
46 .. geese, 33.
47 .. turkeys, 33.
48 .. pigeons, 33.
49 .. pheasants, partridges, and guinea fowls, 34.
50 .. wild ducks, 34.
51 .. woodcocks, plovers, &c., 34.
52 .. hare, 34.
53 .. rabbits, 35.
54 .. fawns or kids, 35.
55 .. sucking pigs, 35.
327 Powder, savoury soup, 98.
328 .. curry, 98.
329 .. for ragouts, 98.
331 .. for white-made dishes, 99.
330 .. for brown-made dishes, 98.
335 .. anchovy, 99.
336 .. oyster, 99.
461 .. mushroom, 126.
   Preserves, 168.
   Puddings, cheesecakes, &c., 145.

INDEX.

551 Pudding, to make paste, 146.
552 .. plum, 147.
553 .. a plain family plum, 147.
554 .. a common plum, 147.
555 .. a very light plum, 147.
556 .. national plum, 148.
557 .. potatoe, 148.
558 .. cottage potatoe, 148.
559 .. rich sweet potatoe, 148.
560 .. carrot, 148.
561 .. black cap, 148.
562 .. sago, 149.
563 .. a very good, 149.
564 .. bread and butter, 149
565 .. almond, 149.
566 .. Kitchiner's, 149.
567 .. Dutch rice, 150.
568 .. rice, 150.
569 .. another rice, 150
570 .. baked rice, 150.
571 .. ground rice, 150.
572 .. rice snow balls, 151.
573 .. plain rice, 151.
575 .. vermicelli, 151.
575 .. tapioca, 151.
575 .. sago, 151.
575 .. Russian seed, 151.
577 .. suet, 151.
578 .. Hunter's, 152.
579 .. Marlborough, 152.
580 .. custard, 152.
584 .. baked vermicelli, 153.
585 .. marrow, 153.
586 .. conservative, 153.
587 .. economical, 153.
588 .. delicate bread, 153.
589 .. barley, 153.
591 .. Newmarket, 154.
592 .. a light, 154.
593 .. Yorkshire, 154.
594 .. a nice suet, 154.
595 .. mother Eve's, 154.
596 .. Newcastle, 154.
597 .. hasty, 154.
598 .. arrow-root, 154.
600 .. a Swiss, 155.
601 .. Oxford, 155.
602 .. muffin, or cabinet, 155
603 .. French and Italian, 155.
604 .. a cheese, 155.
605 .. a very rich, 155.
606 .. chesnut, 156.
16*

607 Pudding, rusk, 156.
608 .. Portugal, 156.
609 .. tansey, 156.
628 .. boiled maze, 160.
631 .. American custard, 161.
632 .. American plum, 161.
633 .. rennet, 161.
634 .. American apple, 161.
635 .. bird's nest, 161.
636 .. American souse, 161.
637 .. American dry bread, 162.
547 Puffs, apple, 145.
548 .. lemon, 145.
549 .. excellent light, 145.
550 .. cheese, 145.

257 Rabbit, to roast, 82.
366 Ragout of duck, or any other kind of poultry or game, 106.
264 Reed birds, 83.
574 Rice bignets, 151.
Roasting, 73.
223 .. spitting before, 73.
224 .. best kind of spits for, 73.
225 .. fire for, 74.
226 .. time for, 74.
227 .. to preserve the fat white, 74.
228 .. how to make a fire for, 74.
229 .. distance from fire for, 74.
230 .. slow, 75.
231 .. dripping-pan for, 75.
232 .. attention to, 75.
.. general remarks on, 75.

Salads, 123.
446 .. general remarks on, 123.
187 Salmon to boil, 66.
188 .. broiled, 66.
189 .. baked, 67.
190 .. pickled, 67.
Salting, 106.
367 .. general remarks on, 106.
363 .. meat, 107.
369 .. quantities for, 107.
370 .. time for, 107.
371 .. hasty, 107.
343 Sandwiches, 101.
Sauces, 52.
109 .. for fricassee of fowls, rabbits, white meat, fish, or vegetables, 53.

INDEX.

110 Sauces, for cold fowl or partridge, 54.
111 .. very rich mushroom for fowls or rabbits, 54.
112 .. for boiled carp, or boiled turkey, 54.
113 .. green, for green geese, or ducklings, 54.
114 .. egg, 54.
115 .. onion, 54.
116 .. apple, 54.
117 .. gooseberry, 54.
118 .. wow-wow, 55.
119 .. curry, 55.
120 .. parsley and butter, 55.
121 .. fennel and butter for mackerel, 55.
122 .. plum pudding, 55.
123 .. anchovy, 55.
124 .. caper, 55.
125 .. mock caper, 55.
126 .. shrimp, 55.
127 .. oyster, 55.
128 .. lobster, 56.
129 .. liver, 56.
130 .. bread, 56.
131 .. for tripe, calf's head, or cow-heel, 56.
132 .. celery, 56.
133 .. tarragon, or burnet, 56.
134 .. sorrel, for lamb or veal, and sweetbreads, 56.
135 .. poor man's, 56
136 .. truffle, 56.
137 .. sharp for venison, 57.
138 .. sweet for venison, 57.
139 .. wine for venison, hare, or haunch of mutton, 57.
140 .. for a pig, 57.
141 .. turtle, 57.
142 .. for all sorts of fish, 57.
143 .. pudding, 57.
144 .. custard, 57.
145 .. roe, 58.
71 Scotch brose, 40.
362 .. collops, 105.
Seasonings, general observations on, 84.
265 .. roast pork, ducks, or geese, 84.
266 .. sucking pig, 84.
267 .. goose, 84.

268 Seasonings, chesnut for goose, 84.
Setting out a table, 177.
Sheep's heads, boiled, 62.
733 Sherbet, 183.
205 Skate, to boil, 70.
263 Small birds, to roast, 83.
206 Smelts, to fry, 70.
261 Snipes, to roast, 83.
192 Soles, to boil, 67.
193 .. fried, 67.
194 .. stewed, 68.
Soups, broths, &c., 38.
66 Soup, clear gravy, 38.
67 .. ox tail, 38.
70 .. cock-a-leeky, 39.
72 .. pease, 40.
73 .. pease and pickled pork, 40
74 .. plain pease, 41.
75 .. Spanish, 41.
79 .. and bouilli, 42.
80 .. a cheap, 42.
81 .. veal, 42.
82 .. calf's head, 42.
83 .. giblet, 42.
84 .. Kitchiner's cheap, 43.
85 .. maigre, 43.
86 .. mock turtle, 44.
87 .. carrot, 45.
88 .. mulligatawny, or curry, 45.
89 .. eel, 45.
90 .. gourd, 46.
91 .. game, 46.
92 .. turnip and parsley, 46.
93 .. celery, 46.
95 .. hare, rabbit, or partridge, 47.
96 .. portable, 47.
339 Spice, spirit of, mixed, 100.
415 Spinach, 116.
206 Sprats, to fry, 70.
413 Sprouts, young, 115.
629 Squash pie, 160.
291 Stew, hearth, 88.
292 .. hearth, usefulness of, 89.
94 .. lamb, 46.
98 .. Irish, 49.
345 .. Mr. Phillips's Irish, 101.
348 .. brisket of beef, 102.
352 Stewed shin or leg of beef, 102.
355 .. rump steaks, 103.

INDEX. 195

99 Stock, first, or beef broth, 50.
269 Stuffing and force meat, 84.
   .. for veal, roast turkey, fowl, &c., 84.
270 .. goose or duck, 84.
271   for turtle, 85.
272   hare, 85.
273 .. veal, 85.
274 .. pike, carp, or haddock, 85.
275 .. heart, 86.
276 .. poultry and game, 86.
277 .. veal cake, 86.
199 Sturgeon to boil, 69.
200 .. to roast, 69.
201 .. stewed, 69.
468 Suet and fat, to clarify, 128.
470 Sugar, clarified, 128.
241 Sweetbread, veal, 77.
654 Syllabub, whip, 165.

538 Tarte de moie, 143.
539 Tart, rhubarb, 144.
540 .. to prepare cranberries for, 144.
541 .. lemon, 144.
542 Tartlets or puffs, orange, 144.
260 Teal, to roast, 83.
217 Terrapins, 72.
323 Thickenings, 96.
662 Thick milk, or flour caudle, 166.
205 Thornback, to boil, 70.
184 Tongues, to boil, 65.
653 Trifle, 164.
179 Tripe, 63.
207 Trout, to broil, 70.
208 .. stewed, 70.
434 Truffles, 119.
37 Trussing, 31.
191 Turbot, to boil, 67.
186 Turkey, to boil, 65.
248 .. to roast, 79.
248 .. poults, to roast, 79.
417 Turnips, 116.
97 Turtle soup, green, 48.

177 Veal, boiled, 63.
239 .. roasting, 77.
240 .. fillet of, roasting, 77.
358 .. hashed or minced, 104.
359 .. to make an excellent ragoût of cold, 104.

360 Veal, olives, 105.
361 .. knuckle of, to ragoût, 105
    Vegetables, 37.
62 .. preparing for dressing, 37.
63 .. asparagus, artichokes, spinach, 37.
64 .. potatoes and Jerusalem artichokes, 37.
65 .. carrots, parsnips, beetroots, and turnips, 37.
   .. cooking, 113.
398—499 .. general observations on cooking, 113, 114, 115.
416 Vegetable marrow, 116.
253 Venison, haunch of, to roast, 81.
    Vinegars, flavoured, 124.
447 .. for salads, 124.
448 .. basil, 124.
449 .. burnet, 125.
450 .. cress or celery, 125.
451 .. horse-radish, 125.
452 .. garlic, onion, or eschalot, 125.
453 .. tarragon, 125.
454 .. elder flower, 125.
455 .. green mint, 125.
456 .. camp, 125.
457 .. capsicum, cayenne, or chili, 125.
734 .. raspberry, 183.

656 Whey, 165.
324 White thickening, 97.
198 Whitings, to fry, 69.
260 Widgeon, to roast, 83.
260 Wild ducks, to roast, 83.
    Wines, general directions for making, 178.
716 .. ginger, 178.
717 .. mead, 179.
717 .. metheglin, 179.
717 .. honey, 179.
718 .. parsnip, 179.
719 .. malt, or English sherry, 179
720 .. orange, boiled, 180.
720 .. lemon, boiled, 180.
721 .. grape, 180.
722 .. raisin, 180.
723 .. raisin with sugar, 181.
724 .. raisin, in imitation of Frontignac, 181.

INDEX.

725 Wines, gooseberry, without boiling, 181.
725 .. currant, without boiling, 181.
726 .. orange, without boiling, 181.
726 lemon, without boiling, 181.
727 Wines, cowslip, or clary, 182
728 .. birch, 182.
729 .. elder, 182.
730 .. damson, or black cherry, 182.
261 Woodcocks to roast, 83.

THE END.

www.ingramcontent.com/pod-product-compliance
Lightning Source LLC
Chambersburg PA
CBHW031954080426
42735CB00007B/395